Director Wisdom

Candid Conversations with Sweet Adelines Directors

Curated by Jennifer Palus

Copyright © 2019 Jennifer Palus

All rights reserved.

ISBN: 9781099385681

DEDICATION

To every singer and Director who looks for fresh ideas that will make each performance even better than the one before. And especially to the generous souls who share their insights with open hearts.

Contents

Forward by Cindy Hansen 1

Introduction 2

Chorus Brand & Culture 12

Do you think a Director's personality and chorus brand are linked? 12
What's your brand (as a Director and a chorus)? 15
Does your chorus brand and culture influence the songs you sing? 20

Inspiration 25

As a young Director, who were your idols? 25
What was it like to meet your idols the first time? 33
Do you remember the first time you realized you were someone else's hero? 39
Thinking beyond barbershop, what music or performers inspire you? 46
Do you have a favorite quote? 50

Music Strategy 55

How is your Music Team organized? 55
Do you prefer blown or electronic pitch pipes? 68
Are you a risk-taker, especially with regard to music? 72
Any bad song choices stand out over the years? 79

Rehearsal 82

Do you provide a rehearsal plan? 82
What's your typical rehearsal like? How do you set the tone? 85
How do you keep everyone engaged through the rehearsal? 89
Do you have regular section rehearsals? 92
Where do you like to fit announcements and chorus business? 94
Do you include music theory in rehearsals? 96
How has your approach to rehearsal changed over the years? 99
Do you have a favorite rehearsal memory? 106
Do you overtly coach your own chorus? 108
What frustrates you in rehearsal; how do you handle it? 110

Expectations & Requirements 117

How do you song qualify? 117
What's your philosophy on attendance? 126
Do you incorporate PVIs? 128
How do you tackle a new song? 130

Authentic Performance 136

How do you balance the need for technical accuracy with the goal of freedom and artistry? 136
When do you fix a problem and when do you let it go? 143
Is it important for all singers to have a shared story about a song? 145
How do you encourage singers to get out of rehearsal mode and perform? 149

Membership 152

What are the keys to becoming a great chorus member? 152
What tells you that a new member will stay and thrive? 154
How do you help new members assimilate into your chorus? 159

Administration 162

Do you engage members in the necessity and value of administration? 162
How much involvement is too much? 164
What's your take on Director involvement in administration? 166
What do you see as obstacles and opportunities for Sweet Adelines in the future? 171
Is there a book that you give as a gift to inspire others? 174

Contest 176

Do you have a theme or mantra when heading to contest? 176
How do you share your contest score sheets with members? 180
Did you have to overcome any negative contest experiences? 184
How do you break through a plateau? 187
Any advice for choruses who are working toward a regional medal? 191
How do you avoid burnout when you're in the International cycle? 195
Did becoming a judge change how you direct? 201
Do you think a chorus can achieve perfection? 203

The Director's Path 206

How should a new Director come into a chorus? 206
How should a Director leave a chorus? 213
What are some things you would tell your younger self about directing? 221
What lessons did you learn only with time? 227
What was an important but difficult lesson you learned as a Director? 229
Do you think the path to Director is different today? 232
What are important characteristics for a Director? 235
What advice would you offer aspiring Directors? 240

ACKNOWLEDGMENTS

I am so grateful to the Directors who took the time to be part of this project and for their candor and generosity in sharing their approach to directing!

Forward by Cindy Hansen

As a 35+ year coach in the extended Barbershop world, Main Street Disney, and A Cappella Education Association, I've been blessed to work alongside most of these talented Directors and come to know and learn from all of them. You can do the same by reading this inspiring book.

Through the years it's been a joy to watch chorus members and Directors alike come to understand the unique chemistry it takes to make a successful award-winning group. This book will open your eyes to key ideas that can make it possible to have that chemistry.

Getting the opportunity to tag-team with 16 of the talented Directors interviewed in this book has changed my life. All of them have inspired me to be a better coach. Their words will change your life as well.

Jennifer approached me after a coaching session with her own Metro Nashville Chorus and said writing this book emphasized to her that "the more successful the Director, the greater the importance of their personal leadership skills." She could not be more correct!

Most all of us in the world of 4-part harmony have been inspired by many, if not all, of these talented individuals. They have come into our lives at one time or another and entertained, educated, inspired, and motivated us. Not to just be better amateur singers and performers, but most of them have challenged us to believe we are capable of so much more than we ever felt possible.

Through Jennifer's interview and creative questioning in this book you learn that each Director uses the gift of great music to inspire lives, offer magical moments, and bring the joy of singing into the lives of their chorus members. Directors don't have to be the most musically talented, educated, or be the most knowledgeable about the art form, or even have the most awards or gold medals. No. They only have to build a chorus of believers, who trust and feel inspired by them every week.

I am challenged, inspired, blessed, and changed forever because my life path has crossed with these amazing Directors.

Cynthia K Hansen Ellis

Introduction

What Were You Thinking?

This book grew out of two realizations.

The first was a moment that has repeated itself many times in my experience as a Sweet Adeline. I'd be in a group of members talking about the organization, and someone would mention the name of a Sweet Adelines icon such as Bev Sellers or Renee Craig. Everyone would pause for an instant and smile as they shared this bond of memory and admiration. I knew the names, of course, but never had the opportunity to meet these women or observe their talents on stage. I could tell by the response, though, that I wish I had known them!

The second was the realization that some of the high-achieving and best-loved Directors of the current Sweet Adelines generation were starting to leave the spotlight (or at least they can see the exit from here!). Of course, the video archive of modern performances is much larger today, so new members will be able to watch performances by today's great Directors and understand why they were admired and respected long after their hands stop waving. But they will have missed the opportunity to chat with these Directors, to get past the excitement of meeting an idol and swap some stories.

I began to wonder: Would it be possible to capture some sense of their spark and wit and experience through interviews? Would members find it interesting to read about how the "marquee" Directors approach running their choruses? What are the common themes and what makes each Director, each chorus, unique?

I made a list of Directors. I started with recent Top 10 medalists, Master Directors, the voices that were shaping our organization, etc. I looked at the subset of that group who already knew me and wouldn't think I was some crazy lady asking them to devote 90 minutes to a squirrelly interview with a stranger.

I am forever grateful to Karen Breidert for being the first interview, for immediately saying "YES" to the idea, and for giving such great responses to my questions that I felt confident readers would be as fascinated as I. You were the "proof of concept" for me, Karen!

DIRECTOR WISDOM

The first list had over 40 names, and I knew not everyone would be interested in the project or available for an interview. As I began to create the transcripts, it became apparent that 15-20 were probably the right number of interviews to include. It took over 9 months to record all the interviews, because I don't know if you know this: Directors are busy people!

You may look at the list and think, "Oh, you missed so-and-so!" Yup. This is not a definitive list. It's just a representative group of great Directors who also share one trait: They were willing and able to talk to me. To those I missed or with whom I couldn't connect, I offer one word: ***Sequel.***

I hope you find this book interesting and helpful. If you ever wondered what it was like to sing for Dale Syverson, Jim Arns or Lori Lyford, this might give you a taste of what life in their choruses is like. If you have sung for only one Director (as I have) in your Sweet Adelines career, you can get a sense of what's similar and different across the organization. If you are considering following a Director's path, there is a lot of great advice from the masters in these chapters.

The interviews have been organized by question, so you can get a sense of the Directors' opinions and experience on different topics. It reads a little like a panel discussion, but keep in mind the Directors were not in the same room and couldn't build on or respond to each other's responses.

Finally, I should mention if you're looking for scandal and gossip, if you're hoping for snarky asides from or about the Directors – you're in the wrong book. There's none of that here. There's humor, humility, and some honest sharing of foibles. There are lessonslearned, and frustrations conquered. There's a strong sense of the Directors' love for every singer on their risers, and there's the confident, competent explanation of masters describing their methods, opinions, and advice.

This book is one part historical archive, one part giddy fangirl scrapbook, and one part love letter to the amazing women and men who do so much more than wave their arms every week.

Enjoy their wisdom!

JENNIFER PALUS

DIRECTOR WISDOM

These are the Directors…

Name	Sweet Adelines Chorus(es) Directed
Becki Hine	Song of Atlanta
Betty Clipman	Scranton, Millstone Valley, Vienna Falls, Houston Horizon, Woodlands Show
Britt-Heléne Bonnedahl	Rönninge Show
Dale Syverson	Northwest, Chicago, West Suburban, Rich-Tone
Diane Porsch	Fox Valley, Riverport, Buffalo Gateway
Elizabeth Davies	Sound Harmony
Jennifer Cooke	Scenic City
Jim Arns	Charlemagne, Chain O'Lakes, Melodeers
Karen Breidert	Melodeers, Choral-Aires, Spirit of the Gulf
Kim Vaughn	San Diego
Kim Wonders	Bowling Green, Metro Nashville
Lori Lyford	Rolling Hills, Scottsdale
Michael Gellert	Elkridge, Harbor City Music Company
Mo Field	Stockholm City Voices
Peggy Gram	Top of the Rock
Ryan Heller	Pride of Portland, Alamo Metro
Tony DeRosa	Toast of Tampa
Vickie Maybury	Skyline

NOTE: In the interview sections, the Directors are indicated by their initials.

…and, boy, are their arms tired.

As of 2019, the Directors who participated in this book had between 3 and 54 years of directing experience, with an average of 30 years.

In his book, Outliers: The Story of Success, Malcolm Gladwell says it takes about 10,000 hours of practice to achieve mastery at a world-class level, to be a rock star, an outlier. He says that chess grandmasters, for example, achieve that rank after 10 years of focused effort. Investing 1,000 hours a year to an interest is about 20 hours a week.

Depending on the demands of their jobs and families, Directors probably spend 10-20 hours per week on their choruses. (YMMV[1]) At that pace, 10,000 hours of focused effort, practice, and growth would take between 10 and 20 years.

It's not surprising, then, that some of the current icons of directing (and again this book does not contain an exhaustive collection of those!) seem to be working on a different plane. What's more amazing is the generous spirit of mentoring and sharing in our organization, allowing less-tenured Directors to absorb the lessons of the past and continue the evolution of the artform.

> *One of the most remarkable things about our organization is that we share so freely. There aren't any secrets. Every time we learn something new, we're anxious to share it with someone.*
> *~Peggy Gram*

---

[1] YMMV – your mileage may vary

DIRECTOR WISDOM

Director Joined	1966 DS	1972 PG	1974 DP	1975 BC	1979 JA	1979 KB	1983 BB	1983 LL	1984 VM	1985 KV	1986 KW	1993 BH	1993 MG	2003 MF	2003 RH	2007 TD	2009 JC	2017 ED
1963	O																	
1964	O			O														
1965	O	O		O														
1966	●	O		O														
1967	●	O		O														
1968	●	O		O														
1969	●	O		O														
1970	●	O		O														
1971	●	O		O														
1972	●	●		O	O				O									
1973	●	●		O	O				O	O								
1974	●	●	●	O	O				O	O								
1975	●	●	●	●	O				O	O								
1976	●	●	●	●	O	O			O	O								
1977	●	●	●	●	O	O			O	O								
1978	●	●	●	●	O	O			O	O								
1979	●	●	●	●	●	●			O	O	O							
1980	●	●	●	●	●	●			O	O	O	O						
1981	●	●	●	●	●	●			O	O	O	O						
1982	●	●	●	●	●	●			O	O	O	O						
1983	●	●	●	●	●	●	●	●	O	O	O	O		O				
1984	●	●	●	●	●	●	●	●	●	O	O	O		O				
1985	●	●	●	●	●	●	●	●	●	●	O	O		O				
1986	●	●	●	●	●	●	●	●	●	●	●	O		O				
1987	●	●	●	●	●	●	●	●	●	●	●	O		O				
1988	●	●	●	●	O	●	●	●	●	●	●	O		O				
1989	●	●	●	●	O	●	●	●	●	●	●	O		O				
1990	●	●	●	●	●	●	●	●	●	●	●	O	O	O				
1991	●	●	●	●	●	●	●	●	●	●	●	O	O	O				
1992	●	●	●	●	●	●	●	●	●	●	●	O	O	O				
1993	●	●	●	●	●	●	●	●	●	●	●	●	●	O				
1994	●	●	●	●	●	●	●	●	●	●	●	●	●	O				
1995	●	●	●	●	●	●	●	●	●	●	●	●	●	O				
1996	●	●	●	●	●	●	●	●	●	●	●	●	●	O				
1997	●	●	●	●	O	●	●	●	●	●	●	●	●	O				
1998	●	●	●	●	O	●	●	●	●	●	●	●	●	O				
1999	●	●	●	●	O	●	●	●	●	●	●	●	●	O				
2000	●	●	●	●	●	●	●	●	●	●	●	●	●	O		O		
2001	●	●	●	●	●	●	●	●	●	●	●	●	●	O		O		
2002	●	●	●	O	●	●	●	●	●	●	●	●	●	O		O		
2003	●	●	●	O	●	●	●	●	●	●	●	●	●	●	●	O		
2004	●	●	●	O	●	●	●	●	●	●	●	●	●	●	●	O		
2005	●	●	●	O	●	●	●	●	●	●	●	●	●	●	●	O		
2006	●	●	●	O	●	●	●	●	●	●	●	●	●	●	●	O		
2007	●	●	●	O	●	●	●	●	●	●	●	●	●	●	●	●		
2008	●	●	●	O	●	●	●	●	●	●	●	●	●	●	●	●		
2009	●	●	●	O	●	●	●	●	●	●	●	●	●	●	●	●		
2010	●	●	●	O	●	●	●	●	●	●	●	●	●	●	●	●		O
2011	●	●	●	O	●	●	●	●	●	●	●	●	●	●	●	●		O
2012	●	●	●	O	●	●	●	●	●	●	●	●	●	●	●	●		O
2013	●	●	●	O	O	●	●	●	●	●	●	●	●	●	●	●		O
2014	●	●	●	O	O	●	●	●	●	●	●	●	●	●	●	●		O
2015	●	O	●	O	O	●	●	●	●	●	●	●	●	●	●	●		O
2016	●	O	●	O	O	●	●	●	O	●	●	●	●	●	●	●		O
2017	●	O	●	O	O	●	●	●	O	●	●	●	O	●	●	●		●
2018	●	O	●	O	O	●	●	●	O	●	●	●	O	●	●	●		●
2019	●	O	●	O	O	●	●	●	O	●	●	●	O	●	●	●		●

O Member   ● Director

Do you know a DAFJIQ?

Perhaps you've heard of the EGOT? It's shorthand for performers who've earned an Emmy, a Grammy, an Oscar, and a Tony. There are only a handful who earn all four (and some of those are honorary awards). I decided to try to create a barbershop equivalent:

DAFJIQ

	Director	Arranger	Faculty	Judge	IBOD	Quartet Champion
Becki Hine	🎖️			👁️		
Betty Clipman	🏆		🗣️	👂❤️	💬	👑
Britt-Heléne Bonnedahl	🏆		🗣️			
Dale Syverson	🏆		🗣️	👂❤️	💬	👑
Diane Porsch	🎖️		🗣️	👁️	💬	
Elizabeth Davies	✋					
Jennifer Cooke	✋				💬	
Jim Arns	🏆	🎹				
Karen Breidert	🎖️		🗣️		💬	👑
Kim Vaughn	🏆		🗣️	👂		👑
Kim Wonders	🎖️		🗣️			
Lori Lyford	🏆		🗣️			
Michael Gellert	🎖️	🎹				
Mo Field	🎖️	🎹				
Peggy Gram	🎖️		🗣️	👁️	💬	👑
Ryan Heller	🎖️	🎹	🗣️			
Tony DeRosa	🎖️					👑
Vickie Maybury	🎖️		🗣️	❤️		

DIRECTOR WISDOM

I understand that Renee Craig and Nancy Bergman are two DAFJIQ unicorns....and that is likely another reason why their names come up so often in Sweet Adelines lore.

Of the Directors interviewed in this book, Betty Clipman, Dale Syverson, and Peggy Gram have achieved five of the six. They are all DFJIQ. None of these three said they have the arranging gift, though Peggy said she considers herself a "re-arranger."

PS: I'm not suggesting every Director should aspire to DAFJIQ status (especially since not everyone <u>wants</u> to be a judge or an arranger, etc.). But it is an interesting inventory of accomplishments.

DAFJIQ Table Key:

CONVERSATIONS WITH THE DIRECTORS

Chorus Brand & Culture

Do you think a Director's personality and chorus brand are linked?

DIRECTOR WISDOM: Chorus Brand & Culture

Each of the conversations began with the same topic: the interrelationship between a Director's personality and the brand or culture of the chorus. Everyone agreed that a chorus and Director reflect and reinforce each other.

Yes, the Director sets the tone for the chorus and it grows out from there. ~MG

The culture is set from the top, <including> who the Director puts in charge of warmups, the Music Team, and the admin leaders. The chorus culture is formed by the leaders for sure, starting with the Director. ~KB

Director personality has a huge influence on the chorus culture. I'm a new Director (six months) in an existing chorus, so I'm trying to let things evolve organically rather than change everything overnight. ~ED

I think the Director definitely has an impact, but the chorus also needs to develop its own personality. A Director can only do so much. You have to capitalize on the gifts the chorus has in its members at any particular time. ~PG

Several Directors pointed out that the chorus can have as much of an impact on the Director as she or he has on it, especially when a new Director comes into an established chorus culture. Each will adapt and grow in new ways.

My first year or two, I was more product-centric: get the music taught, ensure there was good training, etc. Pride of Portland already had a strong reputation, an established culture. But then we started to see a new culture emerge. I think it was Lori Lyford who said to the chorus during a coaching session, "You need to have as much fun as Ryan is having!" She and I had talked a lot about what that means: enabling more things in the chorus rehearsal than just musical skills, finding more freedom, and more fun. So that began the next phase in the journey, and we're at this great place now where they reflect me but are still true to themselves. ~RH

I saw this just the other day. I went to the Region 21 Summer Seminar and I got to watch the San Diego Chorus sing without me for the first time since I retired. (Since retiring, I stayed away on purpose.) And they were <u>wonderful</u>. I am as proud of who they are with Kathleen Hansen as I was of who they were when they were with me because, at heart, they are The San Diego Chorus...with a new twist. ~KV

A few conversations touched on the idea that there is also responsibility inherent to this intertwined culture and brand, and the Director needs to be aware of her or his influence.

Yes, I believe that they go hand-in-hand. Sometimes to my chagrin, because if I'm particularly wired or in a bad mood then my members pick that up. They can get tense because I'm tense. ~LL

We have a dynamic of joy, empowerment, and command through feeling confident in what you're doing. Those kinds of things I'm especially aware of as a male Director in a female organization. It's an honor to be part of that world, and I want to be careful how things are perceived – since I'm from Mars instead of Venus, so to speak. Female Directors may be able to pursue different personality traits or push sensory buttons that wouldn't work for me. ~TD

Chorus Brand & Culture

What's your brand
(as a Director and a chorus)?

After establishing that the idea of brand includes both the chorus culture and the Director's personality, the Directors expanded their thoughts on their personal and chorus brands. Keep in mind that you're seeing excerpts from separate conversations. The Directors didn't hear or see each other's answers, but if they had I'm fairly certain there would have been a lot of "Yes. That!" Some quotes are taken from conversations that were more about Director personality than chorus. Some quotes focus more on the musical brand than the cultural brand. All are valid approaches to the question of brand and, one hopes, all are interesting.

My brand is: Joy. I always try to remember why our members joined in the first place. Why they pay and keep coming out each week. If a Director puts that first and foremost, it colors everything you do – from music selection to running an efficient rehearsal. I guess I always try to keep the members in mind and what their needs and desires and hearts are all about. ~KB

I think I'm known, we're known, for being rather cheeky and highly energetic. And fun, and I think we're sexy too. I think that's who I am, and I think that's who we are. ~BH

There is an honesty in singing that an audience picks up on…or doesn't. From a personality standpoint, I hope that members and audiences sense an honest, sincere approach. But also notice it isn't just happening by accident! It takes focused work, attention and education to achieve artistic results. I would like to think that the personality we embody is joy, but joy in the sense that joy has all kinds of experiences along the way, including hurt. ~ TD

I'm highly energized. I'm fun; I'm funny. I love being a woman. I love to look like a woman and be a little sexy. I'm not a front row person, but the front row on my choruses always look great, like Broadway. I don't mind poking fun at myself. I took a pie in the face at an International Showcase, and many Directors in the audience later told me they would not have agreed to it. But I loved it. I had glasses on and then I took them off to look out through the holes in the pie. It was fun! I like to make an audience laugh and to have fun. ~BC

People say I'm classy. There's truth to that. I respect quality in what I'm doing. I expected our members to respect themselves and what they brought to the process. ~PG

DIRECTOR WISDOM: Chorus Brand & Culture

For me brand isn't something that comes from an external expression of what I want people to see. Brand comes from the ethics and personality of the person. It comes down to recognizing how I can be as humane as I can be, for the creative person in front of me (the singer, the chorus, or even the audience). Everything that happens in rehearsal, in an email, in a conversation, is coming from the same place. When there's consistency in the humanity, in the integrity, in the dignity, I know for sure that those values translate into nuances and subtleties that are embodied in performance. It becomes a collective experience. People in the audience can feel something natural, basic, and decent inside something seemingly complex. It means we've done our work to uncover every stone, so there are no obstacles to human interaction in performance. ~MF

I love the ways people do things, but I have never wanted to be "like" other people, other choruses. I love unique thinking. San Diego has always been comfortable with out of the box thinking and we have prided ourselves on knowing that the quirky and weird will fit right in with us. We make it a goal to not let fear of anything rule our life together. ~KV

I'm a joking, crazy, "ooh-shiny" kind of person, but I take the product really seriously. My goal as a Director is to make sure they have fun, but my end goal is to get them to stage feeling free and prepared because of what I've done in rehearsal. It's hard for me to judge how others perceive us, because I'm inside of it. But I always hear that it's this absolutely solid barbershop ensemble combined with just fun and craziness. People tell me they ask themselves, "What are we going to get now? What are they going to do next?" I just love having fun when we do music, but then I get carried away. I have to say "OK, we have to focus – myself included!" The chorus is really good at focusing when it's time to focus. They understand how to get down to business. ~JA

I think my personality is outgoing, extroverted, friendly, open, sincere, and honest. I TRY to be all those things anyway. I try not to take myself too seriously and I try to enjoy the special moments, the lighter side of life. I love laughing as much as everybody else. I believe those things influence the culture of the chorus. We try to be open and honest with each other. Our chorus culture is about experiencing unconditional love. Loving each other because of our flaws and our mistakes. I think the culture of the chorus is very reflective of that. We also love the expectations and the challenges we're given. I love to be challenged. ~KW

JENNIFER PALUS

Our brand is kindness. We've very nice to each other in our chorus. We have ways of doing things that are joyful and kind. ~MG

We've talked a lot about this as a chorus and with coaches. The key ideas are things like joyful, positive, quick learners. A lot about family. Joy comes up the most. As the Director I wanted "musical excellence" at the top [laughs] - and it is on the list! But "joy" comes up the most. We're very education minded. And we're willing to work with people if we see potential. We have a very young member, 12-years old, who at first couldn't hold her part in audition. But we heard potential and kept her as an associate member for 6 months. Then she passed her audition. We feel like we're training singers. ~JC

My chorus' attitude is one of lots of fun, hard work with an emotional connection to the music. That's so important. I get connected to it, and then they get connected to it. Sometimes it's the chicken and the egg. Sometimes they will demonstrate something so emotionally that I just get swept up by it. Also, I would say what typifies us is that we are high-energy. We have a blast doing what we're doing, whether it is the deepest, most profound ballad or the silliest, little, frivolous pop song. ~LL

The brand? Intensity and humor, a combination of both. We have a great time pursuing musical excellence through a sharing sisterhood. ~DP

Most people say we're passionate and musical. That we're strong, but we're fun. There's a kind of playfulness to us and at the same time a sophistication when it comes to our music-making and performance. I suppose those are all great descriptors for both myself, and the chorus! ~RH

I'm very high-energy. People describe me as vivacious, lots of energy, and extremely positive. We have a very positive atmosphere, very inclusive, tons of energy, and fast paced. We work hard, and we play hard. We attract high-energy members. Probably forty girls in my chorus are under 35, with maybe half of those under 30. These are young women who are independent; a lot of millennials and gen-X ladies. They're single and very driven. Our members tend to have high educational backgrounds, and they're into making a difference in their communities. For example, one member just left to go into the Peace Corps, and she'll be back. We stay in touch even when they are away. We attract powerful young women who are into service and community. ~VM

DIRECTOR WISDOM: Chorus Brand & Culture

I had a picture in my mind for a long time of what I wanted a chorus to be. I wanted the artistic phrasing that Renee Craig always had, and I wanted the dance look of her chorus, Ramapo Valley. I wanted the vocal power of Gem City. I wanted the theatricality that Jim Massey brought to the OK City Chapter. You can see I set a pretty high standard for what I wanted, and for a number of years now I feel like I've got it. I wanted to be that composite of all three, and I feel like that has guided me to the place we are now. If I had to describe our brand, I'd say we are visually engaging, and we tend to do edgy material. ~DS

In the beginning and for many years we had no thought about our image at all. It just came so naturally that somehow, we found people who were attracted to my style or way of being. When people described us in the early days, they sensed that we were fairly sophisticated and oriented to quality and education.

But then a very special thing helped us think about and create our image. It was a Music Team meeting where there happened to be a bowl of fruit on the table, and we were discussing dresses and music selection. One of the members kept asking "Does it fit in the fruit bowl?" That became a clear way to help us find what really fit us, what is really "us." Of course, in those days I was the only Director. Now that we have two Directors, sometimes we have to adjust to our personalities and make sure we all still fit into our image, our fruit bowl.

Understanding who we are influences our music, our costume, and how we advertise. We all know what our style is. ~BB

> *I had a picture in my mind for a long time of what I wanted a chorus to be.*
> ~ Dale Syverson

JENNIFER PALUS

Chorus Brand & Culture

Does your chorus brand and culture
influence the songs you sing?

DIRECTOR WISDOM: Chorus Brand & Culture

One goal of a brand identity is that we all know what our style is. When a chorus has a strong brand or culture, your audience feels it, your guests feel it, and of course, your members feel it. The sense of who you are is so strong that it can also provide clear boundaries for things you are NOT. One place this comes to life for Directors is song selection. Certainly, a song needs to reflect a chorus' skill level, but there are also intangibles that come into play, usually about whether a song "fits" the chorus' and the Director's personality or brand.

Your chorus image has a lot do with, or should have a lot to do with, costume selection, music selection, and the way you run your rehearsals. For example, I'm not fond of male-bashing songs or edgy sarcastic songs. I like songs with a lot of love in them and I'm a very corny sappy person. I tend to go more for the message of love and peace and hope; nothing too new-age-y or weird, definitely something that speaks to the values I believe in. ~KB

Our approach is pretty much an 80% contemporary to 20% traditional competition-worthy selections. We have decided to shake things up a bit and turn over our rep this year and the members are very excited about that! For choruses that are fortunate enough to win or wildcard in their region it makes it difficult to do this…but we're gonna give it a try. No matter what, male-bashing songs are not messages we are comfortable doing. We much prefer loving and joyful messages which are reflective of our culture and attitudes. ~DP

We have a youthful presence. We are high energy. We are positive, warm and engaging, and we seek musical performance collaborations with other artists. We sing music that is upbeat. We don't sing music about putting someone down. Oh, and we're very competitive—we seek musical excellence in all aspects of our performance. ~VM

It absolutely influences the types of songs we sing. We want to be true to our image with the material we choose. When we look for songs that are not contest, we look for songs that have a comedic edge, a light-heartedness. We're not a *serious* chorus when it comes to repertoire or to a performance package. ~JA

We don't do very well with very sad contest songs. It takes a lot out of you. For contest, we like songs that are hopeful, at the least, or happy. We try not to be religious, but we like songs that are spiritual or something that lifts the spirit without choosing a particular religion. ~MG

I refuse to do man-hating songs. I don't think that's who we are. I have a very good-hearted chorus, and I don't think they're into putting anything or anybody down. You can have a song about heartbreak or a broken relationship, but not about "I want you dead and run over by a truck"! I try to be aware of how my chorus will view a song. There are some things they love and some they are lukewarm about. They love to be inspired by the music, and they get a kick out of all the pop songs we do. They're good at pop because they're highly skilled in barbershop. ~DS

As a Director I'm not going to pick a song that I can't wrap my head around. I'm not going to pick a song - I don't want to say that I don't *like* because you can learn to like a song. But if I'm not crazy about a song, I'm not going to bring it to the chorus. I think the Director's preferences and desire to be challenged in turn challenges the chorus. We avoid the "poor me" songs, and we have even changed lyrics to be more empowering. I have a strong personality and have never felt, "Oh, I don't deserve this person." It's more like, they don't deserve me! I have never liked the songs about "he loved me, then stomped on my heart and left with my best friend." I think we have too many women that have dealt with those issues in our society. Also, I don't like "dead momma" songs. Those are songs I prefer not to sing. I think there are many other songs to sing that have stronger, better messages. ~KW

We have a difficult time selling two types of songs. First, the poor, downtrodden, helpless woman song. We're not good at those. As close as we got to that type of song (and won a gold medal with it) was "What'll I Do." Now, we took a more hopeful approach: "I love you; you love me. We've grown apart. We're better people for it. We're going to go on stronger." As a chorus, we could dip into the concern about what are we going to do now that you're gone. Then it's like, "Yeah OK I'm going to be fine, but yes I'm going to be sad sometimes." We made that work, but we don't do those "poor me" songs.

The second type of song that we don't pull off well is super sexy and slinky. I don't wear that very well. For example, one song that didn't work very well for us was "Two Tickets to Georgia." When we stood still and sang it like a rhythm song (because I love rhythms!) it was hot - man, it was good! We could sing the buzzards out of it. But then it had to be choreographed. It became too cutesy, and I'm not saying that was the fault of the choreographer. It wasn't! That's a cutesy song. When we first learned it, Tony DeRosa coached us and said, "Hey, it's just a rhythm song; have fun with it." So, we did. Then we had to try to choreograph that. It just turned into this fluff piece that I couldn't get into. Nobody could get into it, so we put that away. Another one like that was "Put Your Arms Around Me." The whole first part of that was kind of slinky and fun, but it was mostly the front row that did all that slinky stuff. The rest of the song was powerful. ~LL

We wouldn't sing "dear old mom" songs. We like "Zing Goes the Strings of My Heart." We can all agree to that over here. A lot of the really American songs are not us, of course. Since we are so quality-oriented, we try to find songs that really can create good barbershop arrangements when we choose something to be arranged for us. We love songs that have an emotional message and communicate well. Just a cool song that's fun to sing is less motivating to us. ~BB

We changed uptunes and I purposefully chose a happy, upbeat song because I found when we did "Cry Baby" and "So Long Dearie" they just didn't connect to it as much. They had trouble tapping into their anger [laughs]. My chorus loves upbeat songs, they will sing "As Long as I'm Singing" all day long – it has an optimistic, life is great message. ~JC

There are a lot of songs I wouldn't sing. There are some songs I find boring. Some don't fit our culture. I was raised in the era of Women's Lib, Gloria Steinem, the whole bit. When I was young, the separation between men and women and power was dramatically worse. Back in the day, when I first joined, we did songs that said things like (brace yourself) "If you can't tell the world she's a good little girl then just say nothing at all." Um no. And I would never do victim songs. I like to be powerful. I like to show power on stage. So, we sang, "Yes Sir, that's My Baby" or "Deed I Do." You know, we can be flirty. I love men, and I loved my husband, and I never wanted to sound like a male-basher. I hate that. I like to show women with power. I like to empower my chorus. That's one of my biggest goals, to empower all of my chorus members. ~BC

There are definitely songs that I wouldn't have sung with my chorus because they are frivolous or derivative both lyrically and musically. Well, we could have sung them, but we would have had to create a narrative around them, so they made sense in context. When choosing songs, I believe no song is off-limits to me. A good song is a good song is a good song. Yeah, there are certain chord progressions we want to identify that are stronger than others for this genre. Having said that, you can ring almost any chord if you know how to treat it with great balance and texture. You need variety, and if you can say all the right things about humanity inside a piece of music and draw out something that makes somebody in the audience feel a little less alone – then they probably won't notice small nuances that might not satisfy your music category but are still well within the scope of the genre we're singing. ~MF

You have to capitalize on the gifts that a chorus has in its members at any particular point in time. Songs aren't going to work for you as a Director if they are not going to work with your chorus' strengths. At the same time as a Director, you have to have goals for your chorus. You can gradually bring your chorus to different material, for example, to more backbeat songs. You can develop the singers. ~PG

<After we get a short list of possible new songs> we always say, "Is that really us?" We want the song to be driven by who we are, is it playful yet sophisticated and musical? That's how we make our choice. If something's not a fit, my Music Team is not afraid to tell me. They get the music first and they may say, "This is a great song, a great arrangement, but it's not for us." I take that in, because if they're thinking it, obviously the general membership would as well. We've had a time or two where I thought a song was going to be good, but after three weeks we were still slogging through the mud. I asked what's going on and they said, "We just don't like this song. It doesn't seem to fit. There's no energy we can wrap ourselves around." I said, OK. No sense fighting that battle. We tend to stay away from angry songs and sad/poor-me ballads and are drawn towards fun, celebratory, passionate, joyful stories that can excite and inspire our audiences. ~RH

If it isn't joyful or hopeful, then I usually don't pick it! I'm not scared of selling emotion or vulnerability as an artist, but when you're dealing in a mass group, I think it's much harder to center it and be able to focus it in a way that an audience can truly understand without being discouraged or sending the wrong message in some way. So fundamentally, when it comes to repertoire, I work to pick things from a dramatic standpoint that there is a hope message behind it...versus "my love is lost and now I have no reason to get out of bed." Also, think about the months of investment, how long we live in that material. It's a long time to come to weekly rehearsals and have to be in a despairing mindset. My personal choice is to celebrate life. We celebrate joy and celebrate empowerment in most of the titles that I pick now. That leaves a whole lot of stuff on the table.

There might be different colorings in the overarching themes that pertained to a certain song. For example, in "Maybe This Time" in the context of the original show it's an almost downtrodden, defeated message. I certainly didn't want to have that feeling on a week-to-week basis. So, while we talked about that as being a part of the messaging (it's a heavy lyric because this person has certainly seen a lot of defeats along the way) the overall theme for the song is hope. Which is how we portrayed it: "There is light at the end of the tunnel. I'm not dirt. I have something to live for. I have some reason to continue." ~TD

> *I believe no song is off limits to me.*
> ~Mo Field

Inspiration

As a young Director,
who were your idols?

JENNIFER PALUS

When the Directors talked about other Directors, coaches, and mentors they learned from and admired, two things became clear. First, every Director is indebted to others who helped them on their path (both directly and indirectly). Second, there is a collegial attitude of respect and admiration among Directors. They value the differences in approach and continue to learn from one another's performances.

My idols? Well, my very first Director was Dale Syverson; you never forget your first chorus experience. How can you not look up to these people who have achieved so much? Jim Arns, Britt-Heléne, Lori Lyford, Dale, Betty...all those people who have guided me, mentored me, of course they are my idols. But I also look up to people who maintain that balance of achievement and friendship or joy. If you could have a chorus that was guaranteed to win gold medals, but you hated each other, I personally wouldn't have anything to do with that! On the other hand, if you have the most friendly and social chorus, but you never get anywhere...you know I wouldn't want that either. I can have friends elsewhere! To me it's a balance of working hard and achieving but never losing the joy. ~KB

Going back to the 70's. Mary LaMaster was my first mentor. She was the long-time Director of the Choral-Aires and she had also directed the Melodeers. She was my mom's Director. I would go to the rehearsals as a guest and I would take notes. I gave them unsolicited suggestions. You're a kid; you don't know any better! Betty Clipman and Carole Persinger are two important coaches and friends. Betty helped me grow in skill level and understanding the female voice. We've coached each other's choruses over the years. On the men's side, Jay Giallombardo was my first Director of a high-level chorus. I'm a charter member of New Traditions. He was the charter Director and I was Assistant Director. We started off with about 25 guys and become international champions 20 years later. He taught me a lot of skills when I was singing in his chorus in my twenties. ~JA

I loved Jim and Marcia Massey because they helped me become a Director. It was really both of them that did that. Jim knew I had a musical background; he knew I had the chops for it, but I needed direction. My first coaching session after becoming a Director was with Bev Sellers and I was very nervous, but she was kind and extremely helpful. I wish I had known directing was in my future, I would have paid more attention, earlier, but Renee Craig, Nancy Bergman, Carolyn Butler and Joni Bescos each had a direct impact on me as coaches and friends. ~KV

DIRECTOR WISDOM: Inspiration

When I was starting out, and still true today, I admired Dale Syverson and Peggy Gram. A bit later, I think I'd been directing about five years, Lori Lyford went to Scottsdale and I became aware of her. Early on, it was also Renee Craig, because I was always in awe of her musicianship. When I joined the organization, Renee was one of the ones people referred to as "a wall pusher." She would expand our walls as an organization – enlarging what we did. She was an arranger, a Director, a Queen and on International Faculty. She had such success with Ramapo Valley. That was a chorus that I loved to listen to. And I listened to Rich-Tones right from the beginning of my journey as a Director. Dale and Renee really inspired me. ~KW

Always Dale Syverson, because she is…well, Dale Syverson. I sang for her; I was a Rich-Tone for three years in my early twenties. I was just out of college; I had moved to Dallas to start my career in Fashion Merchandising. I was already a Sweet Adelines as a charter member of a chorus in Tuscaloosa. I had heard of the Vocal Majority and went to see them. A guy there befriended me and took me to Rich-Tones. I was floored and thought "This is my new home!" To me, Dale is like the Madonna of Barbershop. She reinvents herself for every International cycle. I really admire that. You have to keep growing as a Director or everything just gets stagnant. Back when I started, I was also really impressed by June Dale and Pam Pieson, who was up-and-coming at that point. And I loved Jean Barford. Gem City was huge back then, always in the top group. Jean had such energy and presence on stage. ~BH

I'm a barbershop brat, so grew up in BHS/SAI. My earliest idols included Jim Clancy, Joe Liles, Jean Barford, and Dale Syverson. I would listen to recordings from international conventions with my mom, and be astounded at choruses like Ramapo, Scottsdale, and Ronninge. I idolized Britt-Heléne and Renee Craig. My mother loved Renee's lead voice, so we would listen to those recordings saying, "Oh, listen to how expressive this is!" North Metro was an unbelievable powerhouse, with June Dale. And Jim Arns, I can still remember the VHS recording, I think it was the Baltimore contest, when they threw "him" over the rails -- I watched that probably 100 times when I was around 13! When I started directing Pride, I said to them, "These are the coaches I want to bring in. We are a top 10 chorus. They have achieved the success that we say we want." In those first two years we were able to get June Dale (she was a great mentor), Jim (he took me under his wing), and Lori Lyford. Lori understood my background from the classical side and helped me make the switch between the two. And then Carol Kirkpatrick, who was still with Pacific Sound, and she had been one of the forces behind helping Pride to create themselves from two mid-sized courses that merged. She was a tremendous resource to me, as was Kathy Carmody in Denver. ~RH

JENNIFER PALUS

There's a huge sweep [of admired Directors] and for a variety of reasons. From a loving standpoint, I'd have to say one of the most loving and giving Directors that I've ever observed would be Tori Postma. From a delicacy and nuance aspect, I would definitely say Jim Henry. For being "so inside the music that you're lost in it" perspective, I would say Joey Minshall. But from a global, how to be emotional in your music, how to put those things together, I would say Rodney Eichenberger or some classical conductors that I've had the privilege to see. I grew up playing French horn in an orchestra and there are things that classical conductors do that vocal or barbershop conductors don't do. For example, a classical conductor is always just a beat in front, but a barbershop Director is right in the moment and responding to it. It's a different, fluid game. In putting those two approaches together, I started to realize there is great emotion that goes before the musically rhythmic event happens [in classical]. I started trying to assimilate those styles and figure out how we can drive that emotion, so that when the event happens, I actually don't have to pounce on it like a barbershop Director - nor do I have to give an indication so that they can sing it the beat afterwards, which is what happens in classical music. Maybe there's a hybrid of the two things. I started directing that way, and it was a game changer. I stopped responding to 'events'. I was able to then get out of the habit of responding to what the chorus was giving me, but enjoy what they were expressing much more. I was 'in the music' and they could come to me instead of me directing them to come to me. I would just be there, and they either show up or they don't. We ended up being in it, together. Very fluid. I have to let go of those results and that requires a lot of trust. It requires leaving a lot of room for the musician to figure out how to solve the problems and add their expressiveness, instead of me directing them to the solution. ~MF

Betty Clipman for sure; she does amazing stuff with her chorus And Becky Hine! Becky is a positive, energetic Director who, and this is something I love about her, she knows where her weaknesses are, and she surrounds herself with people who fill in those weaknesses. She's very open about that to the chorus as well. I really admire everything Becky does. And I admire Dale Syverson because she constantly is learning; she's never complacent in her education as a Director. I think directing a chorus like Rich-Tones and having that mindset is pretty amazing. ~JC

Ann Gooch was my first idol. I could direct when I started; I knew the basics. Ann was the one who taught me how to hold my hands. The one who made a huge impact on me in terms of her directing itself was Jean Barford. I sang under her at an IES. I was mesmerized by her. I understood the powerful position you have as a Director. How you can really get a group together. I wasn't aware of that before. I had probably done it, but I wasn't conscious of it. Jim Massey – not in the way he directed but in the way he handled the music and his creative process. It's more the personalities and their leadership that inspire me…Betty Clipman, Dale Syverson, of course. ~BB

DIRECTOR WISDOM: Inspiration

Very early on, Zoe Thompson was in my region [13]. She was directing the Lakeside Chorus, and she was the first Director that I met. Before I became a Director, I went to an MENC convention, and Joe Liles was at my table. He invited me to go to a Lakeside Chorus performance. Zoe was directing them, and I met her afterward. I held her on a pedestal. The time she came and coached my Rolling Hills chorus - shoot, that was so awesome! She was so generous and kind. Eventually she retired from directing. Then she stepped in at Pride of Portland; they had a time they were without a Director before Ryan came. I was on the books to coach them. I got to coach Zoe! It sort of closed the loop. And I love to watch other Directors. I love watching Rich-Tones. I love the fun that Karen Breidert would have with her choruses. There are different things to appreciate from different Directors. ~LL

In my region, I had Jim Massey, Nancy Bergman, Joyce Stephens (I will always remember Joyce. She had platinum hair and wore a white mink coat. Oh, my goodness. OK. I mean, you want to talk style!) I had Lynn McCord. I also admired Joni Bescos, who was directing Verdugo Hills at that time. Bob Brock was directing the Bountiful Chorus that became Mountain Jubilee. Renee Craig coached us several times. Dale Syverson was directing in Illinois and moved to Region 10 to direct Rich-Tones and she and I became friends. Betty Luckett (now Meinholz) who was the baritone of the Bron's Tones had a very influential part to play in my development as a singer and a Director. Carol Kirkpatrick is another. I didn't know Betty Clipman at that point in time (as a young Director), but I enjoyed her performances and I really liked her comments on our score sheets. ~PG

Jean Barford was one; she coached us to our first International medals. And Jarmela Speta was my very first voice teacher in the early 70's. I used to be a chest-tone-crammer and she taught me there was no wisdom nor longevity in that. Lyle Pilcher was a very popular coach back then. It used to be said if you wanted to win, you would have Lyle for a coach. He was always brutally honest with quartets, but I wanted it so bad I was willing to take the heat. I had campaigned for him to coach the Debutones. (We were a teenaged quartet. We were Rising Stars before there was Rising Star.) The other three members of the quartet were uncomfortable with going to him, but I thought, if I want to learn the most, I need to go to whomever has the most to teach me. We had coaching for 12 of the last 13 weeks before that International. Two weeks before the contest, he heard us sing on a SPEBSQSA show. At the afterglow he asked to hear something - anything - he hadn't heard before. So, all being in the chorus that Larry Wright directed, we sang him every chart of Larry's that was in our chorus repertoire. The next day during our coaching session, he replaced four of our six songs with our chorus songs. With his guidance we moved from 4th to 3rd that year. I think of him often when my chorus asks, "Can't we get our music sooner?" ~DS

JENNIFER PALUS

I started barbershop when I was seven and my first Director was my dad. In fact, the only consistent Director that I ever sang under in a barbershop chorus was my dad. He was my first mentor, and he was the first one to step aside and say, "take this." I was Assistant Director under him. Then I directed the men's chorus I inherited from him.

Another early musical Director was Derric Johnson, who was the music Director for Voices of Liberty. I learned a lot from him about interpersonal dynamics as well as style, sound, how to set up properly, different opinions on a word coloring and vocal imagery, that kind of thing. And then Bryan Harden, who then was also a music Director of Voices. I did a lot of studio session work with him. And Joe Martin, who's a producer I work with and he's a writer and arranger. I've just had a lot of professional experience with him. So as far as being under someone, really just my dad was the only exposure from a barbershop standpoint and then, you know, being able to watch these other men in a professional setting, all that stuff is transferred over to everything I've ever done with any of the groups that I've been in front of. Beyond that, being exposed to coaches like Jim Casey, Jim Arns, Dale Syverson, and Betty Clipman, all of which are also directors, has been so very valuable.

But as far as a Directorship goes, my dad was really the biggest influence, and he taught me some of the ground level things both about conducting and more importantly, about music and how to treat people. Being a barbershop chorus Director is very little about music and very much about people and interpersonal dynamics. I am very honest in saying that I learn a lot at every rehearsal. I've learned a lot about what I should have said differently or done differently to get a better response from the singer. ~TD

When I started…Jean Barford, and she was only in her late 20s, but she was well known. Jarmela Speta, Renee Craig, Bill and Carolyn Butler, Zoe Thompson, Mary Dick, Gloria Sandstrom, Marvin Yerkey, Joni Bescos…I mean I think of all these people, wow; some are not with us anymore. I would see the winning choruses, and we were just starting music schools, so we were exposed to them as teachers. I was a music major in college, but I quit after two years to get married. Sweet Adelines became my continuing music education. I was so enthralled. I could see what these people were doing, and I wanted to copy that. It seemed like it could be accomplished. In my 19-20-year-old head, I thought, "Well, why don't we do that?" And these women seemed so old to me at the time – they were in their 30's and 40's, maybe 50's at most (LOL!). I remember saying to my chorus after our first contest together, "Why don't we do what Racine does?" and they laughed. But that became our mission. And all I did was listen to barbershop 24/7. I was so hooked. And these icons were out teaching classes at music schools I attended. I just wanted to learn. I didn't know I'd be doing it myself <later>. ~DP

DIRECTOR WISDOM: Inspiration

Bev Sellers and Carolyn Butler were two big role models. Bev had a strength and a passion for the organization that I wanted to emulate. Her goal in life was to retire and arrange uptunes (because we needed more) and just give them to the organization. She was a very strong volunteer. And she was like that with her chorus. Everybody has all these facets of their personality. She was very much a competitor and that's what a lot of people saw. But they didn't know the Bev that I did, or a lot of us did, that was playful and funny. She had a passion for the organization and for her members, and they loved her.

Renee Craig is another role model. I grew up in region 15. At my first regional competition, Ramapo Valley was there, and I was just stunned. Going in, I thought our chorus was so good, and I just couldn't understand why we were hoping to be in the top 10 at regional. And I was like "Well, why don't we go to win?" And then I sat there, and I watched Ramapo and Renee. Oh my. And then George Avener was there with Island Hills. Both of those chorus eventually won international, and Ramapo more than once. I grew up in a very strong region with great role models. And I wanted to do that. I wanted to change the room the way they did. I want to be part of a great performance.

And George Avener was one of my role models. He had one side of him that was... well, he would yell and everything, but on the other hand, he had the side that everyone loved about him. Directors always ride that fine line between driving to excellence and everybody having fun. You have to do all different things at the same time. You have to keep them laughing while you're striving for A. These are people that did that very successfully. After my quartet won and I got into the Coronet Club, I sang for Renee on the risers, and I saw how much she utilized her skills of motivating people.

Dale Syverson was a huge role model, even though we competed together. We were on different International rotations, and I watched her. See, I became a Director by accident, by default. They needed a Director when I lived in Scranton, and I said, "I'm not a Director." And they said, but you sing in a quartet. (That makes me a Director because I sing in a quartet? Ha!) My quartet was top 10, but so they thought I must be a Director. So, I had to become one. I used to network with people like Dale and Renee and Bev and ask, "What do you do about this and what do you do about that?" Dale's the one that told me about getting the book, Top Performance by Zig Ziglar. That was when I was directing Vienna Falls. Many things in that book were so helpful. For instance, it says criticize the performance, not the performer. That's what Renee did to a "T." Renee would never say, "You're not soft!" She would say, "That passage needs to be softer this time." She would talk about the performance, and instead of criticizing what the performers were doing, she would tell what she wanted and what the music called for. And we always felt good about ourselves. That's what I strive to do with my chorus members. It might not be exactly the way I wanted, but if it was closer than it was the time before, I try to never forget to say, "That's better." ~BC

Renee Craig was "the" idol. Betty Clipman, Dale Syverson…these were the people in the Sweet Adeline world that I wanted to emulate. I think I had other ideas about who I would want to emulate personally before I even knew any of the Sweet Adelines Directors. Some of the conductors that I worked with and in the opera or somebody like Leonard Bernstein, you know, great, great musicians who you can go back and look at their work. You can watch classes that they've given and emulate that. Of course, I'm not as learned, not as educated; all my education has come on the job.

[Q: In what ways is a conductor different from or similar to a chorus Director?]
A conductor often will have just a few weeks to come in and do the job that a Director does all year. There's a whole lot of preparation for the conductor to come in, and everyone knows the expectations. The expert comes in and everyone is on their toes. That's very different from building the chorus week after week. The chorus and the Director grow together. A conductor usually comes in with great flowing ideas of artistry – they want to layer their sense of the emotion and artistry on top of the product that's already been prepared for them. I try to remember to bring in those big musical ideas to my chorus. ~MG

> *Being a barbershop chorus Director is very little about music and very much about people and interpersonal dynamics.*
> ~Tony DeRosa

Inspiration

What was it like to meet your idols the first time?

JENNIFER PALUS

I asked the Directors if they remember what it was like to meet or work with the icons of the organization for the first time. Some looked upon their idols "from afar" for a long time before meeting them; others literally grew up with them.

I was definitely excited to meet them. I've been in the organization for 44 years. I joined the organization when I was 16, and Joni Bescos was like my mom. I sang in a young quartet, Papa's Girls, and that was before we had YWIH, so we were very unusual. I coached with people like Joni Bescos and Earl Moon from the men's organization. Kim Vaughn was a Queen with High Society when I was singing with Papa's Girls, and I remember gushing over their crowns in a hotel elevator—we didn't know until then that you got a crown as a champion. I grew up in Southern California with all those people in my backyard. I remember when I met Renee Craig. Joni had Renee in as a coach for Verdugo Hills. She said my quartet should work with her, and I was like "Renee Craig -wow!" because she was an icon. And she was wonderful, just like another mom. ~VM

I wanted to absorb everything I could! I'll never forget my first Directors' Seminar. I was directing Melodeers at the time, but I was the youngest (or nearly) member of Melodeers, and I was brand new to directing. I went to Directors' Seminar in Tulsa and had a hard time wiping the drool of my chin! Just hanging out with these people I had heard about and read about! My very first class was taught by Carolyn Butler, who we lost way too early. I think that spitfire little redhead got excited about something and she said, "Hot Damn!" and I thought "What am I a part of here? These are awesome people who get me so inspired!" And their passion rubbed off on me. ~KB

I don't know if Renee remembers meeting me, but I remember her. I went up and introduced myself to her and talked to her for a few minutes. I don't think Metro Nashville had really gotten much exposure in the organization at that point. I was just another Director to her. You meet these people and you go, "Uhhhh. Wellll. Ummm." What do I say? I don't remember my conversation with her, because I was so in awe of her. I met Dale at a Directors' Seminar back in 1991. Dale, Peggy and I took a hotel shuttle to the airport on Sunday after, and I remember sitting inthe van and just babbling like an idiot…and I made Dale laugh. It was back when the United States was involved in Desert Storm. I remember saying to Dale and Peggy that I want to have good singers not SCUD singers, where it goes up and you don't know where it's going to land! Dale knew what I meant and liked my analogy. ~KW

DIRECTOR WISDOM: Inspiration

Renee Craig! I first met Renee in the early 80's at a convention. I mean just standing in her presence, I could have passed out! I've seen Renee both in rehearsal and on stage, and she's exactly the same. She's not what you'd call a conductor. She moves, she dances. She really didn't need to be out front, because the chorus sang at such a high level. Renee would just move and get a body groove going. She wasn't worried about turning a diphthong! She just had an aura that I liked. Now for the technical things: Jean Barford was an idol. When I was starting out as a teenager and young adult, I didn't have a lot of skills. I would just watch a lot of barbershop Directors. Without a lot of knowledge of the "why" I would just imitate what they did. ~JA

It was Zoe Thompson at a music school or Directors' Seminar. Oh, and Jim Massey was there and Renee Craig. All these people, and you'd look at them from afar…slack jawed. And to actually TALK to one of them?!? I remember one time, the Rarities Quartet <International Champions 1970> was at our regional music school. I had a vodka gimlet in my hand loaded with jumbo green olives. I had a brand-new polyester pantsuit, lime green. I can see it now. I was smoking, because we were all smoking then. We were sitting, talking, and two of the Rarities came down the hall and one said "Oh, you're the new Director of Fox Valley…" and I was so enthralled, I looked at her blankly, then turned the whole gimlet over, right in my lap! I don't know what she must have thought. That's what happened when I encountered one of these icons! ~DP

Over the years I think we probably had most everybody who's wonderful in front of the chorus. We tried to bring everybody in and get a taste of everyone. One of my most favorite ones was Renee Craig, who was not known to be a particularly good coach. She's just such a stellar musician! It was interesting because what she taught the chorus was to be flexible at all times. She would be working on something and say, "Nope! Going to change that. Do this instead." If they didn't get it right way, she'd say "What's taking you so long?" You could see the singers work to get it. We learned a lot from her about musicianship. I wanted the chorus to experience this icon. Then I brought in Nancy Bergman because I wanted the chorus to experience what it's like when you have someone in front of you who wrote the song! We were doing the band theme and I needed a ballad to go with it. Nancy invited me over, and I spent the whole weekend with her going through reams and reams of music and arrangements and stuff. We'd pick something out, and she'd sit at the piano and play it. She would interpret it as she played it. It's such a wonderful gift. But we didn't find anything. We tried writing a couple things together (which we did end up turning into songs, but they weren't right for this). I went home. About two weeks later she sends me "Bandstand in Central Park." Isn't that wonderful? I tried to bring in almost everybody. Joni Bescos was my mentor, and she was our primary coach when she moved back to California from Dallas. She had a huge impact on everything we did. Jim Arns has been great, and Dale Syverson. My favorite choreography person is Cindy Hansen, because she doesn't think there's a "box" either. ~KV

It was a particular joy to meet Renee Craig. She was the icon of icons. But really it was just like meeting anybody else. I mean, you meet them, and you tell them that you love them, you talk about things that you have in common and maybe ask for their help in some way. Now some of my idols have become pretty close friends. Dale Syverson, I've probably had with the chorus probably 15 or 20 times. I've learned so much from her. In one way I'm not easily impressed, even by my heroes. But then again, I try to be impressed by everybody. ~MG

At the age of 16, the men's chorus I was singing with (Vocal Gentry in EVG) put me on the Music Team and sent me to a Harmony University/Director's School. I remember being mind-blown having Jim Clancy and Joe Liles giving me feedback on my directing. Keepsake, Acoustix, and Gas House Gang were around and having the opportunity to not only meet these great guys, but to sing tags and receive support and encouragement from them was incredible. Being a barbershop brat, mom would frequently host coaches for her then chorus (West Lake Chorus in Region 24 – long live 24!), so I got to meet and hang out with legends like Sylvia Alsbury and Shirley Kout. At my first international as the director of Pride, I hadn't yet gotten to meet Dale Syverson. So somewhere I was, probably in a hotel lobby singing tags, and she and Kim Hulbert and Susan Kegley (the bass of Acapella Gold) came walking in and I got introduced and thought, "Oh my God, here's all these fabulous people!" Then they wanted to sing a tag, so that blew my mind. But of course, once you know what it's all about, of course we do that. But in that moment, I remember just being so shell shocked and starstruck. These women were walking in and then, oh sure, it's nice to meet you and let's do a tag! ~RH

I have always made it a habit to go to other people's shows and sit up close but up to the side, because I was less interested in hearing the chorus than I was in watching the Director. For quite a number of years, I would "try on" other Directors. You should have seen me try on Jim Clancy. My arms are not near as long as his are; I looked really funny! I was using all these other Directors I would see (and didn't necessarily know) as role models. I used them to experiment with conducting styles trying to find my own. I don't look like any of them now, but they all helped me become who I am. My hands evolved as I developed my choruses' sound. I would say I wanted a phrase to move like this (and I'd move my hands) and they would do exactly what the chorus in my head was doing. I would find a way to put that movement in my conducting. My chorus and how they respond vocally has been a big part of the shift in my conducting. If you imagine your chorus' sound in front of you, you can't brutalize that sound and expect artistry. You can't karate chop it – you'll get barber-chop! There is a strong relationship between what you look like as a Director and the results you get. ~DS

DIRECTOR WISDOM: Inspiration

Before I was a front-line Director, I was directing a camp chorus at a regional event and Betty Clipman was the faculty. I was directing as Betty was coaching the chorus. She turned to me and she said, "Oh, this girl has great hands and she'll be a great Director." Betty doesn't remember that, because I asked her, but I remembered. It kind of inspired me to continue on to become a Director. ~JC

I've been around a long time! We didn't have International chorus competition until 1973. I came in in 1965, so I would get the Pitch Pipe with regional competitions pictured. There would be Gloria Sandstrom with Mission Valley Chorus, and St Joseph's Chorus, and Jarmela Speta at Racine Chorus. There were about 15 regional winners, but you only saw their pictures. My quartet had won regional in 1971, so we sang at International in 1971 and 1972. And then in 1973, I got to watch the very first international chorus competition. Oh my! These people would walk out: "Oh! There she is! There he is! There they are!" I couldn't stand it. And then they would start to sing. It was a revelation. No one had ever seen each other before, live like that. Unless you were a judge, and I certainly wasn't anywhere near a judge in 1973. I didn't go into the program until 1981. Then as my quartet was competing and moving up, I would meet different icons at the Coronet Club reception. Mary Dick, she directed a chorus in Minneapolis, City of Lakes. She was fabulous. I met her. "Oh my God, it's Mary Dick!" I'm trying to act normal and not act starstruck. But I was! I met a lot of them through those things. Then at International where people would come up to my quartet because we were doing well. We were in the top 10, and then we went into the five, and then we won. I'd be like, "I can't BELIEVE so-and-so just talked to me!!" So yes, I remember those times.

Then we started Directors' Seminar and I had become one, so I could go to those. I was also able to meet people through quartet coaching. Freddie King was a huge huge role model for me. Freddie directed Dundalk Chorus. He coached my quartet in the beginning. My second husband was our very first quartet coach. And he told us at one point that he thought he had taken us as far as he could, but he wanted to take us to sing for Dundalk Chorus because he wanted to introduce us to Freddie King and he wanted him to hear us sing. So, we went. We were good at the time, you know, we weren't champions yet, but we were very good. We were regional champions and Freddie took us under his wing. We came into the top 10, seventh or eighth, with Freddie coaching us. Then Freddie said, I think you ought to go to Jarmela Speta. We started coaching with her and we came in fourth, then we won. But Freddie was huge in there and his chorus, Dundalk, came in second at the first international competition. He had a great year. He was terribly funny in front of his chorus. He could also be also tough. We've all seen that side of a Director. ~BC

Nancy Bergman was singing with the After Five Four and they got as high as third internationally. She did some absolutely wonderful music for them, you know, some of it really needs to be revisited. I would sit at their feet every time they would start to sing; I would be the first one sitting on the floor in front of them aping everything that they did. After I started directing, Nancy came and coached the chorus and basically taught me how to direct. She has been a long-time mentor for me. And I loved the Bron's Tones and sat at the feet of the Bron's Tones at many a show and listened to them. At that point in time I sang baritone; my mother sang bass. I was aping everything Betty (Luckett Meinholz) did. Nancy was a baritone, so I had good role models, absolutely. ~PG

Carolyn Sexton was a wonderful mentor to me. I was the Choreographer in Song of Atlanta for seven years and sang for Roger Von Haden. He took us to International in Miami and then Baltimore. Roger died in 1993. At his final Regional with the chorus, he had actually checked himself out of the hospital to direct us in the contest (we won) and then I directed on the Show of Champions. Carolyn was a long-time coach for the chorus, and she was a big help at that regional. After Roger died, I was the interim Director. I went to the Directors' Seminar in 1993. I was pregnant with my daughter Melody, and I didn't really know anyone except Dale. Carolyn took me around and introduced me to all these people. That was great. ~BH

> *I wanted to absorb everything!*
> ~Karen Breidert

Inspiration

Do you remember the first time you realized you were someone else's hero?

JENNIFER PALUS

Now the tables have turned, and these Directors are admired, respected and revered by today's members and Directors. I asked them about their first experiences as someone else's role model.

I still find that kinda hard to swallow! Even your book title "Director Wisdom" is very humbling. If I have anything to impart, I am happy to share it. But I don't consider myself like that. ~KB

I still think, "really?" when people say, "OMG I got to drive Vickie Maybury to the airport!" I don't see myself like that, so it's always a surprise …and kind of fun. ~VM

It took a while – in fact, I'm still not quite used to that! I started to realize I better watch what I'm saying or doing…because people are looking at me. 30 years ago, I could nod off in a seminar. No more! I learned that what I say is going to be quoted and respected…just the same as I did to the people I looked up to that we talked about earlier. ~JA

Probably that happened on a regional level first. After we came in 10th at International and made such an impact in Orlando in 2000, people would come up to me. That was our go-go set, and it was hilarious. We became globally recognized after that package. We made fun of Rich-Tones, Melodeers, and North Metro in an "Our Day Will Come" parody that Clay wrote, and we got 3 standing ovations in that song because it was so funny. I don't think of myself as different than anyone else, but I do like when people recognize me and say hello. Gives me a chance to connect with lots of talented, wonderful people! ~BH

It's very humbling. It also puts things in perspective. It's kind of like when you're a kid and you envision being popular or famous. I remember as a kid imagining when I'm popular I'm going to be signing autographs, signing my name. Well, I realized after 25 years of teaching I was signing my name a lot on notes for students and on report cards! But it is humbling when Sweet Adelines come up to me. Sometimes if the person isn't a Director, she'll remind me that I coached her chorus. When they tell me the chorus, if I don't remember the person specifically, I try to remember the session and what we did that day. I try to make a reference back to the day I was with them. I try to make a connection, even if I can't always remember their name. I want to be respectful of that person, acknowledge the fact that they were there when I taught or I coached somewhere. I want to thank them for their generosity and graciousness towards me and acknowledging the fact that they are an important person as well. ~KW

DIRECTOR WISDOM: Inspiration

It just kind of blew me away because I don't hold myself to be something, you know, some treasure of information. It would always surprise me when they would do that. I tend to be more "of the people." I'm hope I'm approachable and not set apart. I will smile and talk to anybody. I'm kind of like my mom that way: I don't know strangers. Sometimes that doesn't help me get from place to place in a hurry at contest! My quartet or Jana will say "Just keep your eyes down!" as we walk. But, I'm respectful of the fact that others enjoy what I do …. but the attention is not the thing that makes my world go around. It's a nice push on the revolving door, but you have to keep it going yourself. ~LL

After all these years, it's still strange. You know those things happen to you in tiny little pieces. Once I was standing talking to a group of people somewhere at an international and I felt somebody move up. I tend to be an inclusive person and I'm outgoing, so I tend to widen the circle once I feel someone come up. So, this young girl, who I have never seen again as far as I know, touched me. She just touched me on the arm. I turned to say something to her, and she said, "No I'm good" and walked away. I never saw her again. I thought, isn't that fun? Little tiny moment. In my own region, I was awarded the Regional 21 Hall of Fame award in 2001. My friend Linda said to me, "This is the first award you've ever gotten that wasn't about singing." She was absolutely right, and it did something to me inside. It made me feel like I was influential. Not iconic, I don't mean that at all. But influential, and the influence has been good. That's the first time that really clicked for me. And I had been a Queen three times at that point. But you don't think about yourself that way. I remember when Marcia Pinvidic called me and said, "I'm calling from the International Board meeting" and I asked, "Oh no, what did I do?" But she was calling to say they were awarding me the Lifetime Achievement Award. I was just stunned. I got off the phone and cried. That's not an award you work for. ~KV

It's a lot of responsibility. I think about, like the thing with Betty [complimenting me at a regional event]. She doesn't remember it, but I do. It really makes me think about choosing my words carefully. Because something you say to a person they may remember for a long time. ~JC

I still have trouble with that. I don't see myself that way. I think, "Stop; why are you nervous around me?" I feel pretty good about the choruses I've directed and what we've accomplished, but you can't do that alone. I always question myself. Maybe that's what makes a person good. When I go out to teach or judge or coach, I'm not insecure; I just want to get it right. But I see myself just the way I am at home, the way I dress at home. Flannel shirt, Green Bay Packers sweats, nothing matches, someone who goes fishing and gets worms on her hands. I don't see myself the way other people see me. ~DP

JENNIFER PALUS

Perhaps the first moment that I realized that was probably in 2008 right after our Amelia Earhart package at IES (International Education Symposium) in San Antonio. I don't think anybody was expecting little Stockholm City Voices to say something - to have a heartfelt approach and voice it, but it was the last IES, and so many of the people in the world-wide region were very upset at the loss of IES. It was the one place where we felt that we had some solidarity and we could figure out where we were in the larger process. So, we wanted to address that, and that idea branched into [the package around a strong woman, an innovator] . . . [the character] informed the entire package and it informed all the work that we put into that package. We did our vocal warmups in character. We rolled that into the culture of the chorus and so what was onstage there, in that moment, was a cohesive expression of who we were and how we hoped to speak to our friends. Hopefully a statement that women in the audience could relate to. And it was after that moment when people came up to me and said, "Wow." ~MF

When people started asking me to coach them, I was like, are you serious? I was very shocked and flattered. Then I started doing it, and everything shifted. My whole reason for being there was to help them get what they wanted. It was like I could make a difference. I will sit in the audience and watch people that I've helped that I know have wanted whatever it is for a long time. I sit there and just cry, I mean, I can hardly stand it. When Lustre won, for example. I mean I've been coaching them since. . .before they won regional. They're wonderful people. When they were putting the crowns on their heads, I was just like a puddle out there.

To help people make their dreams come true…as people helped me. It was very humbling to me that people would ask me to help them, because I'm just out here trying to be the best I can. And one of the things that I've so admired about many of my heroines and heroes, like Dale, is that Dale never stops reinventing herself. She's craving knowledge and craving to know more and to learn. You can see many of us that wouldn't miss an educational event, unless we absolutely could not be there for something outside of our control. Dale's always trying to learn more. For example, if she has a certain style and it stops working, she works out what she needs to do to change her approach. I try to say to my chorus when we're working on choreography, these are "enhancements" not these are "changes." I think that's Dale's approach. She enhances the way she does things. One of the advantages you have when you spend lots of volunteer time getting educated as a judge: You're seeing what's working now. You think, "I want my chorus to sound like that. I wonder how they got that." And that's what Dale does. Rich-Tone has always been way up there. Sometimes they win, then they're third, then they win again. They come back with a new sound, a new look, a new approach. I've always aspired to be like Dale. She never says things like "Huh. They're not rewarding good sound anymore or we would have won." I've heard people make excuses like that! That's the ego getting in the way. Be like Dale, see what's working, find ways to enhance and re-invent. ~BC

DIRECTOR WISDOM: Inspiration

JENNIFER PALUS

It's always a surprise. Some Directors in my region that I coach have a tendency to be "in awe" and heap on the praise. It's a bit fun and a bit humbling. ~MG

No, I just walk around like everybody else. If that's there, I don't get it. I mean I remember when I was a kid at a barbershop convention thinking "oh wow!" when I saw my quartet idols. But now that I'm on this side of life, I just sit back and think, hey everyone's here for the same reason: we love barbershop and singing in general. Let's just get in and party together. ~TD

My reaction? Total disbelief. When someone says they want to be like me, I still say, "Aim higher, honey!" ~PG

I'm probably very naïve. I still don't grasp that people are looking at me as an icon. I think it's also a cultural thing. Here in Sweden we don't have the worshiping of the leader that you have in the States. We don't have that. We don't keep our leaders on a pedestal. We are more democratic. Although people are saying wonderful things about me and say they have me as an idol. I just say, "thank you very much and let's do this now." I have a hard time with that. I don't look at myself as something special. I just love what I do. ~BB

This happened after The Tiffanys had won. The Tetrachords were a much-loved quartet in Region 3. They were working hard to move up at International. One of them came up to me at a regional meeting and asked me to coach them. I turned around to see who she was talking to! It was me. I had coached some, but that was the first higher level coaching I had done. Later when I moved to Dallas and had done some local in-region stuff, I was at a summer music camp. I was in the lobby and we'd had a faculty meeting and the region was starting to arrive. I was standing and visiting in the lobby and somebody walked in and said "look, over there, there's a big shot!" and again I turned around to see who they were talking about. To this day it's still uncomfortable for me to think of myself that way. ~DS

DIRECTOR WISDOM: Inspiration

It's still hard to understand that anyone might think of me as an idol. I often say it's a great honor to be a director/coach and it's a humbling one at that!

One of my favorite memories is from around 2006. Pride was competing at that international as was Melodeers. I got onto an elevator and several women said, "Oh my gosh, that's him!" I turned and smiled and said, Hi. They said, "We just think your chorus is unbelievable!" And I thought, well thank you, but do you really know who I am? Sure enough, they thought I was Jim Arns! We had a nice laugh about that. Then finally, a few years later I would get comments like, "Hi Ryan, it's so nice to meet you, we loved your chorus …" So that's nice.

I think back to how excited I was my first time meeting folks, I want that to be the same. I want to know about their choruses. If they're singing, let's sing something together. Whatever kind of positive impact I can have on people is a blessing. ~RH

> *Whatever kind of positive impact I can have on people is a blessing.*
> ~Ryan Heller

JENNIFER PALUS

Inspiration

Thinking beyond barbershop,
what music or performers
inspire you?

DIRECTOR WISDOM: Inspiration

I love Southern Gospel. It's so close to barbershop; I just love that close harmony. I like Broadway. I love the resurgence of a cappella groups like Pentatonix or Voctave. I'm a Voctave junkie. I don't know how many millions of hits they have on YouTube, but I think it's mostly me! A cappella music, I just find myself gravitating to it. ~KB

Bernadette Peters, for sure. Ella Fitzgerald always. And someone you've probably never heard of, her name's Fleming McWilliams. She was a classical music major at Belmont and does this eclectic rock-opera hybrid with her husband. They're called "Fleming and John" and I love her. She's just so talented! I tend to listen to Broadway and jazz and swing, but I tend to go towards some more modern type things for the chorus, because I feel like that draws in more members. Just because I love Ella doesn't mean everyone does. -JC

I had a wonderful time with Maureen McGovern. She's a great singer with lots of recordings, probably best known for the theme to the Poseidon Adventure (The Morning After). Rich-Tones had a master class, and Maureen was the guest. Dale invited me to be one of the singers. I was so thrilled. It was very exciting to work with her. When she talked to us, she didn't talk to us about our technique. She didn't talk about our vowels or our dynamics. She asked, "What are you singing about and how do you want to get that across?" It was about the meaning. I love to listen to her. I like listening to big bands - swing, traditional, instrumental. I'm not very familiar with most popular music, music my kids like at school. So, I will say, "Help me understand why you like them." The kids play something for me, and we talk about it. Sometimes they walk into the classroom with their headphones on, and I'll ask what they are listening to and they share. I'm open to listening to new things. It's interesting, with music in my life all the time, at school and in my hobby, when I have downtime I often don't listen to music. When I sit, I sit hard. ~LL

I recently saw Mannheim Steamroller in concert. It was magical. I've always enjoyed them, and I think they were better than I ever heard them. There's a comedy group here that does fast-change comedy. It's a husband and wife and another guy. The three of them will play 25 characters in a 2-hour show. They are hysterical. I've gotten so many character ideas just watching them. ~PG

I love watching figure skating and dance contests. Love vocal jazz. I go to the theater all the time. I love opera, rock, pop, be-pop. I love all kinds of music and I'm inspired by all types! I think the more you can broaden your horizons and learn about different kinds of music the better it makes you as a performer and a leader, and in our art form you're going to be more successful. ~VM

JENNIFER PALUS

The honest ones. When I was younger, it was always about the voice. As I've gotten older- well that hasn't gone away, and I'm still struck by amazing instruments – but storytelling is much more what captures me. You look at Frank Sinatra. If you mute the band and listen to his accuracy and such – yikes! But he had a certain swagger and style about him. I don't think it made the audience less aware of his inaccuracies as a vocalist – it just didn't matter. The way Barbra Streisand crafts a song. I'm a huge David Phelps fan because of his raw instrument. He's a great storyteller, but I listen to him more for the voice than how he draws me in emotionally. It's easier to teach someone to be a better storyteller than to have someone say, "Well I'm never going to have that kind of voice." I'm more interested in the individual and what they're able to bring. Personally, I'm not an innate soloist. I love singing harmony and supporting a strong lead. When I had to be a lead, I had to learn what would work for me. I had to be honest with my strengths and weaknesses. ~TD

Broadway performers. I love The Real Group; I think they're great performers. I saw Red Skelton live in Nashville. I was just out of college and he was like 72 or 73. He did an hour-and-a-half to a two-hour show without an intermission. Stood up; told jokes. He would say to the audience, "Are you getting tired? Do you want a break?" They'd say, no! So, he kept going. That impressed me. It wasn't about him. It was about the audience. He always had energy and electricity when he performed. I think when you see somebody live that's different than when you see somebody on video or on TV. A live performance speaks with more volume. You see that person as they are. Celine Dion, I've seen her twice live. It's not what I expected. There's a lot of energy. I like performers that have energy and sincerity in what they do, that are authentic. I'm going to carry this answer just a little bit further. I love to watch baseball, and I also admire athletes because of their performances. Yes, they make a lot of money, but you can tell the athletes who perform for the love of the game. That speaks to me. It's not the paycheck that makes them dive after the ball and injure their shoulder; it's the love of the game. ~KW

Barbra Streisand always; she's incredible. Manhattan Transfer is a group that I really love. And just about any group that sings a cappella accurately and well. I'm not into vibrato fighting choral music, so I don't tend to listen to it very much - unless it's Mormon Tabernacle Choir or something like that. I usually am drawn to acapella. Oh, Voctave – love them! They're amazing. Barbershop harmony has created an extra-special appreciation for what they do. ~DP

DIRECTOR WISDOM: Inspiration

I'm a fan of musical theatre. I'm amazed at the people who can act, sing, and dance all at the same time. I was at the Lion King and Finding Nemo shows at Animal Kingdom recently. Those performers do that 5-6 times a day! They're doing the same thing over and over with great success very time. That's huge inspiration for me, for a chorus. You can't just come on a Tuesday night and phone it in and think you're going to be great the next time you step in front of an audience. I'm a big fan of Madonna and disco. I love groups that do harmony: Queen, The King Singers, The Police. Even with rock groups, I'm a harmony lover. ~BH

I'm very much into classical music. That's my background, my whole life. I like musicals. My absolute favorite singer is Barbra Streisand. I get inspired by her expressive way of singing. I'm not specifically fond of singers who are extraordinarily technical; I cling to those who really touch my heart. ~BB

If anyone takes on directing and doesn't expect it to change them, they won't be a very good Director. There's too much of what we do that, to do it well, it takes a piece of yourself. You must be willing to dare greatly, do things you've never done before, never thought of doing. All things I thought I would do I've done already. I don't have the imagination to come up with the next thing or I would have done it. That's why many of my role models nowadays are not barbershop. I get inspiration elsewhere. One example was when I was listening to Sarah Brightman on a soundtrack of Phantom of the Opera. She's not even my favorite soprano, but she does this exquisite thing on a high note. She changes the color of the note, not just loud soft but she changes the texture. I was so entranced, I listened to it repeatedly to understand the mechanism of how she did that. Then I taught it to my chorus. You can hear it in our performances, it has to do with vocal textures. Another thing I picked up on the Phantom soundtrack was from Mandy Patinkin. Now I don't think his is the strongest voice, but his delivery is so emotionally evocative. He speak-sings some of what he does, and it works, especially in Broadway. He did this thing where he was holding a note and the word ended with a "T". He did a decrescendo and the pitch stopped and THEN he executed the T. I thought "We could do that!" Why wouldn't I want a judge to think, oh my gosh they can sing so soft I can't even hear them!" I practiced that with my chorus, and we've taken that technique to contest successfully several times. It struck me as so incredibly artistic. I call this "vanishing." I haven't shared that with many people (but you can share it here). A chorus really must have their breathing coordinated to pull it off. It will be perceived as a trick if you don't layer it on top of good skills. ~DS

Too many to name. I read a lot of biographies of performers. I love people who can talk or write in an analytical way about their craft. Robert Shaw is a great one for that. ~ED

Inspiration

Do you have a favorite quote?

Learning what quotes inspire and amuse other people is like a little glimpse of their approach to the world. Not everyone had a quote at the ready and some have so many favorites they could not choose, but where quotes were offered, they are shared here.

> Note: With the rise of the internet, great quotes are frequently misattributed. The pages that follow reference the source given by the Directors. Some effort has been made to validate or correct them, but:
> **If you use this section for a term paper,
> I am not responsible for your grade!**

DIRECTOR WISDOM: Inspiration

Becki Hine

"Shoes never lie."

Betty Clipman

"A coach is someone who tells you what you don't want to hear, who has you see what you don't want to see, so you can be who you have always known you could be." ~Tom Landry

"You will get all you want in life, if you help enough other people get what they want." ~Zig Ziglar

Britt-Heléne Bonnedahl

"Entering the Positive Zone"

We've been working on mental training for more than seven years, and that's a reminder that our culture is positivity. We enter the rehearsal hall and we're supposed to have great posture and a smile on our face. I've taught the chorus how important that is and how it affects your brain. Every rehearsal we have mental training: relaxation, goal anchoring, visualization, etc. We like the law of attraction and we are attracting A+ performances. Two long-time mantras for our chorus:

"It's all happening perfectly." & *"Practice your best."*

Dale Syverson

"It is not the critic who counts; not the man who points out how the strong man stumbles, or where the doer of deeds could have done them better. The credit belongs to the man who is actually in the arena, whose face is marred by dust and sweat and blood; who strives valiantly; who errs, who comes short again and again, because there is no effort without error and shortcoming; but who does actually strive to do the deeds; who knows great enthusiasms, the great devotions; who spends himself in a worthy cause; who at the best knows in the end the triumph of high achievement, and who at the worst, if he fails, at least fails while daring greatly, so that his place shall never be with those cold and timid souls who neither know victory nor defeat." ~ Theodore Roosevelt

Diane Porsch

"The pessimist sees difficulty in every opportunity. The optimist sees opportunity in every difficulty."

I find it very difficult to be around people who see the dark side of things as it requires much more energy to share time with them. It's so important to have a positive attitude in order to enjoy life!

Elizabeth Davies

"What an honor it is to direct these people."
~Don Rose

Jennifer Cooke

"Be the change you want to see in the world."

Often attribute to Gandhi but I don't think he said it, but still it resonates.
I feel if I want things to happen that I must be a part of the solution and not part of the problem.

Karen Breidert

"No one ever regretted being kind."

I've thought about that so much. Have you ever gone to bed at night and said to yourself, "Gosh darn, I wish I hadn't been so nice today!" On the other hand, I have thought "why did I have to say that?" or "why didn't I do that differently?"

Kim Vaughn

I love quotes! I love them and get a new one every day from Real Simple.
Maya Angelou is one of my favorites; she said,
"You can only become truly accomplished at something that you love."

And I'm not sure who said it, but I like
*"Life is not measured by the number of breaths you take
but by the moments that take your breath away."*

Kim Wonders

I remember Vickie [Kim's sister who passed away in 2008] told me she was looking through her yearbook and this guy had signed her yearbook, "Your best is your best until you do better." Vickie said, "That's dumb!" and we laughed. But the more I thought about it, the more I liked it.
"Your best is your best…until you do better."

Another one I like that Vickie made up is:
"If your output exceeds your intake then your upkeep will be your downfall."

DIRECTOR WISDOM: Inspiration

Lori Lyford

"Fake it till you make it" has helped me. When I was so tired, and I really didn't want to go to chorus or I didn't want to go to school or whatever. I'd tell myself, OK I'm just going to act like I want to do this. I want to be here. Soon you end up with enough energy coursing back to you and begins to feed off of itself.

But my favorite all-time music quote is:

"The magic lies not in the communication of sound, but rather in the sound of communication." ~Ned Rorem.

I came across that, and I thought: That is just it! Because you spend so much time typically working on sound, focusing on this vowel or that diphthong. Sometimes you just have to say, "What would it sound like if you delivered it as if you really meant it? What if these words were coming from your heart? What would that sound like?" Invariably the sound is improved - because it's coming from a different part of, what, your brain? Your soul? It's authentic.

Michael Gellert

"Freedom First."

Nothing should ever feel like it's difficult. There should be no pain, no stress, no discomfort, no violence in the music. Everything should feel like it's flowing, and it should be freeing your soul.

Mo Field

"There's nothing more contagious than enthusiasm."
~Carlos Santana

"I know nothing...eventually"
~Manuel on Fawlty Towers (BBC TV show)

Peggy Gram

"All of us are smarter than any of us."

Ryan Heller

"Shine bright"

I saw this on letter stationery and stole it and now it's a chorus mantra.

*"Champions don't go to get everything they want.
They go to give everything they have"*

Someone found that on a meme on the web and we latched on. It must be about the audience. That shifted our culture to stop thinking about WHAT we're doing and think about WHY we're doing it.

"Keep the main thing the main thing."

Tony DeRosa

"Singing's easy! Singing's fun!"

I think a lot of times we miss the big picture that singing should be an easy, easy thing to do. It should be about release and joy. In theory then, because of that, it should be fun. It shouldn't be done with a scowl on your face. It shouldn't be done looking as if you're taking an exam or having an exam at the doctor's office or whatever. I have started saying that when I see people working to be 'perfect' on the risers. Release; have fun. This is easy.

Vickie Maybury

"Whatever you expect with confidence becomes your own self-fulfilling prophecy"
~Brian Tracy

Music Strategy

From a distance, most choruses look similar. There's a Director and singers and leaders who work to support the goals of the chorus. Look a little closer, of course, and you find differences in structure that may have been put in place as a thoughtful strategy or just accepted as precedent.

How is your Music Team organized?

We had one Associate Director. I hate to say it this way, but she was directly under me (just doesn't sound nice!). She and I would do a lot of talking and planning. Then we had Assistant Directors that were "under" her. It was her job to use them and train them and assess them and coach them. I liked doing it that way because for instance on a show, if you had every Assistant Director direct a song, there would be none left for me! So, the Associate Director did songs on the show and was in charge of any rehearsal I missed. But she could delegate to her staff in any way.

I like to fill the Music Team positions with square pegs for square holes. There are people who are fabulous at running a section rehearsal but are not necessarily the voices that you want the section to imitate. There might be someone who can plunk out notes on a piano but is not good standing in front leading. It's finding what someone does really well and not forcing them to do something they don't do well. I also think there is a time to say to a section leader, "Next year at this time, I'm going to bring in Suzy. She is your assignment this year. I want you to groom her, and a year from now she is going to take your place and I'm going to give you a little rest from the MT." If you say it like that you can circulate people in a positive way. It's good for them too. ~KB

I have a directing team of four; two of them are co-education managers that sit on the Management team. Then I have section specialists, two per section with one in training. Everything that we do is built on teamwork. Everybody brings different strengths to the team. The other person on my Music Team is the Music Coordinator (also on Management Team). She handles clearance of music, learning tracks, etc. The total Music Team is 14 people. Our Management team is about 10. I have a Cast Team; they manage the shows. The Cast Team has two project managers, two production managers who produce the shows, people that handle the casting and work with actors, costume people, the tech person, two people that handle sets and design, two people that handle location and contracts with venue and performers, and a script group.

I did a big change up a few years ago and had my Music Team mentor a lot of new people to bring them on and change things up. If I feel we need to make changes, I generally go and talk to the person to ask "I think it's time to change your role. Do you have suggestions for someone who could step in and you could train?" ~VM

DIRECTOR WISDOM: Music Strategy

I have a manager of the Music Team; I am not the "team captain" of the Music Team. Of course, stuff doesn't just happen that I am not going to buy into. But the Team is led by someone who will organize the team, who will make sure the meetings are scheduled, and make sure there's an agenda that gets out to people ahead of time. This person will touch base with the management team.

I have section leaders and Assistant Directors and a choreographer. And then special jobs like someone over the song re-qualification requirements, a music clearance person, someone who handles ASCAP/BMI, a visual coordinator, mentors who help members re-enter the chorus after an absence, someone who voice-places guests, someone who coordinates the star quartets (qualification program).

Usually everybody who's on the team gets another job, versus saying you have that job, so you should be on the team. ~LL

Sometimes being the musical Director felt like a lonely place. Having a Music Team around for support helped me hugely with that issue. Our Team was me, an Associate Director, Assistant Directors, Section Leaders, and a Director Trainee. The trainee reported to Kathleen, who was my Associate Director for several years. Kathleen has a master's degree in conducting so she was perfect for training and teaching others. She is now the front-line Director of San Diego.

One of the things that I would sometimes do is have the whole chorus direct something. We'd be working on something and I'd say, "OK you direct," and they directed it. You begin to see the people who are good at it. Some of those people may not have the musical background to support it. That doesn't really matter. They're really good hand wavers! A good hand waver is a good Assistant Director. ~KV

We have Assistant Directors, and they are usually people who've completed the DCP and, more importantly, they are people who pump the chorus up when they are out front. Then we have Section Leaders and those who listen to recordings. There are more people on the team than there are positions, because we have the DIY program <*a self-assessment and mentoring process, described later*>. We don't want anyone to be inundated with so many mentees they can't get it done. If people have been in a quartet and sung on the International Stage, then we call that a SME (subject matter expert) and they are invited to be part of the Music Team because of all the coaching that they've had. They have enough in-the-saddle training to help others. They are invited; not everyone wants to do it. And we invite those who've completed the DCP. If anyone has really aced the DIY program, we feel like they should be helping others, so they get invited. When we have Music Team meetings all of those are invited as well as Visual Team (which is also part of Music Team). There are always people who can't be there. Everyone is invited, and we meet with those who can attend. ~MG

JENNIFER PALUS

DIRECTOR WISDOM: Music Strategy

Over the past two years we've changed our musical leadership format which I'm prone to do every 6-8 years. Change out who's on the Music Team and how we do things, because it gets stale. I don't get the same results anymore. You can't get A results without using your imagination. As an example, when I pick leaders from my chorus, I have learned to pick people who are comfortable with the music. By which I mean: people who understand and can share their understanding. I look for people who have exhibited leadership qualities in relation to working with others before I'll consider them for the Music Team.

There are only two people in history I've put on the team the minute they walked in the door. One was Joni Bescos and the other was Peggy Gram. They don't have to prove themselves, and I'd have been crazy to delay adding them to the Team.

I also require my Team members have a servant's heart. Tomorrow night I'm meeting with a member that has been proposed as a member of a Section Team, but I am uncertain of her servant's heart. So, I'm not sure how it will work out. I'll be honest with her.

In every section we have a team with one to three Section Trainers and one or two Section Coordinators. The Trainers are out front working with the section on music. The Coordinators work with the Trainers to make sure all qualifying is done in a timely manner and if someone needs help, they get it. We have another new person on the team who doesn't know that she can do it, but WE all know she can. That's part of her servant's heart, that's so important. It doesn't take much to make a singer feel unworthy. I can't have anybody abusing any of my people, even if they don't know they're doing it. If a section reacts negatively to someone on the team, there's something missing. We keep an eye on that. ~DS

JENNIFER PALUS

I have an amazing, an amazing overall coordinator named Carol Singleton. She and I had been teamed up now for all the years. Carol is my, you know, my right hand and sometimes my left hand. She keeps everything kind of aligned for me. We have an Associate Director, Assistant Directors along with a staff of section leaders and visual team coordinators. I try and have more than one section leader, especially for the size chorus we are, but even if we were 40, I like the idea of collaboration and having varied personalities and positions to help the varied personalities on the risers. If for some reason someone doesn't relate well with someone then there is a backup. There's also constant support along the way. Some of that also comes with just the personal checks and balances that I have. The section leaders have a lot of autonomy. They can call off-site section rehearsals. Carol is one of the only people in my chorus that I will have consistent ongoing one-on-one communication with. If I'm texting with someone else in the chorus usually it's part of a group text. Again, the whole male/female thing; I try not to have a lot of one-on-one conversations. So, with the group texts everybody knows what's going on. As far as an official meeting, we usually have an end-of-the-year meeting about what's been going on over the last year and how we want to position ourselves for the following year. It's probably not as efficient as it needs to be by any stretch, but it is working for us. We don't have any official meetings; we just have constant communication. ~TD

We have Director, Associate Director, and Assistant Directors. This is over-simplified, but you could say the Associate Director works "with" the Director; the Assistant Directors work "for" the Director. The Assistants do a lot of the warm-up, rep songs, if we want to split the chorus in half they direct while Renee (Associate) and I coach. The Associate knows all the rep and could do a performance. The Assistants could do parts of a performance.

I'm so lucky: I have eight frontline Directors singing in the chorus, six of them are actively directing other choruses. (I can't get away with anything! <laugh>) Then we have Section Leaders, which can vary with the size of section, but most have 2 or 3 Section Leaders. The song qualifiers (we still call them TE for tape evaluator, even though no tapes are involved!) are under the Section Leaders, but it's a floating box (they are not on the Music Team; they are activated only when we do qualifying.)

That's the musical part of what we call the "Performance Team." There are three parts to the Performance team. If you think the Music Team is in the center, then to the side of that, there is "Showmanship Team" with a Showmanship Chair (which is also a position on our Management Team). That group has hair, makeup, costume, choreography, anything that has to do with the visual aspect. Then on the other side, we have the administrative gears, "Director's Resources Staff" and that Chairman is also on the Management team. They handle pitch pipers, legal, music librarian, performance coordination and other music admin roles. There's a lot of communication between these teams, it's all the tentacles of the musical side of the chorus. It balances the administrative side. ~JA

DIRECTOR WISDOM: Music Strategy

Our Music Team is comprised of Director, Assistant Directors, Choreographer, Section Leaders, Assistant Section Leaders, and sometimes a Music Team Chair. The Team is in place to create and implement musical programs that challenge individual singers and the chorus as a whole. They help select music, select coaches, determine expectations for the chorus. They set goals and direction for the chorus and support the Director and the administrative side of the chorus. Most importantly, they help our singers be successful. It's a yearly appointment. I usually send a letter at the end of the year and ask if they want to continue, but it's not a lifetime appointment. I evaluate where we are and if I need to make changes on the Team. ~KW

Working with a small group, you have fewer resources. But the benefit is that there's a bit more room for people to flex laterally. Part of what we built into our vision was developing a sense of independence and autonomy with the individual and with the sections. So, my direction to my section Directors was: bring me one voice. I want section unity, absolute section unity.

And the only requirement is that as a leader you use the language and the sentiment from the Vision Statement to achieve your ends. If you're stuck, ask me for help. If you're not stuck, then have at it; do your own thing. Talk to one another, solve your problems. And let's do this in a loose, informal way. So, if you're having a problem, call me and we'll solve the problem. Of course, we did a lot of group musicianship and leadership training, but then leaving room for autonomy was paramount.

If I had an idea for some music or if we needed to talk about a specific project, we would get together. I'd get their feedback. Or, when choosing music, I'd say 'let's play this for the chorus, you know, not tell them what we want to use it for - let's just play it for the chorus, for maybe warm up music or something, and see how they respond'.

No big meeting once a month to plan or micromanage. None of that stuff. I rotated people into different roles or assignments sometimes, and some things I kept consistent. Like, vocal skill building, there were one of three people in charge of that activity. I would try and stay out of that on purpose. I would step in and add small things every now and then. I would let other people mainly be in charge. I would coach the person giving warmups, if a useful teaching opportunity presented itself.

As I didn't want the chorus to look at me as a person that was going to give them technical clues when I stand in front of them to direct the music, we separated work session from the music. I want the art. I didn't want them looking at me like a technician. I wanted other people to be in the role of teaching them the technical necessities. ~MF

JENNIFER PALUS

The Music Team includes my Assistant Directors, of which I have five. Then the choreographer who's also one of my Assistant Directors. When I have had arrangers in the chorus, they were on the team. And all my section leaders, but again they overlap on some roles. We also have a team member who maintains our Finale music files and is a big music theory resource. So even though I just named a bunch of roles because there's so much overlap, it's not like a huge Music Team. It's probably 10 or 12. The members can move on and off the team, based on what's going on in the chorus. The only time I consult separately with the Assistant Directors is about a performance. Otherwise it's me and the full Music Team. The Assistant Directors are all either in the DCP or have passed the DCP. As people showed their interest and aptitude, I've invited them to be on the directing team. I am a distance Director (I live in Nashville and direct in Chattanooga), so that allows us to take performances we otherwise could not. All the Assistant Directors do warmups, and if I miss a rehearsal all five of them take some part of the rehearsal. -JC

We've changed the title over the years many times. We used to have Section Leaders, but it got to be too many on the Team as we began to grow. So now we have Section Directors and Section Mentors. The Section Directors are the group that meets. They are the people who can sight read and know their way around the music. The Section Mentors help evaluate and are assigned the task of helping their assigned singers. Our Directing Team is comprised of two Assistant Directors and me and often times meet in advance of Music Team meetings in order to set the agenda and make recommendations to the others. Technology allows us to meet via Skype, Facebook Messenger video, etc. Years ago, we met physically every month. Today we probably meet in person 3-4 times per year. We can do long-range planning without having tons and tons of meeting. I don't think we need to ask all these women, who are already busy, to have a monthly meeting when there's another way to get it done. Our Music Team consists of any job involved with our music product and/or performance. As a result, there are many opportunities for singers to be involved in the creative process of the chorus. ~DP

I was a co-Director for seven years. The real advantage is you can step back and both coach and direct. Being a Director is a big job. We require so much of our Directors. If you can have a relationship that works as Co-Directors, that's a good situation to have. If not, then you need a Director and some "Director's Assistants" <not the same as Assistant Director>. There is administrivia that needs to be taken care of, working with arrangers, doing copyright work, all the follow up. The Director must be responsible for the grand vision. But keeping track of all the threads that lead to the culmination of the final product is more than a full-time job. You're the CEO. The music is what drives the organization. You have a team or Board over here, but the Director is what drives the chorus. ~PG

DIRECTOR WISDOM: Music Strategy

The Music Team includes all my Assistant Directors – and I have five – and the Choreographer, the Arrangers in the chorus, all the Section Leaders, and our Finale expert. Many people have multiple roles, like my Choreographer is also an Assistant Director. It's about 12 people, I think (and the chorus is about 60). I don't formally re-appoint every year, but people move around and rotate as people change roles. I'm a distance Director <lives in Nashville; directs in Chattanooga> so the only time I consult with the Directing Team separately (as opposed to within the context of the full Music Team) is when we're talking about local performances. All the Assistants are either in the DCP or have passed it. All of them do warm-ups and when I must miss a rehearsal all five of them take a part of the night. I didn't set out to have five, but as people showed their interest and aptitude (or transferred in) they took on the role. We get a lot of performances and having many people who can direct makes that work. ~JC

We have 15 section leaders, one in each part is what you'd consider the "executive level" Music Team, along with the visual leader, and three Directors. We meet regularly. One full day each semester we gather with the full Music Team for a meeting and some kind of education. We work on developing the team. Recently I did a little demonstration on how to give feedback during the voice in focus (small group) singing. ~BB

We had the Assistant Director, Section Leaders, and the Visual Team Leader. That was the Music Staff. The Staff was responsible for getting the chorus musically ready for what we were doing. Then we had a Visual Team, that was responsible for choreography, costumes, and makeup, and any coaching having to do with choreography. Then we had a Director's Resource Team. They were a creative team that did scripting, concept for show packages, technical scripts, and they drove what the chorus did overall. I had several Director's Assistants to whom I could delegate tasks and follow-up. It's a role I don't see very often, but it's very effective. The first place that I heard of it was Joni Bescos. Dale put out a call for people who wanted to audition for Rich-Tones Assistant Director. Joni put in an application, but she said, "I don't want to be Assistant Director, I want to be Director's Assistant." Dale asked what that meant. Joni said, "I'll go over all the arrangements with you. I'll do the soundboard, so you don't have to, decide where to stand, etc." Dale said, yes thanks.

It's like I said, there are all these pieces of the Director role, and you must find out who can help you do them and keep up with everything (and many Directors have other jobs, real jobs, as well!). ~PG

I have a Creative Team of four people. It's handy because now we can Skype and get together without someone having to drive 2-hours. I have a Directing Team, with all the people that are out in front of the chorus. Our Section Leaders are fabulous, very experienced (top quartets, Directors, etc.) and they are very strong at vocal production. Our section rehearsals are amazing. I think I'm in heaven. It's the most fun I've had as a Director. My chorus is in an area that love the arts and we have attracted a lot of very strong talent. We have three judges and a judge candidate, and I use them all the time. We have voice teachers and lot of voice students. The person who does all our warm-ups was a professional voice teacher who spent 3 years with the Mormon Tabernacle Choir.

And so, one of the things that I've been challenged with is: I have a bunch of people who could direct. How do I use them so that they're part of my team, using their talents and part of the solution? How do I utilize them so that people don't get bored and also feel empowered and that they're helping to take our chorus to the highest level we can be? So that's a challenge, if you have a lot of talented people, to give them an opportunity to use their talent in the areas where they shine the most. I don't do the warmups, unless there's a very specific thing I want to address; we have a person who leads warmups. Another manages all the PVI program. We're training people to do PVIs. We have about 10 people now who can give PVIs. First, they observe PVIs, then they start giving them and getting feedback.

We have a lot more people doing stuff that I used to do (in previous chorus). I'm at the helm – I'm not a figurehead, don't get me wrong. But I'm not in all the day-to-day. When I came back as Director, I had had the time to reflect and work with a lot of really good choruses. I realized it's not good to have a "one-man band." Sometimes you don't have as many trained people as you would like. Well then, train them! But sometimes we think, "Well I'm the best, so I'll do it." I think when I came back, I focused more on the long haul for this chorus. I've already picked my successor and I've been grooming her for five years. Of course, the chorus makes that decision, but they adore her. I make sure they see her talent, and the talents of all my team. I want them to know it's not just me up there. We shift around the talented people; it keeps things interesting and keeps me more vital. I think the strongest Directors empower other people. ~BC

DIRECTOR WISDOM: Music Strategy

In addition to describing his Music Team, Ryan Heller explained that his chorus is broken into quads, four quarters of the risers with about 20-25 people per quad. This approach helps them organize tasks and goals and is also a shorthand in the chorus, e.g., "Let's have Quad 1 and 3 perform for Quads 2-4."

We have the Directing Team – one Assistant Director and two Associate Directors. They're all under contract. At our installation every year they get re-contracted. My time is divided between Austin and Portland. In a six-week window I might miss one rehearsal and that will be a Music Team led rehearsal. The Directing Team is the first tier of leadership and they'll break up warmups, repertoire, etc. to have that sense of cohesion without me. All three are certified Directors and two currently direct other choruses. There's a deep pool there. Beyond them we have three more certified Directors on the risers.

Then we have the Section Leaders. One Section Leader per section. They identify people in their section for their team to help with sectionals, give PVIs, etc. I say that I don't want that to be my choice. I want them to identify people I might not normally go to. They also put together the team of listeners for our evaluation process. I'm not micromanaging all the details and gives them more autonomous leadership. All of those people are the Music Team. I might meet with just the Director Team or the Section Leaders and Directing Team.

Once a year we have the DREAM TEAM which is all of the Music Team and the management team. Usually in February or March. We go through the round table discussions *(*defined on next page)*. Are there systems we need to change? Things we need to be aware of? What are we doing well? We look at the near- and long-term plan. We make sure management and music sides are aware of the issues. We might have one other meeting for a Saturday 6 months later. They also have their email lists for ad hoc interactions.

The Choreographer is part of the Music Team and she has her own team. She and another member are Front Row Captain. Then we have "Quad Queens." There is 1-2 people in every quad who's responsible for the members in her quad for visual evaluations and such. The Quad Queens give feedback to their quads. All of that is under the Choreography and I'm not involved at all unless there is an issue in communication. Our big rule is: It must be done with positivity. Even if you're giving constructive criticism, let's be certain it's constructive. I might get involved to coach someone on language. The choreographer has also identified people she might want to pull off the risers to demonstrate so it's not just her.

As always, things change and evolve. People are always coming and going, and we understand that life happens. As always, I think it's paramount to stay flexible, positive, and open-minded! ~RH

Round Table Discussions
Shared by Ryan Heller

Ryan also said that the idea of the Dream Team and the Round Tables were brainchildren of a past Pride of Portland Team Leader who clearly had a lasting impact on the chorus.

After International, every member of the chorus is invited to participate in Round Table discussions. The goal is to gather feedback from members about the just-completed International contest: What did they like about the journey, what do we want to try differently next time, etc.

There are 8-9 different tables, each with topics such as performances, rehearsals, education, communication, finance, fundraising, etc. Each person on the Dream Team (all musical and administration leaders) decides what questions they want to do.

Two leaders are positioned at each Round Table, one to lead the discussion and one to take notes. The leaders stay, and the members rotate. All of the notes are compiled and shared with chorus. The Dream team distills the common themes and priorities.

When we have our annual Dream Team meeting, our agenda is largely based on feedback from the round table discussion feedback. What are the common themes? Are there action items generated? What most needs the attention of the leadership?

The Round Table encompasses the entire 18-month run to next International. At the 2016 Round Table, as an example, one big take-away was the chorus wanted to do more performances. They put together a plan to do about 20 performances during the year. The leadership has heard feedback that was too many. This will be discussed at the 2018 Round Table to get input. They will ask members question like:

- What's the right the number of performances? What's too many or too few?
- Do we only want to bring the entire chorus to a performance that is paid or has great P/R potential?
- If only 25 can show up, should we take the gig?
- If there is only space for X singers at a performance, what is the best way to select a roster? How do we avoid hurting the feelings of those not selected?

DIRECTOR WISDOM: Music Strategy

We have the same break down that I inherited from Roger; we've had the same one for years. We have a Visual Performance Coordinator and a Music Performance Coordinator. So, it's two sides. The Music Performance Coordinator is the President of our Music Team. She and I run all Music Team meetings. She's the boss of all the Section Leaders. We have one Section Leader in each section, and then 1-2 Assistant Section Leaders per section. Those aren't set numbers; they are in place based on the talent we have in a given year. If we have four great people, we'd do that. Or some years when people were too busy at their jobs, we had co-Section Leaders.

We also have what we call Section Mentors (used to be called "tape listeners"). We changed the name because no one used tapes anymore and because they really are mentors. Quartet Promotion is on this side too. That person does activities that promote quarteting and makes sure we celebrate quartets when they go to contest. We have a Music Librarian who takes care of the guest books, keeps them up to date.

I just added a position for Music Clearance, now that you have to clear arrangements for each ensemble and the clearance only lasts for three years. I didn't want to try to keep on top of that, so we created a new role. Under the Visual Performance Coordinator is costume chair, makeup chair, choreographer, front row captain, riser choreographer, assistant riser choreographer. The creation of any makeup look is me, makeup chair, and the Visual Performance Coordinator. I'm on the Choreography creative team because I like to be involved in that. ~BH

> *I am not the "team captain" of the Music Team.*
> ~Karen Breidert

Music Strategy

Do you prefer blown
or electronic pitch pipes?

DIRECTOR WISDOM: Music Strategy

We use electronic. In a chorus of 140, you'd have to have 10 blown pipes for everyone to hear. The problem was we had to replace them frequently and had issues matching them. Today we use 6 electronic pipes. Aesthetically, the blown is more "real." I'm not a fan of electronic anything, really, because it's synthetic. The blown is more instrumental; it's more like the voice. ~VM

We use the electronic and have for years. I wish that the ones that we used to all use, the Franz brand, were still available because that was a decent sound. I find that there's so much variance with the blown pipes. It could be the operator error that bends the pitch sometimes on the ones with the reeds. When we use a blown pipe for my kids at school, we use the Tombo (the outies!). They seem to stay in tune better. A lot of people were like purists when the electronic pipes came out. They'd say, "I just don't like the tone of it." I say, get the right pitch and make your own tones! We use the electronic because it's loud enough. We use four pipes for our chorus (of 120). ~LL

I actually like both, and I like them both at the same time. I like the electronic, and the bigger the chorus the more you need it. It's hard to get five or seven pipes to match. I prefer acoustic on ballads and electronic on uptunes. Because most ballads don't start hugely. They started in a more beautiful quality. I don't want to hear the loud "ehhhhh" of an electronic and then begin a gentle ballad intro. I want the pitch pipe to match the sound I want to come out of us. ~KV

We've done both, and we have gone back to electronic pitch pipes. The subtle differences in the blown ones was just becoming too much of a headache. I couldn't stand hearing just those little differences. Even if it was just ten cents <fractions of a tone> I was freaking out. We have a bank of eight electronic ones. The baritone section leader is in charge of the pitch pipe blowers, to be certain there's enough of them and to be certain they have everything they need. That's totally off of my plate that way. She also sends out a breakdown list: here are the most common places that Ryan will start in a song and the key to blow. They have all of that information broken down. She'll send that to me now and then to confirm it's accurate. That was her idea; I didn't think of it! ~RH

We graduated to electronic. I know there are pros and cons. I really like the electronic for a rehearsal technique, so people can thumb that pitch to work tonal center. Very annoying – but it works. Try to do that with a pitch pipe and somebody's gonna hyperventilate! Also, the reeds on pipes can go funny and then the chorus is starting in two versions of the key. ~KB

I like electronic. To me they are they are truer to pitch; they are more consistent. With the blown pitch pipes, I don't care what people say, it's how it's blown, and everybody has a different technique. I can line up four acoustical pitch pipes and have four people blow the same pitch and they would all sound different. The reeds in the old pitch pipes would also deteriorate. Personally, I'm not impressed by the Tombo either. I've heard some of those get out of tune, too.

Long ago we had to use the acoustic (before electronic ones were available). We used four or five, and I had one person over all the pitch pipe blowers. She would often get with them and practice blowing pitches together. She was very good about that. There's a skill to blowing pitch, even the electronic ones. You know, the timing, knowing when to do it and to be ready to do it.

The first time I heard electronic pitch pipes was after Toast of Tampa won International in Indianapolis in 1993. Either at a Directors' Seminar or the next year at International, they gave an educational class. I was sitting in the audience and kept hearing the pitch, but looking around, no one was blowing a pitch pipe. I realized they were using electronic pipes and I liked the sound. I investigated and we shifted to electronic. We were one of the first choruses in Region 23 to shift, I think. ~KW

My preference is the acoustic one. Absolutely. But do we use them? Not anymore. For two reasons. We have a lot of people, so we need a lot of pitch vibes just to make sure that it's covered either live on stage or in a rehearsal. Also, the acoustic ones are never in tune with one another. The electronic ones are <in tune>. I like the way the acoustic ones enter your ear better. It's because we're an acoustic instrument as well. But then there's so much more functionality available when you want to do things like tuning or have a pitch piper hold down "DO" as another part sings above that. I've kind of surrendered to the technology, even thought my preference is absolutely acoustic. I would say that to quartets; if you can make it work use an acoustic. It weaves into the sound of a cappella group better than an electronic tone. ~JA

Blown. We had one for a while and now we have two. We use Tombo, because it works better for matching. I have two really good pitch pipe blowers who can hear if there is a discrepancy and actually adjust their air flow to correct it. ~JC

DIRECTOR WISDOM: Music Strategy

I prefer a regular pitch pipe to an electronic pipe. Perhaps because they are reed instruments there is a sense coming from the person blowing it, a certain color and warmth. I find the electronic ones, if they are blown too long, tend to lose their sense of center because they are almost too centered. Like if you put your foot under a stream of really hot water in the tub, it is so hot it almost feels cold for a second. If you repeat a sensation too much, you lose your sense of its effect. Also, we don't teach people how to listen to a pitch pipe no matter which kind it might be. People get the area of the pitch, but they're not really listening for the variations, it seems. All pitches are sound waves with peaks and valleys. Some people hear the lower part and gravitate to it, downward. Some gravitate to the upper and some the middle. The acoustic pitch pipe gives more variation of color, which has a benefit. The electronic pipes are too narrow. If you're a person that listens to the bottom, you can't hear the top and you think you're close enough. I know it sounds strange, but when you have more flexibility and can let your ear hear the lower and the upper part, you can make a choice. Your vocal coordination will go where your ear goes. There's an exercise I do about listening to pitches and I've found you have to work harder to get that experience with an electronic pitch than you do with an acoustic pipe. ~MF

We switched to electronic ones when they came out many years ago, because of pitch pipe blower error and differing pitches. But after a while, we just ignored that electronic sound, because it doesn't sound musical. I have been amazed through the years that the Vocal Majority would use one blown pitch pipe for over 120 men, so we went back to the blown pitch pipe, and only used one for many years. That exercise certainly helped us to develop our listening skills. Since Tombo pipes have come out, we use those now, and we have three that usually match pitch. ~BH

I like the electronics for rehearsal because they are always in tune. But we use the reed pitch pipes for contest performances. We have a huge box of them, because they don't stay in tune. We've figure it out: we go to International and we buy 4-6 pipes on-site, make sure they're matched, and use them on-site that week. I like the sound of the reed pipe. It sounds more like the human voice and it cuts the audience noise a little bit better. One of our Assistant Directors has the dubious job of coaching the pitch pipe gals in order to ensure that their approach is unified. There's no doubt that pitch pipe gals have a thankless job, so I try to make a point of mentioning and thanking them often. ~DP

> *I want the pitch pipe to match the sound I want to come out of us.*
> ~Kim Vaughn

Music Strategy

Are you a risk-taker, especially with regard to music?

Most of us are risk-takers at times and cautious at other times. When it comes to your chorus, where or how do you take risk and where do you want to have a safety net?

DIRECTOR WISDOM: Music Strategy

We took a lot of risk in Spirit of the Gulf (SOG) in that we had so many Snowbirds. It was quite typical for us to have half the chorus missing until just a few rehearsals before international. You talk about taking a risk! But that is the culture of that chorus. It's south Florida, people go away for 6 months. I always felt if we can't make it, then we have no business making it. You know, we have to live with the culture that we are given. That was risky even to be doing packages and expecting that the Snowbirds did their homework, and those who stayed did our work, and we could come together and make it happen. The Snowbirds worked SO hard. We would also have a Snowbird retreat. I would go up somewhere north like Boston and most could meet there. We'd have an intense retreat. But in a way I found they might have worked harder than those who stayed in FL, because they didn't want to come back and be holding the chorus up. So, you know, it's that "where there's a will there's a way" thing. People thought "How is SOG gonna work? When they only have a few rehearsals together and go off to International?" But I was a Snowbird <u>Director</u>! You talk about asking how is this gonna work?! But when you think outside the box, you can make stuff work! ~KB

I love to take a risk AND there's a part of me that doesn't want to take a risk BUT there's a part of me that thinks I should. You know there's a whole inner battle going on. Throughout my life, I've played some things safe, and I've taken risks with other things. I think the chorus is the same way. I think that they are open to taking risks. But it's kind of like. "Let me put this one foot out here first and make sure that the ground is solid before I shift my weight that way." ~KW

I said to Bev Sellers one time, "I need to get rid of my inhibitions"
She said, "Betty – keep the ones you have." ~BC

I take risks in the music that we sing. I will push the envelope. I've been told in some of the judge's comments that a song is outside the lines of being a good competition song. There have been a couple of songs that I've brought back after a couple years – and the comment that it wasn't good for contest went away. Some of the best scores we've ever gotten were on a song that originally, we were told we shouldn't do. I took that as a challenge. There's a time to be safe and a time to risk when it comes to music choice. ~MG

JENNIFER PALUS

I'm not sure that I would think of myself as a "risk-taker" when it comes to the performance of the chorus. Yes, we've tried new things and have sung music that hasn't been sung before. But at the end of the day, I'm hired to enable success, primarily in performances and the competition arena, so I try to choose music wisely, with an eye on what will be most successful for the chorus.

On a more personal note, the rehearsal hall is where I take more risks. I am not afraid to try new things when it comes to rehearsal strategies, conducting gestures, or anything else that might facilitate a better experience/performance for the singers.

For us the biggest risk has been to explore freeing up our performance energy. My default is always sound based, always coming back to vocal skills. Erin Howden is our primary visual coach and she suggested to just take 10 minutes in the middle of a rehearsal and have a dance party and play these games. That for me is a huge risk! I want to use that time! But then of course to come back on the other side of it and hear the results, the freedom in the room, the positive impact on the product. Of course, some of those things fall on their face. But we've hopefully introduced it in a way that says, "we're going to try this and if it doesn't work, we'll try something else." ~RH

That's a great question and I'm not sure I know the answer. I will often say to my chorus and when I'm coaching, "I don't know how that's going to score, but I know how it makes me feel as an audience member." We're in a competitive venture, but I don't have the judging handbook memorized every step of the way. I assume that could be a risk. <chuckle> For me, I feel as someone whose been up to bat and taken a lot of hits, there are some things that might not be the norm from a creativity or vocal production standpoint or might not be aligned to get the best number. But I don't feel that's a healthy way to go about a musical, creative venture. You do what feels right – not breaking any rules (I will not risk breaking rules), but I have a vision instinctively of what looks and feels good to a general audience member, even if that audience member is not the one writing down the number. I'm not very risky when it comes to song selection. From a personality of our chorus, with the spectrum of members (and because my mom, sister, daughter, and niece are in my chorus) … for every song, visual, and costume, I feel I have to pass that litmus test. Does it fit the chorus? Is this selling something that we don't want to sell – in how we're presenting ourselves or the thematic content? I tend to be more conservative from a visual perspective. Maybe that's not taking a risk I should take. But as a male in front of a female chorus I want to be above reproach when it comes to personality choices, song choices, how we're selling our message. I never want people to think, "Is he tapping into an emotion or a society hot button?" I won't take those risks. If it's a good solid message of joy, then I might be riskier with vocal production and that kind of thing. ~TD

DIRECTOR WISDOM: Music Strategy

I would not take risks as far as contestability of arrangements. I always chose good barbershop arrangements with strong barbershop chords. But I would take risks in staging, choreography and interpretation. ~PG

When I first started directing, there was another chorus in Region 23 that were technically great singers but, frankly, a little boring. I was directing Song of Atlanta and my ears weren't trained yet – so I was willing to do things that had cool visuals and were fun to sing. I wasn't aware that I was taking risks with vocal production. I just didn't know better. Because of the types of characters we've portrayed in the past, people think I'm a risk-taker in asking my singers to portray certain characters. "How did you go from being pirates to being fairies?" But it never dawned on me that we couldn't do that! I just had an idea for a package and Clay had ideas for songs. People think we're taking a risk by having over-the-top characters, but to me it's just a cool character. I don't think I really am a big risk-taker. We choose music and characters because they're fun, they're great ideas, and they fit my personality and the chorus personality and so we can do it. ~BH

We took a risk with our (distance) swan set in Las Vegas in 2017. It was really out of the box. When you do a swan set with your chorus you have total control over most of the parameters, but we had to rely on tech people and timing and hope that the jokes would translate. (That is a challenge for us, because what we think is funny is not necessarily what you think is funny. It can be a cultural difference). We got lucky and it hit the buttons with the audience. The idea for that set was brainstormed about 10 months before. We weren't sure if it would work and we were so relieved when you started to laugh. ~BB

Some people take risks by singing music that they thoroughly enjoy but that doesn't have as many opportunities for chords that lock and ring. Compare a song like "Pal of My Cradle Days," a very strong contest ballad, and one like "How Deep is the Ocean," which isn't as strong in terms of its chords. But if you feel passionate about the song, it can be a risk worth taking – as long as what you're doing is thrilling! I'll never forget, I was in the pit when "the BUZZ" came out and competed in the first round with "How Deep is The Ocean." I think it's one of the most dramatic songs Irving Berlin ever composed. The lyrics are so dramatic. That's how "the BUZZ" felt about it. They sang it, and they won the international competition because they sang it so dramatically. They embraced the song and they sang it in the style it was meant to be sung in and absolutely blew the audience away. ~BC

I'm definitely a risk-taker but I have learned my lessons well, so I became less and less of a risk-taker musically and more of one visually and artistically. The right music has a life of its own. The wrong music is a battle every single week. The right music is magic. The wrong music is worry and constant struggle. It's the toughest decision we make as Directors, but it's also the most important. ~KV

I'm very conservative when it comes to contest music selections and definitely try to avoid arrangements that are questionable. Back in the late 80s when Joe Liles' arrangement of "My Buddy" was made available, our chorus (Riverport) decided to compete with it before anyone had really sung it as a chorus. We sang it at regional contest (and won!) but the Music judge said it wasn't a strong vehicle. Jarmela Speta advised me by recommending, "Don't listen to that. Your chorus does it well and it's a good choice" So I listened to her advice and we took it to International, and *that* panel felt it was a strong piece. So that was probably the biggest risk I can remember taking…but I'm so thankful to have listened to Jarm in that instance. She was right! ~DP

Because I make learning tracks the song selection process can be inverted. I'll make tracks and say, "oh this sings really well, and I love this." Then I give it to my Music Team. It's almost backwards in that I've sung all four parts of a song before I think about it as a vehicle for us. On the other side, sometimes I'll make tracks for a song and realize it would not be good for my chorus. It might be too rangy or have widespread chords. Those always sound hollow to me; I prefer tighter voicings. ~JC

We have a responsibility as artists to expand why we choose the music we choose and how we negotiate the conversation of the music: the lyrics, the chords, and the four individual melodies. A good song can come from anywhere. Older song writers were saying exactly the same thing as contemporary songwriters. They just use language in the vernacular of their time. Peel down any old lyric and you'll find many of them were written to be the "pop" of their day. But there are gems from the 20th century and even earlier that speak to the same human condition that we experience, and suffer, and triumph with, and are challenged by, today. If we, as barbershop musicians, can find value in the conversation inside the music, we can absolutely draw out the contemporary message from a dated vernacular. The nuanced treatment of the chords can enhance a modern expression and depth, greatly. But we must train ourselves to look deeper, to negotiate the meaning. ~MF

DIRECTOR WISDOM: Music Strategy

I've always leaned toward risk taking, doing something a little avant-garde, a little different. When it comes to contest, I take calculated risks. As a judge I know what that looks like. Years ago, we did Thriller (back in the '80s) and it was very out-of-the-box for that time. Another one we did was "Hey Big Spender" with stools and fishnet hose, and it was very risky to get into that persona in an organization that's always been pretty conservative. People loved it. There were probably a few people who might have made comments at the time <since it pushed the envelope>, but it was about the character. And that's been a real strength of my chorus. ~VM

Usually we will sing cutting edge music. We don't like singing music that everybody has done. One exception to that, where we went the safer route, was "He Was There at the Mardi Gras" Nancy Bergman's arrangement. It was part of our gold medal round in Las Vegas. But I feel like we were able to find some juice in it that maybe others overlook. One of the risks that didn't pay off (and honestly, I think we were ahead of our time) was at the Hawaii International, the one after Detroit. In our finals package, we did our first song, and then we took a little snippet of the first song that had words that would lead up to the second song. All the connective tissue was music. No spoken words. Everything flowed into the next, and we didn't blow the pitch pipe again. It was incredibly creative. But the audience didn't get it. The audience was like "meh." We had never felt that before. We have enjoyed having the audience like what we do. The judges did not like it either, because there is a rule that there must be speaking parts in the package. But now fast forward several years, and you may remember Rönninge did a very similar thing, but they spoke the words to one of the verses between songs. So, it worked for them, but it was a risk we took that did not pay off. We sang well. We did a good job. It just wasn't up to code, at the time. The organization evolves. ~LL

I'm extremely pleased with the fact that Sweet Adelines are going more and more into the genuine musical expression, that is true to you and not so manufactured. In early days it was more stereotyped and "this is how we do it in barbershop." It had almost no connection with the musical world outside of barbershop. Today it's truer to the music itself. We're going more to the natural way from the inside out. It has a higher level of freedom. ~BB

I think innovation comes from realizing there is no box! San Diego has used black light and a marching band and tear away costumes - all the way back in 1975 - and costumes people still talk about today. And songs like Quiet Please There's a Lady on Stage and I Didn't Raise My Boy to Be a Soldier and Auld Lang Syne and real Irish dancing and costumes that were made of only blue and white cotton or purple fringe or green velvet. I hope people want to be in the room when we perform because they just don't know what to expect! ~KV

The music has opened up a little bit more. We're still fairly conservative compared to, say, the men's organization. But we have opened it up and we're pushing the walls to be able to bring more innovative things. How does that help to preserve the artform? Because there's a whole book in the artform we can't or don't want to sing anymore. You can sing anything in barbershop as long as it fits the mold. Over the years in my arranging, I've been told by judges or arrangers that we weren't singing barbershop, but I knew that everything I arranged was barbershop. It just didn't come from the same old fashioned mold. I did a barbershop arrangement of Beatles songs – it fits all the criteria. I appreciate that we are looking to bring more of the music that's happening now into our artform.

If we don't do that, if we're sticklers for the old fashioned style of song, we're going to lose our audience. The most successful groups do the most modern music and they have their "chestnuts" of the classics. It's like how names become old fashioned then they come around again. Or clothing goes out of fashion and then is back in fashion. My grandfather was named Harry, then for years there was no one named that, and now it's come back. Or it's like restoring a beautiful old piece of furniture… those old chestnuts of music should be in your repertoire. But you'll lose your audience if they are the whole thing. Keep them in the middle and educate your audience that doesn't know anything about barbershop, give them some history and context. ~MG

> *If we're sticklers for the old fashion style of song, we're going to lose our audience.*
> ~ Michael Gellert

Music Strategy

Any bad song choices
stand out over the years?

Sure, both too easy and boring or too hard and we couldn't really achieve. I don't think I chose music the chorus didn't buy into, because I think I had a pretty good handle on them and they on me. There was a song that become a joke with SOG, because I really grooved on it. It was called "White Wings" and they did NOT like it, so it became a joke. Whenever there was a lull someone would say "hey let's do White Wings" Make a joke from your mistakes – turn 'em into a funny experience. ~KB

The chorus did not care for one of my all-time favorite songs, "Beside an Open Fireplace." It was just too morose for them. They thought it was a real snooze. And I learned a lesson when we tried to sing "Forgive Me" at contest. My chorus did not like saying "I'm sorry. I'm sorry. I'm sorry" – and that's what that song is. It's a great barbershop song, but the message is, "I'm sorry." I had to drag them through the weeds for that one! ~DS

Some songs we abandoned because I was overly ambitious for where the chorus was at the time. The great thing is, they're kind of clamoring for some of those songs now. They want to try them again. There an 8-part arrangement of Neil Diamond's "America" that is just crazy. We might try that one again. Every once in a while, there will be a song that I love that the chorus is not crazy about. We do "Girls Just Wanna Have Fun" and it's not a favorite. I think the chords are too repetitive. That's a problem with some of the modern songs. ~JC

<After we dropped a two-song contest set that had flopped at International> I realized it's not the responsibility of the arranger to tell you that you're making a mistake, BUT they do try to tell you in such nice ways. At some point during the journey, both of the arrangers I had work on these songs said, "This is hard. This is very challenging." But I said, "the chorus can do anything." I still believe that, but it has to be at the right time. The songs were not badly sung! They weren't good songs for contest; too much Broadway. Even Cindy Hansen tried to tell me in a coaching session, and she's not responsible for that either! But I'll say it again: you learn a lot from failure! ~KB

There have been a handful over the years. I tried to teach "The First Time Ever I Saw Your Face." A lot of songs I choose are because I think there is a skill that could be learned. Roberta Flack sings this so very softly, and I thought it could be a great skill to be able to sing so tenderly all the way through. It just didn't get off the ground. We worked for several weeks and it started to be a drag. It wasn't a good fit and we let it fall away. There have been some quartets in the chorus that used it, but it didn't work for the chorus. ~MG

DIRECTOR WISDOM: Music Strategy

We had Brian Beck do an arrangement of "That Old Gang of Mine" and it was a great arrangement. My current chorus sings better when the leads and basses are higher. I probably should have given him more information about us. So, we were preparing it for contest, but I kept thinking it sounded like a dirge not realizing that it wasn't the arrangement but that the arrangement wasn't as well suited to our vocal skills because of the low bass and lead lines. So, we learned it, coached it and try as we did we ended up shelving it. We also attempted Joe Liles' arrangement of "My Buddy," which got Riverport to 10th place in Salt Lake but was a poor fit for Buffalo Gateway. We learned it, coached it, used it on a show or two and ended up shelving it. Because the tessitura of the song wasn't as good with this chorus, but it was great in Wisconsin.

[Q: How do you know when it's time to dump a song?] I think it's the way the chorus members react when we work on it. If there's a sense that it feels like work, then it deserves a second look. It's the same with choreography. You can tell when a move isn't right. We're drilling and drilling and they're not getting it. They're not joyful about it. It's a pretty good sign. There're little things you read off of the members. They'll try hard, but it doesn't stick. Or the same passage keeps coming up. It haunts you. When the chorus really loves a song... I throw stuff out that is very difficult and if they love it, they learn it! It may be related to skill set but I think it's more than that. Perhaps the message of the song doesn't reflect the chorus culture or might be offensive to some? The question is, do they embrace what we've chosen? The longer one directs a chorus and understands who they are and what they like, the better we get at choosing the right music (not an easy task!). ~DP

I was having trouble with a new song. I was trying to approach it from the Expression category. I wanted to hold this thought and emphasize this idea and the arrangement wasn't working with what I wanted to do. Jim Arns was coming in and I warned him in advance. We were at dinner and looking at the music. I'm showing him how the music goes and I'm singing this love song to him in the restaurant. Suddenly he looks around and said, "Please don't sell." We laughed! And of course, he modified the arrangement that night for me. ~BC

> *...They try hard, but it doesn't stick...*
> ~Diane Porsch

Rehearsal

Do you provide a rehearsal plan?

DIRECTOR WISDOM: Rehearsal

I was just getting into sending those out before rehearsal (when I retired). I think Spirit of the Gulf does that now. It's so smart. My <private> agenda would be minute-by-minute, but I'd send a skeleton of the evening to the members. It just makes so much sense. They'll be prepared, they'll bring the right music, their recording equipment, they know what to work ahead of time. ~KB

No, I'm not good at that at all. But I had great help, and I had people who would do it. But they never did it to-the-minute, because I can't stand that. I think it's wonderful that other people do a schedule. As a coach, I think it's great. It's so much easier for me to know the schedule. Once I started coaching sessions, I'm very likely to not stop. Somebody will have to tell me it's time to have lunch, because I'm going! We'd just keep going all day. I really love it so much. So much fun! ~KV

I don't send out what songs we're going to work on. Though I might mention it the week before, "We're going to continue on this song next week." I used to have a member help me with that, but she's not in the chorus now. I probably should send it, but I don't. I do send out the songs for POD, Performance on Demand. At the beginning of rehearsal after warmups, we will do a 3-4 song set with emcee work to keep the repertoire up. It also helps folks qualify or re-qualify on their music (they can step to the side and sing to their listener). We have a lot of guests - and if we start working right away and all they see is us drilling into one measure or one technique, they don't get a sense of our performance. (and we don't get to perform!) It's good practice for me to direct and perform (and not interact or correct). It's discipline building for them to stay in character. We can also practice the emcee work and give different people a try. ~LL

Yes, I have a long-range plan and rehearsal plans. It's important to share the rehearsal plan with members in advance. Our rehearsal are Wednesdays, so I try to send it out Friday or Saturday the weekend before. That allows members to focus their personal practice on the right things. When I'm out of town, I email the Directing Team about where we are on the long-range plan…and what the big picture ideas are for this week. Then they put the rehearsal plan together. They created a tool called Speed Dueting. It's on a song that's already been learned when we're working in section duets. We take 10 minutes to do all 6 duets – lightning fast. Identify the cool elements and rotate. They started this one night I wasn't there and now I include it too. ~RH

When the scope of my job changed, I had to be more cognizant of the planning I was doing to get things done at rehearsal. I became very aware of having a schedule for rehearsal and posting it in front of the chorus on a big white board, so that they had a responsibility to know what we were going to accomplish that night. When it was just in my head, I had a plan. But until I put it in front of the chorus, they didn't have responsibility for it. ~PG

We use HarmonySite and that allows me to create a rehearsal plan and share it with all the members (on the site; no need to email it). If I am not going to be there, I can assign different parts of the night to my Assistants. I used to say "you all just run it" but I got feedback that they would be more comfortable with specific parameters. They can trade out if they want to, this is to provide some guidelines. ~JC

My rehearsal is being prepared for next week while we're rehearsing this week. I jot down notes for how to follow up the next week. It's also based on whatever event is coming up: a CD recording session, a show, a contest, etc. I put the songs in order of which ones need the most work based on the previous week and what we want to accomplish with them ~MG

One of the things I liked best was use of a red binder with our music in it that I kept on a music stand at rehearsal that was just for the use of our section leaders. Using their own colors, they would mark music with areas that needed specific attention. I took that binder home every week for review. It helped me focus on areas that I might not have heard or where we had not yet solved our problems. ~KV

I've learned to be flexible – my long-range plan allows me to see where I'm going. If I don't get something done in one night, it's OK, I can see how things will shift. Also, I've learned the strength of the team. There are still some in our organization, even some legends, who want to do everything themselves. "To be a strong chapter, you should do everything, and it will be exactly as you want it." That for me, didn't work. Empowering more people, having more people involved makes for a happier strong chapter. ~RH

> *My rehearsal is being prepared for next week while we're rehearsing this week.*
> Michael Gellert

Rehearsal

What's your typical rehearsal like?
How do you set the tone?

JENNIFER PALUS

I want rehearsal to begin happy, lively, and on-time. All of that sets the stage. I read this book about "the rule of eleven" and it basically says the first 11 of anything are the most important to set the stage. The first 11 words you say, or the first 11 minutes of a rehearsal. I think for a lot of choruses those first 11 minutes are either boring or scolding: *"c'mon we're late! get to the risers! where is everyone?"* I would like rehearsal to start happy and lively. ~KB

There's always some kind of physical release time. Get yourself ready mentally and physically. There's always vocal warmup time, whether it be craft session (Hey we're having problems with this vowel or these intervals) or good, general vocal technique. Then, personally, I don't like to get right into working unless we're really pressed for time or I've come up with something that I know we need to knock out. On a usual chorus night, it's "let's sing." Let's celebrate being together. It sets the tone for the evening. We're going to have a great time together. We want to be here. Let's sing well and enjoy and shape the sound to improve it if needed. Then shoot into things that have more need from the standpoint of choreography or vocal technique. ~TD

We have a three-hour rehearsal, and we've been trying a new format. I learned about it from Theo Hicks when we did a class together at Harmony University. About 1.5 to 2 hours is actually singing songs (not counting warmups). We are front-loading the education, because my thought is: If I want them to use these skills, I need to share them before we get into singing the songs. We also changed so that we do business at the beginning. That allows me to control how much time it gets (10 minutes!). I've had mixed reactions to all this format, but we're trying it for now. ~JC

It varies, but currently a typical night might include: straw phonation; vocal warmup; cold run-through (since contest is looming), followed by reflections on cold run-through; work specific problem areas of songs, break/business, quartet activity (pickup quartets performing a chunk of contest songs), whole-group performance of whatever the quartets just sang. ~ED

We discontinued the term "Warmups" and refer to that portion of rehearsal as "Vocal Education" or "Enhancing Our Craft". We rarely do this portion of the early rehearsal on risers but rather on the floor in harmony groups, section circles, etc. The members LOVE this and we have a full house at the start of rehearsal rather than watching folks trickling in a tad late. ~DP

DIRECTOR WISDOM: Rehearsal

I have tried to stay focused on including three elements in each rehearsal: education, rehearsal, and performance. Understanding that these three things are different, and that each needs time, help to keep the pace of rehearsal moving, and our adult learners engaged. We start the night with physical movement, and many years ago made the change from "warmups" to "skill building." I believe the first 30 minutes of rehearsal are the most important as that is primarily where I do the bulk of the teaching with regards to vocal skills, musicality, etc. ~RH

We have a physical warmup person. A check-in procedure person, usually myself. The check-in is a focus exercise to get yourself balanced and make an intention for the evening. We have a lot of personal physical triggers we use to give ourselves permission to be here and now. (You can see the check-in procedure on the education class that is on the Sweet Adelines site.) We also practice the whole breath technique where you breathe in through your nose for three counts, hold for twelve counts, and slowly breath out for six counts. This technique immediately increases focus. We call our vocal production time "a weekly vocal lesson," and that's usually two different people working within a theme for that week. My co-Director and I take turns working songs, and we have visual work and the mental training. It's a lot of variety of topics and people. ~BB

Like most, we do something physical at the beginning. But boy, I think whoever does those physical warmups needs to be charismatic! It needs to be so super-fun that people don't want to miss a moment. When I'm off coaching, I've witnessed warmups that were just boring. No wonder people stayed in the parking lot! ~KB

My Music Team takes care of the physical and vocal warmups. They start at 7:24pm. I always joke that rehearsal starts at 7:30 that's an area, but 7:24 is specific with more chance of starting on time. I did vocal warmups for the first 18 years, but I have since found that by telling them what I expect from the warmup and giving them the freedom to design their own works well. I decided it was good to have more, different people in front of the chorus and warmups was a good place to start. I can monitor it and step in if needed. ~MG

I feel there is a difference between vocal warmup and vocal production work. Vocal warmups, in my opinion, are to have fun, to sing, to look at your sisters, and laugh. I like to do a lot of silly rounds and little ditties. I take a TV jingle and turn it into a vocal exercise, you know, silly stuff! People laugh and don't get bored. And frankly, so I don't get bored.

I think some Directors do vocal production too early in the night. <Singers> don't care about matching a vowel until they had a chance to sing a few songs and get happy. I see Directors all the time that start with "We're gonna work on an OOH vowel" and right away they start correcting, "Nope! That's not right!" and that's such a downer. The culture of that rehearsal is a downer right from the start!

I also like to weave in vocal production exercises during the night. Instead of starting with an OOH vowel in warmups, wait and do the exercise later. Then you can immediately say "we're going to apply that in this song" (e.g., the ooh vowel in What'll I Do). The key is application – then the vocal work makes sense to people.
~KB

> *I want rehearsal to begin happy, lively, and on-time.*
> ~Karen Breidert

Rehearsal

How do you keep everyone engaged through the rehearsal?

A big ah-ha for me was the importance of moving them around during the night. It breaks things up, and as they move there is a moment of social time and a chance to check in with their section or their quad.

I've come to appreciate the power of play – like a dance break. Or the power of warming up in one big circle and having section leaders give small groups individual attention, rather than warming up on the risers and me diagnosing the full unit. I didn't think like that in the early days. I've learned the importance of variety and pacing. ~RH

After everyone is warmed up, the meat and vegetables of the evening has a lot to do with the pacing. How long do you stay with one thing before moving on? You can kind of read people's body language and if their eyes are glazing over, it's time to move on to something else. And yet, if you move to too many things in one evening, if your agenda is too busy, then you end up feeling discombobulated at the end of the night. I heard a great saying, "Don't confuse activity with productivity!" Just because you did a lot of stuff doesn't mean you accomplished a whole lot. ~KB

It has definitely changed from being a "one-man show." Nowadays we have a lot of variety in our rehearsals. One person seldom does more than 30 minutes of anything. We have a continuously paced rehearsal, so members' awareness and focus can be on top all the time. We know how the brain works. We know most of the time it's only 10 minutes you have at peak focus, then it starts to wind down.

It's devastating for someone to think they can keep a group's total attention for three hours at a time by themselves! ~BB

I believe in starting on time and ending on time. I want to respect people's time.

It's very important to me who's out in front of the chorus. I start and end the warmups (other people may lead a portion in the middle) because I know the tone I want to end on. Then it depends if we're working on something new. If so, I'll often do that right at the beginning while everyone is fresh. I might spend 30 minutes on a new song. I try to always touch on contest, even for 15 minutes, in every rehearsal. Often the flow depends on what we're working on and how intense we're working.

I try to break up rehearsal. Sometimes reviewing a rep song can revive the energy if it starts to stall. I try to vary from week to week. I try to put choreography review in the middle to change the pace and get people moving. I try to give members a chance to reset - emotionally, physically, and mentally during the night. ~KW

Over the years, we sometimes did breaks and then we didn't. The problem with breaks is: Sometimes people leave in the middle!

The bigger learning for me is that we needed a break in what we were doing, a change of activity. Sometime just moving to a different configuration on the risers – step down put leads on the floor facing the risers, tenors on the left and baritones on the right and basses on the back center of risers, like a big square. Or give them five minutes but be sure to give them a reason to come back, say "we're going to qualify right after the break!" ~PG

We need to end with a bang – just like you begin with a bang. Whether it's a song you always sing or a tag or a chant or a cheer or a poem or a quote or something that makes people leave rehearsal just glad they were there! ~KB

> *We have a continuously paced rehearsal, so members' awareness and focus can be on top all the time.*
> *~ Britt-Heléne Bonnedahl*

Rehearsal

Do you have regular section rehearsals?

DIRECTOR WISDOM: Rehearsal

It's more ad hoc. A section leader can call a session any time they want to. They need to tell me that they need it. "We need time. This is why." Deal. Then that could be on a Wednesday night rehearsal, where they just go into the other room by themselves and three parts stay on the risers, or it could be on another night, or it could be that all four parts need section rehearsal at the same time. Or it could be that we put the chorus in sections and put the section leader down front. Then run something. Stop. Let them talk to their section. Run it again; talk again. So, you have kind of the section rehearsal at the same time as full rehearsal. Now I just happened to believe in all of those things. I firmly trust my section leaders. I just absolutely have to. ~KV

The Section Directors are empowered to call a special rehearsal if need be. We draw from a large geographic area making it difficult for everyone to attend extra meetings. So, we try to get as much done as we can within the regular chorus rehearsals. There are breakouts for sectionals, duet sectionals, small ensembles, etc., built into every rehearsal. The Section Directors are encouraged to send out emails to their section singers in order to encourage and provide input for essential areas of the music to be improved upon. The members trust their input, which is essential. ~DP

Rehearsal

Where do you like to fit announcements and chorus business?

I don't like it at the end because I'd rather end with a big bang. I think in the middle somewhere, reading body language. When people need a little break for their knees, that's a good time to throw in some business.

But wow! Over the years our business meetings have changed so much! If we are not taking advantage of electronic bulletins, Groupanizer, websites, all those things, then we're wasting a lot of precious rehearsal time.

I've been in long enough that I remember when we would sit down, have coffee and cookies and discuss EVERYTHING! They would discuss costumes, they would discuss eyelashes, it was ridiculous. I almost left Sweet Adelines in my first year because of a 40-minute discussion about eyelashes! I was a college kid thinking, "I came here to sing!"

Definitely how we use our rehearsals and trusting our teams has changed. Now we trust our committees, and they give reports electronically and we don't have to take time in rehearsal. If it's time for a new costume, we trust the committee to present to the board/team and the chorus members don't get into "I don't like blue" or "that's too many ruffles." We don't have to ask for a show of hands of who's coming to a singing engagement, because that's all been done online.

So now a lot of the business meeting time can be used for applauding people: "These people have sold the most show tickets, let's bring them down for a round of applause." Spend time on the joy, the face-to-face things, rather than sharing information (we can read that stuff). ~KB

I think we've learned to use technology to great effect in our choruses. I recall when we used to teach music by rote…and announcements! It still amazes me that we would stand up in front of people and call off the announcements. How did people remember anything? We know now that most people are visual learners. Today we have the ability to give it to them weekly in a document they can see and refer to and actually show up on time, and in the right costume…well, most of the time. ~PG

Rehearsal

Do you include music theory in rehearsals?

DIRECTOR WISDOM: Rehearsal

Yes, I think little educational moments are great: Judging categories, what key is this song in and how to tell. Maybe have someone else do brief educational nuggets. As long as they're FUN moments and fun people. I don't want to turn even a <u>moment</u> of the rehearsal over to someone who's boring. ~KB

Not as a specific topic, but Anna (Co-Director) is a music teacher and we have a couple of other music teachers. When we did the bell chords in "Zing Went the Strings of My Heart," they did some specific lessons to help us execute that. But most of the time, not so much. ~BB

Yes. My education coordinators (both on the directing team) drive that. One rehearsal night when I was gone, they put together a whole educational night. There was a class on theory, one on breathing, how to read notes, performance body movement, how to do characterization, a class on choreography, etc. Members got to move around to different 40 minutes classes for in depth education. I have a lot of depth of talent and wonderful, brilliant artists and singers on my team. ~VM

We have two current members who were former Directors of the chorus. I look for ways to make sure they are connected and utilized. One of them is in charge of our "education time" – ten minutes every rehearsal. She might talk about reading music, explain a barbershop seventh, or review the Judging categories. We always buy the leveling category videos and we watch those at retreat and focus on hearing the difference between B and B+ or B+ and A-. ~JC

I try to weave in music theory; we don't have a specific "music theory time." We've tried that, but it doesn't seem to work for us. It seems like a break in the trajectory for us. I don't want people to think "Oh, here comes the blackboard" and people start to disappear. I try to do it in action. I'll point out a section of a song and say, "here's where you can see the barbershop 7th and understand which parts are more important." We were working on an exciting section of a contest song and we needed to make it better. The only way to make it better was to have everyone understand where they were in the chord as the chord changes. I drew a chart and explained, "You're on the same note, but you're going from the 3rd of the chord to the 7th. You have to know that. And this person is on the root of the chord, but it's the highest note. It's OK for them to be singing loudly." The chorus found it very helpful and it made a real difference to the song. I try to weave that stuff in – it's more fun that way. ~MG

I think education is the only successful pyramid scheme I've ever known. Because if I know it and I teach you, now we both know it. We can both teach someone else. We're spreading the word. In a small or medium-sized chorus you can touch everyone very quickly that way. Every single singer. Find out what everybody needs. Can you imagine if you and I are both good at teaching breathing or checking breathing to see if everybody's doing the right thing? You and I each take half the chorus. If we each teach one more, we can break that into fourths. You have four people out there who are working with 30 people, let's say. Well seven or eight people apiece, that's not a big job at all. Especially if all you're doing is just checking: "How are you doing? Do you understand?" Of course, then you find the people who do understand, and now they become teachers. Part of my Music Team meeting is education. There has to be a good portion of every Music Team meeting that is focused on education, about something to make somebody better. I expect the section leaders to do the same thing. I expect people to come in knowing the music and let the section leader help with anything that is challenging. If someone is dragging behind, they meet with an assistant section leader in another room. Let them catch up on their own at their own speed, but you can't hold everyone else back for that. Then each time you bring them together you say what you're going to work on today. I feel that same way about vocal warmups. Why can't we take 10 minutes during the warmups for teaching? Teaching staying in the key; teaching key changes or rhythms, or vowels. Always educating. ~KV

Music Theory might be a part of skill-building. Or I might share a physiological thing like a picture of the tongue or the head or an MRI to help with skill building. Another educational thing that we've done we call Summer School. During the weeks of the summer, there'll be a like a little half hour class before rehearsal. There might be three different tracks of courses. One of those has been very basic music theory. Here are the lines and spaces. Here's a treble clef and bass clef. Another track might be about the judging levels or categories. Usually the topics were driven by things we heard at the round tables. ~RH

> *Education is the only successful pyramid scheme I've ever known.*
> ~Kim Vaughn

Rehearsal

How has your approach to rehearsal changed over the years?

It absolutely changed…because I grew up! When I started directing, I was very new to Sweet Adelines and I was very young. I was getting a degree but not in music (my degree is in foreign language and my masters is in guidance and counseling). I was learning as I went. I was an Assistant Director at Melodeers, and when the Director quit one night, they hired me as interim Director and then I became Director. But it was by the seat of my pants! I was learning as I went, talk about baptism by fire! I definitely learned rehearsal techniques and people skills. I look back to those years and things I would have done differently. But I was young; I was learning. Then with Choral-Aires I was able to try some of these new things I had thought about. I was older and wiser. And Song of the Gulf was like the culmination of the greatest blessing of Sweet Adelines for me – that and "the BUZZ"! ~KB

I think one of the biggest lessons I learned was from the Directors' Workshop in New Orleans when Jim Henry was our faculty. He said the most important thing that you as a Director can learn are these three words: **It's my fault.**

That changed my life. I don't like how they're singing? It's my fault. I don't like how the baritone section leader interacts with somebody? It's my fault. All the way down…I don't like how someone's costume fits? Guess what? That was revolutionary to me. It's completely shifted my approach. I've always been a leader who wants to be involved, but I don't want to micromanage. I do want people to feel comfortable coming to me. With that awareness, it created a new feedback loop. ~RH

I think I had more fun as the years went by. I was very intense at the beginning wanting everything to be perfect, including myself. I got more comfortable with when a good laugh was important.

I learned a lot from Jim Arns. I don't think anybody has the kind of pacing he does. He's a monster. He doesn't waste a second! The first time I watched him come and coach and thought, "Look at how much we're getting done!" He just goes and goes, and people don't interrupt him because they know he's going! So, I changed the pace of our rehearsals because of him. I also learned how to make work fun.

I think success is fun. This may sound trite, but I think it's true: Successes can be so tiny but be so good. You know? Turning a word together for the first time as a chorus, learning how to turn a diphthong as a 50-50 turn when you've never done that. It's really fun, and you have to celebrate those because you're going to want it again later. ~KV

DIRECTOR WISDOM: Rehearsal

I can expect more now, because I've been with them so long. Just the other week they did a sort of off-hand start to a song. I stopped them and said "Hi, I'm Dale Syverson. Who are you?" I didn't have to instruct them on what to fix. They started again and got it right.

That's part of what we do. That's part of the human condition, not just my chorus. We get in this nasty habit of seconds starts. The problem is we don't get a second start on stage! Unless you want to psyche your chorus into thinking the first start is in the warmup room and the second start is on stage. ~DS

Being away from directing a while and coaching other choruses and seeing what works or doesn't work helped me a lot. I use much more variety in rehearsal now. We change activity frequently. Moving around; sitting down to watch a video; different motivational things. It keeps the chorus energized. Just realizing that it is not a lot of fun to stand on the risers for 3 hours without moving around.

The other part is more variety of who's out in front of the chorus. It adds excitement and fun. Back in the old days, we just listened all night long. Maybe you had a blackboard or a flip chart. But NOW you can project. I put the music up there and I show them the pivot chords in a key change. They're SEEING what I want to HEAR! It's a huge advantage for those who don't read music because they can begin to understand. ~BC

In the beginning I had no idea what I was doing. I had been an Assistant Director, but the first time I directed a ballad was at a coaching session when Roger was too sick to stay after lunch. The singers were so patient with me.

I learned everything that I know about barbershop and conducting from Sweet Adelines International. I was always in choir as a kid. I took piano lessons and guitar lessons and I played the clarinet in junior high. But everything I learned about conducting I learned in Director training. I'd go to everything I could. ~BH

The things that haven't changed: I have a specific set of goals and I communicate the rehearsal plan. Early on, I approached it from the mindset of my training. The early days were very... linear. I have this set of skills. I know how to do this. I'm going to get this done. I hated to veer off course. If I was 10 minutes behind – OH MY GOD! I was less flexible than I am today. I didn't understand the importance of giving other people more time in front of the chorus, not just me. That's equally true of visual team as much as Assistant Director and Section Leaders. ~RH

JENNIFER PALUS

As a person, I tend to fly by the seat of my pants. I like that; I like thinking on the fly. At first, I tried to run rehearsal like that. But I've learned to be more focused. I know what we're going to work on. I still try to maintain flexibility because it is needed. But I'm more focused during rehearsal. I'm thinking more ahead of time rather than showing up and seeing what happens. ~JC

I'm the type of person (A green brainer if you know that system) who likes organization and agendas. 30 years ago, I had agendas for every rehearsal. I would isolate a skill – diphthongs for three weeks, then breathing for 4 weeks, dynamic awareness. We would work craft a lot. Those were building years, and that effort grew the chorus and got us to the first championship.

Since then it's been maintenance and adjustment for how our art form has changed. These days, we'll have little workshops on topics, a quick review. The work we did 30 years ago has allowed us, this is an odd way to say this, to stay in a "high level rut."

They are an open chorus and we could ask them to do most anything and they would just do it! ~JA

A while back we needed to revamp things to make more interesting rehearsals. I can get bogged down, or hyper-focused on one song or one part of a song.

There was a chorus member, who had recently retired from teaching, and she had a real strength in pacing. She helped me break things down and focus on 20-minute blocks. This gave me a different structure and I had to be more cognizant of variety. I can still be spontaneous - it's not like I can't vary from the plan. But prior to that I never really had a plan.

That also helps me keep track of when I'm working which songs. I've found working targeted areas of songs and working on more pieces in a night allows you to keep everyone engaged (versus really drilling into two songs).

I also take myself a little less seriously. I really value the connection I have with my members. There are no barriers between us. ~LL

DIRECTOR WISDOM: Rehearsal

The greatest change in my approach to rehearsal was with Jan Carley training. She started coaching Song of Atlanta before we went to international in Hawaii in 2008. We came up from 12th to 6th. That was the pirate package. That was the first time that we were really a cohesive unit because everybody had the same goal. Everybody knew how everybody else felt. We were all supportive. We changed our approach to the "appreciative approach" from Jan's first book (Harmony from the Inside Out). Instead of looking for what's wrong and what to fix, you look for things that are right. You build on things that are right.

You still find yourself, as a Director, helping people to finish phrase endings together, turn diphthongs simultaneously. There are always synchronization issues both vocally and visually to address, but you really come at it from a different approach. To me this was hugely instrumental. I mean, I'm a positive person anyway. I always have been. I always thought that I approached everything from a positive point of view. But this changed how I do everything.

Jan is not a vocal coach, but she has helped our musical product. She mostly did exercises with us that were speaking not singing, to help us realize things about ourselves. But then when we sang, again, she's not coaching the music, but she will ask question about your intention for the song. Like, here's a line in the ballad. What's your intention? How do you want the audience to feel when you sing that? What do you bring to mind to get yourself to that intention? So, it really made people think about what they're doing. Not just getting up there and singing words and notes.

On the very first visit, each one of us got one of those little plastic ducks, like kids play with in the tub. She has a chapter in a book called "Shut the duck up," and the whole concept is that as a performer you have this little inside voice that says to you, "Hey, you didn't sing that high enough." You tell yourself these kinds of things while you're going along singing. The whole concept of the exercise is to shut the duck up, for your inner voice to stop talking to you while you're performing, for you to become totally focused as a performer. Part of the concept is as a human that duck is going to talk to us, but as a performer the question is: how quickly can you recover? If everyone gets back to the full focus more quickly, you're going to have a higher rate of success. That was just one of the exercises she's done with us.

She's just been instrumental in turning around how I think and how I word what I say to the chorus. The Music Team trained with her also. Our section leaders and everyone who stands in front of the singers has had training in how you form a sentence with appreciative words. ~BH

Years ago, we started at 7:30 and went until 10:30. When I moved here from California, I found the culture in Colorado is more about early rising and the news is on earlier (10pm versus 11pm). We moved rehearsal to 7:00 to 10:00. Today we usually do 7:00 to 9:30.

There's usually something early at 6:30 that changes every week (sectionals, choreography, etc.), but we're out of there by 9:30. Some may think you have to work 3 hours because "everybody" works 3 hours. My philosophy is more work smart, work fast, don't waste people's time and get it done.

Rehearsals are extremely fast-paced, and I change my teaching focus every 20 minutes. The time flies for everyone. We've gotten really smart at working efficiently. I found I can get a lot done from 7-9:30. It helps with young mothers who need to get home for babysitters or professionals who have to get up very early in the morning or people who drive long distance. ~VM

I'm not as prepared as I used to be. 20 years ago, I made sure I knew what areas to work on and I wanted to be as efficient as possible. Now, I run as many as 10 rehearsals in the course of a week. I'm actually a lot better at inserting the human element.

There has to be a contour and arc. Sometimes it's 9:40 and you hit that great chord and it's like, "yeah we should go home now, we only have 20 minutes left." Or maybe that happens at 8:15 and I'm like "oh, we really should leave…we're not going to!"

I feel like I read the room much better now as a coach and as a Director. Because of all the experience. The same personality types are on every set of risers! They belong to different people, but it's the same personality types. I learned that as a coach. You pick up on signs, physical countenance, body language. Sometimes I'm wrong, but often I can zero in and think, "Oh! You're that person." Not always a bad thing – could be "you're the joyful person who's so glad to be here." Every chorus has them.

I'm better at knowing when it's time to change to something different or when it's time to dig in and get through something. ~TD

DIRECTOR WISDOM: Rehearsal

On a personal note, I've learned the importance of really being my truest, most authentic self. My second year directing, Sandy Marron asked me (prior to her coaching the chorus), "Does the chorus know you're a gay man." I said no, and she said, "That's too bad." I asked why. She said, "If you don't feel you can share that with them, that might be prohibitive of some energy and some artistry."

It took me probably a year to really reflect on that. I wouldn't say I ever had a "coming out" night. But I did start including language that was obvious. If I was talking about my partner, I would use a "he" pronoun. That subtle shift started to open thing up. Nowadays I make jokes about Carlos and things he said and it's a non-issue. It does indeed impact our level of intimacy with each other in the chorus. I am very authentic and true with the chorus. ~RH

I allow myself to be vulnerable. I am not afraid to make mistakes and I acknowledge them. They are forgiving. ~MG

> *Jim Henry <once> said the most important thing that you as a Director can learn are these three words:*
> ***It's my fault.***
> ~Ryan Heller

JENNIFER PALUS

Rehearsal

Do you have a favorite rehearsal memory?

DIRECTOR WISDOM: Rehearsal

We have an open and friendly atmosphere, and you get to know the members and share in their ups and downs. We try to do "Good News" each week where they raise their hand and say, "my son's home from deployment." Or we have a lot of younger members who might say "I got my driver's license" and an older member may be celebrating a great grandchild. Everyone loves that. We hold each other up in love and concern.

We've had folks with serious illnesses who needed to leave the chorus. For instance, we had a former member who had cancer in her throat, and she had to leave the chorus. She came back to visit with another former member. We learned that her cancer had come back, and she would have to have her larynx removed. She would never be able to sing again. She asked if we could sing "How We Sang Today." I said, absolutely. She climbed up on the risers and we started singing. Everyone surrounded her and sang to her in a huge chorus hug. It was very special to give her all our love. ~LL

Every night something wonderful happens! Last night I was doing riser placement. I had all my leads on the risers and was restructuring for better ring and clarity. What I took away from that was "wow I have amazing singers!" so it was a huge moment. Every week, there's something I could talk about. ~VM

I have a favorite retreat memory. Our contest ballad was "At Last" and we were at a State Park with lots of other people going in and out. This young man came in and said, "I want to propose to my girlfriend. Do you have a song that you could sing?" (I'm getting goosebumps just telling this story!) We had a chair set up, because we have open rehearsal at retreat. They came in to watch, we sang "At Last" and then he got down on one knee. (She said yes.) The whole chorus was in tears. That was our story for contest that year! ~JC

Rehearsal

Do you overtly coach your own chorus?

Do you ever find yourself behaving differently when you coach another chorus versus working in a regular rehearsal with your own? Are you able to put on your "objective coach hat" for your own chorus?

DIRECTOR WISDOM: Rehearsal

That's why you have to bring in coaches of your own. I go coach other choruses, but I need coaches because you don't see the forest for the trees. Even Jim Arns, Lori Lyford and Britt-Heléne bring in coaches. You could be the greatest coach in the world yourself and still need a coach.

With my chorus, I found I had to train myself to look DOWN sometimes because I was so in love with them. I would look across the chorus at these fabulous women and then the song would be over. I'd think, "Oh rats, I'm supposed to say something intelligent right now!" and I hadn't really been listening. I'd say to them, "OK, I'm going to look down to listen." ~KB

I can flip between Director and coach. Sometimes it's easier if another member of my directing team directs, so I can be more in coach mode. Generally, I do both. To make the shift, I take off or put on my glasses. When I'm directing, I don't wear my glasses, but when I'm coaching, I do. ~VM

When I coach, I make a habit of not directing the chorus I'm coaching. I learned that lesson quite a number of years ago with a coach I brought in who asked to direct my chorus when I was really frustrated about my lack of success. I let her do it and the sound of my chorus changed immediately and surprisingly (to me, at least) to just how **her** chorus sang at that time. I thought, "Oh, no" because that wasn't the sound I wanted.

This was a clear example to me that someone's hands can change the sound immediately. So, I really make a concerted effort NOT to direct someone else's chorus. It's more important that I teach that director how to get better results....to get the chorus closer to the chorus in HER head. I may show her (or him) some examples of conducting options, but usually with my back to the chorus. That director has to wear it in her skin. ~DS

> *I really make a concerted effort NOT to direct someone else's chorus.*
> ~Dale Syverson

Rehearsal

What frustrates you in rehearsal; how do you handle it?

DIRECTOR WISDOM: Rehearsal

You have to learn to have a survival technique for those things that frustrate you. I'd say to Directors about the things that frustrate you: start by looking in the mirror. What are you doing to cause them or what could you be doing to fix them? I think every Director's list of frustrations would include attendance and the fact that you get some progress one week and the next week you look up and it's like all different people. I had to learn a survival technique for that, especially in south Florida where people were missing all the time.

My technique was: Take who's there. Turn them into the very best performing group we can be THAT NIGHT. I think we get too future-oriented in Sweet Adelines, and we panic because we have a singing engagement, we've got contest, we've got a show. I used to get frustrated with all the people who were missing. Instead I learned to say, let's just be the best we can be <u>tonight</u>. Forget the guilt! I really tried to run a guilt-free chorus. Which does not mean responsibility free! The people who missed had homework to do. We had the obligation to provide them tutoring or mentoring to get them caught up. But we're not just going to sit and twiddle our thumbs when they're gone. We're going to keep progressing and when they come back, we won't make them feel bad about it, but they've got some expectations to live up to. ~KB

I get very frustrated when people decide they need to have an important, life-changing conversation with me right before or right after rehearsal. I am not in the frame of mind for that. I'm a "fixer" by nature, so I can't just take it in and think about it later. I try to get in and start solving the issue. To alleviate this, I've instituted 'office hours' with my chorus. Every Tuesday evening (the night after rehearsal), I set aside 4 hours where any chorus member can contact me to talk about any issue. This has helped catch some minor issues before they become major ones, and it gives members a chance to have these conversations when I can give them my full attention. This has really worked well for us.

It also frustrates me when I'm in the zone teaching music and I feel like we're all together and someone raises their hand with a non sequitur, like "Where are we staying for retreat?" ~JC

I finally came to terms with the fact that I would never, ever have all of my chorus together at one time except on contest stage. Some are working backstage, some are emceeing, some will miss this last thing, something will happen… I never ever saw all of them until the pitch blew for the contest. You just have to get over that. But that's not easy to get over. You would like just once to hear everyone at the same time - but you know it's not going to happen. Not going to happen. Just when you think you've got it together, somebody's off doing something else! ~KV

The biggest thing is when people allow negative thoughts to come in and say, "I can't do this" or "this is a difficult piece of music." Well if you've decided you can't do something, you won't. If they are negative on the risers, they become like a disease and that's the most frustrating. I try to approach them individually and help them learn to reframe from "I can't" to "I can," and what is it you need to get to the next level? I ask, how can I help you as a Director or the music leadership help you to be successful? ~VM

Some nights are just really chatty. I don't know why that happens, but it does. It's frustrating. Also, since I've started getting Botox injections in my vocal cords my chorus knows in advance when I'm going to have laryngitis. On those nights, I expect more respect. I expect them to be quieter since they know in advance, I won't have much voice. If one of those nights it's chatty, I get my feelings hurt. It feels disrespectful. I know they don't mean it; it's just a chatty night. But those nights, I'm injured, and I can't do anything about it. I still have to do my job, and I feel like I can't do it. And some nights we just have low energy. Sometimes it's difficult to get things going because people are just tired. ~BH

My frustrations are the normal ones. I've told them what to do and they're still not doing it. The thing that works best for me and them is to think of several different ways of saying the same things. I may be frustrated in my HEAD, but outwardly I'm smiling and saying, "let's re-process what we did last week." I've learned to tap dance in my head when I'm frustrated, but outside I show that I realize everyone is human. Years and years ago, I was in a class in Tulsa about adult learners with Sally Eggleston. She talked about a baby learning to walk. "What happens the very first time the baby takes a step and they fall down? You don't say, 'You stupid baby! I've been telling you for months how to do this!' No, we clap and praise them. Well, adults are taking their first steps in every rehearsal." That really stuck with me, and I want to show them I understand. I say, "Let's review what we talked about, and when this becomes more consistent, we're going to be at the level we want to be." ~BC

Talking. I'm not a naggy person, so when that would happen, I would stand still and wait. Let me say, I respect excitement about what we're doing. I love when the chorus gets excited and they chatter. Give me that anytime and then we'll come back together. I don't want to stifle that. But there's the schedule and we have to kind of stay with it. ~PG

DIRECTOR WISDOM: Rehearsal

That the chorus that is there this week doesn't sing as well as the chorus that was there last week! It doesn't happen often, but you think "where did you go?" Maybe it's weather related – that full moon thing?

The chattiness makes me crazy. There are some nights that are chattier than others. I've learned it has to do with how *I'm* pacing things. If there's an opportunity for white space, there's chattiness. It is always good chattiness – talking about music, celebrating a success. But it can get out of hand.

I have to look at myself or whoever is out front and think about the opportunities provided for the disruptions. By the same token, I don't want it so disciplined that they aren't having a good time! Sometimes, when coaching other groups (and maybe they were told to be on their best behavior) I've noticed such incredible riser discipline…as if they are afraid to talk. It's an uncomfortable quiet. I like to see them celebrating things we've done well ("Hug a bass!"), and we need those little micro-breaks. Management of the excitement without stifling it is key and not always easy to do. ~DP

Attendance. I know things come up in people's lives – including my own. But as a Director I am responsible for making sure we are achieving our vision at every meeting, that our goals are going to be met. When I'm given too many variables, I'm unable to provide the most successful opportunities that the group demands. When you have a whole bunch of people, some think "One person doesn't matter." But it matters to the spirit. When there's a hole there, people feel it.

And whether it's voiced or unvoiced, it sends out the message: you have to be accountable if you're a leader but not as accountable on the risers. If I need to go away for coaching, I have to make sure the show goes on. I do a whole bunch of work behind the scenes to be sure I'm not missed …and I still get the message "you're missed; when are you coming back?"

I've had some chorus members say, "You're not going to be here, and attendance looks low, let's just cancel the rehearsal." So how about if every week one person couldn't be there, should we cancel the rehearsal because we can't go on without you? What if everyone on the risers felt the success on the chorus was on their shoulders too? What if we all felt that way? This may be why I feel that fostering autonomy is so important to a strong culture. ~MF

I have found if I am in a not-great mood, even if I try to hide it, they will sense it. I'm grateful for my two-hour drive because I can mentally prepare and adjust my mood. If I had a ten-minute drive to rehearsal, I'd have to find some Zen time to get myself prepared. I've noticed with my chorus and in my classrooms at school there are other things that affect everyone: time change, barometric pressure, etc. Those things really do make a difference. Sometimes I think a rehearsal was not great, but then people come up and say, "that was an awesome rehearsal!" Usually that's when I think I've been too hard on them and I worked them too hard…and they are like "This is great!" So that's a lesson for me! ~JC

My frustrations are probably the same as every Director: Attendance and talking. Attendance really comes down to: Provide them a reason to be there, period. Make sure the reason they are not there is not that they just didn't want to be there. I want them not to want to miss anything! It's our job to help them get the most out of their dues dollars, their attraction to the music, their connection with others. It's on my mind so much. I have members who spend a lot of time and money on the road to sing with us. As leaders, we need to be sure their reason for being there is fulfilled (and mine too!). When it comes to talking…our chorus goes through phases with the talking, burst of talking then hard work. Sometimes it takes a while for every person to re-focus.

Years ago (and this was a carryover from before I was Director) they used a bell. A member had the bell and she would ring it if SHE thought the talking was excessive. Like a friendly Sergeant at Arms. We got rid of that. I used to be a high school teacher. One of the most effective methods is just to stop and wait, but not with any disdain or annoyance. Let them have the interaction, most of which is about the music and making the product better. Sometimes I get really detailed and they come right with me – so I understand when they need to have that burst of talking sometimes. I will say sometimes when I'm out coaching, I get frustrated when I work with a chorus that has the skills to do something, but they don't actively engage in the process. They're not focusing themselves. ~JA

Hearing wrong notes that are having trouble being fixed. I know everyone in the chorus is able. So, if I hear that, I know someone is singing without proper preparation and attention. That can annoy me a little bit. I try not to be frustrated at all, because they can sense my frustration. My frustration does not look good or feel good and doesn't help the rehearsal be a joyful, positive thing. Rather than be frustrated, I try to find some humor in whatever I would be frustrated about. I make a joke about it. They get the message, but they know they've been busted. I use humor where ordinarily I would be frustrated. I think I showed way too much frustration early in my directing career. I learned better ways to deal with it over time. The members want to make me happy; they want to see me happy. So as much as possible, I try to be happy. Everything goes so much better when people are smiling and laughing. ~MG

At times it can be a little bit of everything. If I'm honest with myself, the question is sometimes: What doesn't frustrate me? When that happens, my natural instinct is to say, "you're so much better than that." It confuses me when people are thinking so much that they forget to enjoy along the way. People say, "I'm just processing" and I want to say "well, process with a happier face because you make me feel bad about trying to help you."

There's no such thing as constructive criticism. That's a myth. Especially the idea of constructive criticism about their voice – their voice is their identity. It's what they have. It's who and what they are. Constructive criticism still involves "criticism." No matter how wonderfully you wrap it, there's the personal element. That's a frustrating thing. I don't know a week that goes by I don't say "This is not a judgment of who you are. You're beautiful people. But this is what I'm hearing."

I could be wrong, but I feel like as a male in a female environment I have to at least acknowledge that reality. And it's not really male-to-female, it's the same thing with the men. They embody the response in a different way, but you're still speaking to their insecurities. That's probably the most frustrating thing as a Director of a vocal ensemble: the fact that I can't say "Hey that's flat. Fix it." I'll say that every now and then for a reason. If you hear me say that it's because I've gone through the proper spectrum of approach to no result or I'm tired of the fact they've decided to not achieve. If I'm that coarse, it's fairly calculated. I don't want to crush anyone's spirit!

So much about directing is not about music. It's about managing people's expectations. It's about fighting for their security along the way, so that I can bring the best out of them. Usually my frustration about that is at MYSELF – not being in the right mindset to take those things on with great responsibility and great respect and the heart it deserves. ~ TD

I think if you analyze the rehearsals that are NOT so magical you can learn a lot. Sometimes it wasn't in your control at all. Maybe the AC broke, the riser setup guy was late, a member is very ill, or it's just a full moon. Who knows, sometimes it's nothing you could do anything about. But when I had those rehearsals, I would go home and say, let me analyze this. At what point did it turn south? Did I arrive in a bad attitude? Was my plan not right in some way? Again, looking in the mirror first. Did I say something snarky early in the rehearsal that turned everybody off? Did I stay too long in one song? I really think there's a lot to learn from analyzing those nights. As well as analyzing the magical ones. Ask: what made this magic tonight? Because I want to replicate this! ~KB

When I expect the chorus to have a higher level of retention than they do. That's a hot button and it goes to a deeper level, which is trusting that each individual musician is doing her best and actually rehearsing outside of rehearsal night and bringing her A game to the risers. But who knows what happened that afternoon or what's distracting them! Or maybe they spent two hours working on it, but, as someone recently said to me, "It's different with the chorus." So, I continually remind myself of that.

The other hot button for me is attendance. I know it might be illness…and life happens! Family should come first. But when you're an Olympian training with your team, you prioritize the team. You have to build in a support system for the reinforcement of that. If you have people around you who are not supporting you, they may need to go.

Earlier on, I would get frustrated that it took the chorus a while to learn music and get off the paper. I'd give them 2 weeks to learn something. We'd come back and maybe half of them would still need the music. Lori Lyford said "why are you doing that? Let them hold the music longer and learn it at a higher level." And of course, she was right. The other thing I've learned is it depends how much they love the music. If they love the song, they learn it much quicker. ~RH

> *When there's a hole <on the risers>*
> *people feel it.*
> ~Mo Field

Expectations & Requirements

How do you set expectations for your singers? What kind of requirement or qualification do you use for songs, choreography, PVI, etc.? Have these expectations changed over the years?

How do you song qualify?

JENNIFER PALUS

Song qualifying: I hate it. But I also believe in it. I would love to tell you that we qualified on every song, but we just didn't have the time, especially with the snowbird chorus. When I started directing Melodeers nobody was doing SQ. So that was a matter of weaning them in gently, so they didn't get scared by the process. Now I think almost every chorus does some version whether singing for section leaders, or the Scottsdale technique, which maybe means you can get more songs done and the section leaders don't go home with a bag full of recordings to listen to. Electronic recordings have made this easier too.

I do believe in accountability. And what an ideal world it would be if you could just know that people wouldn't be on the risers if they didn't know the song perfectly. But that's utopia. I believe in having people prove they've mastered a song. ~KB

We qualify on every new song. Many years ago, we started this thing called "Gold Medal Taping" (now it's "Recording"). It was an idea we borrowed from Joe Connelly back when he was directing Toast of Tampa. We set a date for qualification, and there's a first date that you're allowed to record. People who qualify on the first try are recognized in front of the chorus. We call them down front, and they get a little piece of candy and applause. They know weeks in advance when that first night will be. Prior to that they can record on the risers and take it home to critique themselves, so they know how they're doing.

We change the name based on our package. During the pirate years it was "Gold Doubloon Recording" and they would get a chocolate doubloon. During the fairy years they got a Pixie Stix candy.

We have one song that was really good, and it was hilarious. When they started calling out the names there were very few people left on the risers. It was epic! It was obvious that people loved that song. Usually about 30-40% of the people pass that first night. ~BH

I put everything in writing. We have a document for song passing that says very specifically what is required. Song passing has been a challenging topic for us. We've lost people because of song passing. One of the goals we decided, as a chorus, was to pass all songs and at the same level. For contest songs, we record on the risers. For rep songs, the Assistant Directors will get ensembles singing before rehearsal and they can pass the song live (or record if desired). They can pass with a quartet outside of rehearsal, but they must have a live song qualifier. We don't yet have a choreography qualification process, but it's in the works. ~JC

DIRECTOR WISDOM: Expectations & Requirements

For songs for an upcoming contest or our annual show, we have mentors and mentees and a do-it-yourself program.
We call it DIY.

They record themselves and listen to it themselves.
Then they try to self-correct.
Then we ask them to send it to their mentor with their comments.
The mentor will listen and comment on the commentary (agree, add other ideas).

We came upon this idea because we didn't want to do the cut-throat qualification where you make it, or you don't. We wanted it to be based on improvement. If everyone improves the chorus goes up. Very rarely we come across someone who is just not able to improve, but that is usually weeded out during the audition process. If that type of singer makes it into the chorus, we work with them and support them...and if it just isn't working, we make them understand that they are the one who will pull the plug. It's their choice. We do it in the nicest way we can. We want everyone to have dignity.

For most of our members though, the process works, and the focus is improvement. If someone is just not where they need to be, <u>they</u> would decide not to come with us to contest, for example. In 15 years or more, we've never told one person they can't come. If someone says, "I really want to go but I'm having trouble" and we say, "We're pulling for you; here's what you have to do." If ultimately, they can't do it, they're going to understand, and they will take themselves out. ~MG

We qualify on every song. We've tried different ways, but we have found that the most logical way for us to record is the reality of where they stand on the risers. They are going to be impacted by those singers <that stand near them>. So, we want to know the reality. It's not perfect, but I don't think any of those situations are perfect.

We did 1:1 for a long time. It seemed to be a good idea in the beginning. But then we found there were singers who could sing by themselves but couldn't sing with other people.

Over the past two years, I've given the Section Trainers more leeway. They make the decisions on the qualifying process. They also make decisions on if a certain singer needs 1:1 or a different method. I expect it to be done and done to our standard, but the methods they use are at their discretion. ~DS

We qualify only for contest songs. We refer to pass as "OOO," all notes, all words, all breaths. We used to only do pass/fail for the non-contest songs in a performance package, but with the new rules for the final round (where the package itself is 100 points and not just 10) we add song qualification on all performance package songs.

We never do song qualification on rep songs. Not now, not ever. We really dig in on qualifying contest – not as a way to keep people off the risers, but to ensure everyone can be on the risers. I like to lighten the load when it comes to general rep. Every now and then a section leader might have her section record and submit if they hear issues on the risers. But there's not a formal process. ~JA

We tried the Star Qualification (singing for evaluation live down front) and found it to be effective but time consuming. And some of the listeners seem to need more time, they want to go back and listen again or work with someone. We offer options. You can record at home with a part-missing learning track (non-contest). You can find three other people and make an appointment with your listener to sing in a quartet. We're changing things up regarding "qualifications" this year and I'm looking forward to the end result. Less "recording device," more small ensemble opportunities; more "coaching" and "instant feedback" being offered by Section Directors, etc…The chorus is excited about this because we are approaching things much more from a "we trust you" vs. "finding errors." ~DP

We do a qualification program on all our contest music. Sometimes we qualify on our general rep, but generally not. I have high expectations and they have high expectations. We've done strategic planning to really focus our efforts and make sure we're on the same page. I have expectations of them and of myself. They have expectations of each other. It's a team process. Currently (but we're in the process of revamping this), for qualifications they must bring their music with personalized breaths marked and someone listens to be sure they have and are following their own plan and are 100% on words and notes. We do a live qualification – that's more immediate feedback. We are in the process of returning to some form of recording that includes a self-evaluation in addition to a check from a musical leader. We also do selfie videos on the risers. Singers record themselves performing and singing and then evaluate their facial expressions. They put the camera to the side so it's not distracting or blocking them from seeing me. We've done this for a couple years and find it more effective than videoing the chorus. They do self-analysis and exchange videos with partners. ~VM

DIRECTOR WISDOM: Expectations & Requirements

We went through different models to see what worked for us. As we grew in ability, what we needed changed. In the beginning, when they needed a lot of education to get to a sense of unity, I had a recording excellence review. Everyone recorded, and it was compared to specific criteria against which they were mentored and coached. This was also an opportunity to train the Music Team staff on how to be analytical and give appropriate feedback. I would coach them as they were coaching other people using a form that covered 101 stuff (notes, words, macro stuff). This approach was more about craft education than qualifying.

As the craft education increased, the need for qualifying decreased. Then I shifted to a model of peer review. I used the quick descriptors from the Judging Categories, and we did a lot of analytical viewing as a chorus. We watched performances and used the descriptors to describe what we saw, what we heard. For peer review, you exchange recordings with the person on the riser beside you, regardless of part. And highlight the music as to what level the person was singing measure by measure. The person getting the feedback can say "OK I need to polish up this area." We identified tools to help each singer sing consistently at the same level within the song. Then we can work on consistency between the singers in a section and across the chorus. I want it to be consistent, because then we can move as a block. I can refocus everyone as a block where we need to go. If we had someone leaning or falling behind, the Section Director and I could have a conversation, "What's your plan? Where are you having a barrier?" The musical product not being in place is not the problem, it's the symptom. ~MF

We have visual and vocal qualification. We song qualify all songs (contest and rep). We allow people to qualify with the learning media. That's to see if they know the piece, words, notes, breath plan. Then visual there's a similar thing "do you know what you're doing" visually. A few times we've gone up a level to one-on-ones or group things.

Last year in July/August we did a new row experiment for our contest uptune. The pass/fail was if you participated, so it wasn't qualification per se. So, for example, Row 4 is on the floor, singing the song and performing full out. Out front they had visual people watching and audio people listening. They got real time feedback. Row 1 and 2 were up on row 4 and 5 singing along (so they were still in an ensemble, since so many people are not comfortable singing alone or in a very small group).

We did 6 runs of the song (one for each row on the floor, then everyone in normal spot), 4 weeks in a row. They got 24 reps. The last run of each night was so wonderful; everyone was so empowered. It worked well. I think we maybe should have pushed that a little closer to contest in the calendar. I've never been a huge fan of full run-throughs (there's always so much to work) so this was a departure for me as well, to have so many straight runs. ~TD

We are very outspoken about the expectations for qualification since we're aiming for A+. But we are never excluding people. We are helping people. If they don't fulfill the requirement, we offer them help instead of saying "you can't be with us." So far, we have never excluded anyone from performing with us. We are very clear in what we expect. If they feel "I am not able to fulfill the requirement" they make the decision themselves. For song qualification, we have a "middle management" group that listens to the song files and provides feedback. The visual team video tapes and we analyze ourselves and send to a visual person who gives advice on visual. It's an ongoing thing. We have tried different methods all the time to build for success instead of excluding. We try to support instead of criticizing.

Recently we were very short of time and section leaders were very burdened (no time to review). We tried something new. We took two people in the same part and had them evaluate each other. We chose the pairings; they couldn't pick themselves. It has been very successful because the chorus members are so fond of it. They sharpen their own listening skills and their way of giving feedback in a positive way. We use this in combination with other methods. For instance, three weeks into a new ballad we would do this "partnership checkout" just to be aware so we don't have members learning wrong words and notes. Then later there would be a more formal qualification method.

There was a period of several years when we did not qualify songs. Qualifying caused such a trauma and members felt "oh I'm so awful!" We though, this is not fruitful! The section leaders were over-burdened, and the members felt bad, it was a downward spiral. We worked on ways to build self-confidence and reduce the negative aspects. We worked on strengthening each singer using a "voice in focus" program. We have 14 small groups across the chorus, and we will do rehearsal where they sing in these small groups with a musical leader. They get used to singing in a small group and dare to make their voice heard, and they get advice for vocal development. If a singer fails in that environment, we give very specific feedback on what they need to work on. We make it clear that what they are doing now is not fulfilling the quality frame we have. For example, right now I have a couple members who are not as accurate as we want. I will give them voice lessons and work with them about what we expect and what they can develop. I try to be as positive as possible, and clear at the same time. ~BB

We qualify all songs. We have several options and the singers can choose the one they like best. They can do 1:1, singing it to their section leader in groups of 5 singers of the same part. Sometimes we do pods of quartets. They can record on the risers. They can do a small group. We even allow members to record at home. We also have someone stand in front of them on the risers. Some people are terrible at taking a written test, but they could thrive in an oral exam. So, we offer different options. ~BC

DIRECTOR WISDOM: Expectations & Requirements

There's a lot of teaching and training at a San Diego chorus rehearsal. Yes, there are always expectations and that doesn't change. The method we use may change and has changed over the years but never the goal. We want to always give the world our best. That's the goal of every performance no matter where. ~KV

For song qualifying, it's 100% correct words and notes for repertoire songs. For contest songs, we also add effective execution of a personal breath plan. For visual plan, we use video and live evaluation. We expect members to execute the plan, but with their own personal physical expression and characterization.

Our requirements have evolved over the years. We do our best to help singers understand that the expectations are NOT in place to keep people off the risers. They're there to help us all do the same thing at the same time - or attempt to.

I've been talking to the chorus about the difference between rehearsal errors and performance errors. Rehearsal errors that are not corrected BECOME part of the performance. Taking the time to identify and correct them is valuable. Performance errors will happen. In a performance the key is to not be distracted by passing errors, but to focus on the audience and the message

I saw a great t-shirt "You don't have to be perfect to be awesome" and that resonated with me. It's not about being perfect. It's about being a performer with authenticity.

As far as how our requirements have changed over the years. . .When I first joined the chorus in 1979, I can't remember that there were any qualifying elements. Not long after, we started qualifying with cassette recordings. Now we use a combination of digital recording and live song qualifying, adopted from the Scottsdale method. We like live qualification for ballads, but our Music Team prefers digital for uptunes or songs with a lot of chromatic passages so that you can hear the notes more clearly and more than once if needed. Both have benefits. Live qualification gives immediate feedback and sometimes you can knock out the whole chorus in one night. On the other hand, digital allows the song qualifier to go a little deeper and give positive and encouraging coaching in her written evaluation. ~KW

We qualified all songs – notes, words, rhythms, and breaths. If you do everything at the same level you've always got the same chorus. The Section Leaders set the requirements. Some wanted their section to individually qualify standing next to their qualifier in rehearsal for instant feedback. Some wanted digital recordings. ~PG

We want the membership to feel as in charge as the leadership (or as they perceive the leadership to be). We are "singer driven" – we can't do anything beyond what they bring to the risers. At our Round Table discussions last time, members told us they wanted an on-going evaluation process without the borders of what had been our qualifying process. The leadership team said "OK, but we still need some parameters." So, for regional, 6-8 weeks out, we want everyone to have recorded the two songs and gotten feedback, but not been evaluated. We're finding that's been mostly successful. Some people didn't submit until the very end and we had to remind them "there is no qualifying, but it is a requirement to do it." We're learning as we go. It feels a little looser and it makes me nervous as the Director. I'm hoping the handful of singers aren't thinking "if there is no requirement, why bother." And I'm hoping the 95% of the chorus who gets it will exert peer pressure. It's an educational tool and we want to learn more about our performance to have a better performance. This is a risky undertaking, but we're finding it creates a sense of freedom in rehearsal. When we get ready to do a round for recording, there's not that tension you get with qualifying recordings. The freedom and release to put more energy and message into the story is helping with internal dynamics and colors and textures (versus I can't breathing in this no breath zone). There may be some inaccurate intervals, and someone may breathe in a no breath zone, but the performance has more risk and more abandon. Exactly what we need right now. The qualification was creating a rigid box that wasn't allow us to catapult up where we want to go.

As part of our rehearsals we do something called "unity circles." This can be one section or multiple circles. I would take all the baritones and they circle up. The section leader stands in the middle. Every part is singing, but the section leader can give real time feedback to the section or individual singers. This is also a great technique to break up the rehearsal. We use it on new songs we're learning and songs where we are polishing the interp.

Another exercise we like (from Erin Howden) is break into small groups, e.g., 10 groups of 10 for us. They choose a leader and start the music. The leader moves them around the room in a free, physical fashion. They don't know what type of song. In fact, Erin suggested a 3-minute mash-up of 30 second clips of all different styles. In that 3 minutes, everyone in the group has to have a turn at being the leader. They learn it's not always easy being out front. The group learns to be quick on their toes to follow. Everyone sees that we all have different styles in how we respond to music and how we move and that they are ALL right! There's no wrong way, except to stand still. Then we go back up on the risers and they are performing with more abandon and not worrying if my hand is here or here.

It's so interesting, as one coach said to me: The things that get you into the Top 10 will keep you out of the Top 5. ~RH

DIRECTOR WISDOM: Expectations & Requirements

When we first started "Star Quartets" for qualifying, the idea was only four people would be singing for four listeners. We divided up the chorus, with equal numbers in four different rooms. I'm fortunate enough to have at least four qualified listeners on each part, to make that work. But most people didn't sign up to be in a quartet; they wanted to be in a chorus! And when you are thrown into a quartet, if one person doesn't know their part, it can mess you up on your part. Jana said in her room, "everyone sing." That made it work better. The listeners can still hear their specific person, but we're singing as an ensemble. That creates more of the atmosphere that is authentically us. We are a chorus. We're not a chorus of quartets.

For me qualification is about, "Did you learn the song?" There might be a little word bobble, but I want to know you know the song. Some people ask "Well, how many mistakes are there? I mean 3 mistakes per person times 120 people...yadda yadda." I just want to know if you learned the song. Because, let's be honest, you can spend weeks and weeks trying to get people to record on the risers to pass a song, but most people still wait until the end. And with a tape, they don't get real-time feedback. I love that we give face-to-face feedback, they take their music with the marks their listener made and go back to sing additional reps with the group.

Some people are very concerned about the wrong notes, but if they pop up, I WILL hear them (and fix them). To me the bigger question is: Do you feel singers can deliver free and expressive singing into a little box six inches in front of your face? I doubt it. People get so freaked out about mistakes. I say, learn the song, let's check that you learned it, and we'll get to musicality much faster. Finally, even if you get to 100% words and notes with taping, there's no guarantee that it will stay that way!

We do everything live; we don't tape at all. I would rather have freedom in the sound. But each chorus has to do what's right for them. Try something new, modify it to work for you. ~LL

> *As a coach once said to me:*
> *The things that get you into the Top 10*
> *will keep you out of the Top 5.*
> ~Ryan Heller

Expectations & Requirements

What's your philosophy on attendance?
How often is enough to be a contributing member? Can someone be successful even if her schedule precludes weekly rehearsal?

DIRECTOR WISDOM: Expectations & Requirements

No attendance policy. Come when you can. It's my job to create compellingly attractive rehearsals. ~ED

We have an attendance guideline for prospective members. They are expected to visit a minimum of six weeks regardless of singing skill. Our chorus votes on incoming members, thus six weeks provides a snapshot into who they are, what their attendance pattern is like, do they arrive on time, etc. It's rare, but we have had a few singers who have passed the audition but have not been recommended by the Management Team because of a not-so-successful behavioral past with the chorus, etc. ~DP

We don't have an attendance requirement, but we do hold all members accountable for everything that happened when they're absent. We Vimeo all rehearsals and anyone who misses is required to watch before the next rehearsal. We've also started using Facebook Live so those who can't be on the risers can experience the rehearsal in real time. The chorus votes on how many rehearsals someone can miss in the last 12-15 weeks before a contest and still compete. ~VM

There's no question that a person can be successful and not attend every rehearsal. Yes. That can happen…however, rehearsing a consistently attending "ensemble" is important.

Of course, life happens and not every member can be at every rehearsal. We have "snowbirds" who evacuate Buffalo from late October until mid-May. Amazingly, these women are some of the most prepared singers in the chorus! They follow the live stream of our rehearsals on Facebook Live and they learn their music while they're away. They don't take for granted that they can postpone their commitment. We DO miss them, however, because they are not there in their spot in the risers – sharing their voices and energy with the rest of us.

Personally, I have always felt that regular attendance is critical to the success of any chorus. The more who are there regularly, the better the product. Most importantly, if there is trust in "why" people are missing and trust that they are doing their best to be a part of the team, then attendance expectations are understood and can be quite flexible. Chorus culture is key here. - DP

Expectations & Requirements

Do you incorporate PVIs?

(Personal or Private Vocal Instruction, a.k.a. one-on-one voice lessons)

DIRECTOR WISDOM: Expectations & Requirements

PVIs are important and there are folks within the chorus who can handle assisting others with many elements of good singing. I've also made it a point to offer them to each member of our 90-member chorus. I find this invaluable because it's a chance to touch base with each of them in an individual and personal way.

I don't believe in 20-minute PVIs as a result...so I will take 45-60 minutes with each singer. Admittedly, I've not done this during the past 3 years or so as it requires many, many hours in order to get it done. I can't do that very often, of course.

Sectionals are focused on vocal production...not "notes & words" ...so there's a certain amount of vocal attention given to each singer at that time. As I've shared with the chorus, "Our purpose is to rehearse a prepared chorus, not to teach you the music."

As a result, we can focus much more on vocal production vs. the basics that should be covered at home. If a singer is not prepared, she is expected and asked to listen until she knows her stuff. The prepared singers appreciate this very much. ~DP

I don't require PVIs. I started doing PVI's in front of the chorus. We have a signup sheet and two people each week will stand up and do their PVI with me. I've had a huge amount of interest. People on the risers can see and hear what's going on, "Oh she adjusted her posture and it made a big difference." And the people getting the PVI get a burst of positive response. It's only 10-15 minutes for two people. It's a mini PVI; I only give them one thing. ~JC

JENNIFER PALUS

Expectations & Requirements

How do you tackle a new song?

DIRECTOR WISDOM: Expectations & Requirements

We would work three weeks in a row in sections on a new song. One of my pet peeves was section leaders having to teach notes. The first night, everyone was expected to know words and notes, so we could work in sections. The objective for sections was to lift phrase endings and breath together. If it was an uptune, maintaining tempo and lifting the phrase endings.

They would start with just an open vowel (la, ba, va) so that the consonants didn't interfere and the confirmed the note patterns cleanly. Often consonants will take you to a different place, but if you work in the neutral space you can retain the resonation space. And if they are looking at the music, they are seeing the words even if not singing them, they're getting some rep on words too. Mostly what you're paying attention to, as the Section Leader, is tempo, interp, and note patterns. We can use a metronome to help with tempo and slow it down and bring it back up if that's helpful.

The second night is putting words in gradually to the open space. They would start with the la/va/ba – and you notice that doesn't require the jaw to do anything (the lips move but the mouth doesn't). Then they would alternate: sing "ba" for a phrase then words for a phrase. Make sure the words are not getting in the way of the space. Then shift to all words.

By the 3rd night working on the new song we would work as duets so that they got a better understanding of how their part interacted with the other parts. On each of the nights, after section work, we would come together and see how it was progressing with the full chorus. ~PG

For a new song we start with good tracks. I try to avoid teaching songs in the rehearsal. I like to work on them when they are learned. We set a goal to be off paper in so many weeks. It comes together pretty fast. I count on my Music Team to put together the actual deadlines for learning new songs. I'm somewhat oblivious to that. I'm more the Big Picture Guy. ~MG

We try to have learning media and the arrangement come out at the same time. People are expected to have worked on it before the first night at chorus. Sometimes we work with a keyboard, so people can hear the chorus. Sometimes we work in four sections, with a keyboard in every sectional. It usually takes 4-6 weeks to get a new song learned. A really simple song would be faster, and a more complex song could take longer. ~BH

I would hand out a ballad and say, for five minutes, go work on these 4 bars as a section. Then they would come back, and I would help the chorus understand that a vowel sound has a feeling attached to it, rather than focusing on the formant. How do we layer the different levels of excellent performance? How do we draw the humanity out of this music? The singers have time to percolate all the technical elements down to one idea or one sensation and repeat that until that sensation is part of their fiber, their story. It's what they put behind the lyric of their own experience that makes the lyric come to life for them. They have the chance to repeat that feeling as a physical experience until you can't separate them anymore. Then, move on to the next 4 bars. They are going to be SO excited about wanting to have the next 4 bars feel the way the first 4 bars felt.

It seems like a slow process at first. Some Directors I work with say "but I want to get through this song tonight." I'm sorry, but you're shooting yourself in the foot. The idea is not to get through things to check it off a list. The idea is to work with the musicians so that they can make higher level decisions and make flexible movement more easily in the future. So, you do four bars, and the next four and the next four. Then repeat those 12 bars and you look for where there's still low hanging fruit to address.

Because ultimately, we are not here to serve technique. Technique is here to serve us. Sometimes in barbershop the tail is wagging the dog on that one. ~MF

This has changed a lot over the years because of where the chorus is and the level of expectations. Many, many years ago we made the decision to no longer teach words and notes in rehearsal. We're going to go ahead and work this, this, and this and not teach words and notes. Then there was a time when we would use cassettes to make our own learning tapes. I'd get together with the Music Team. We'd have four people holding cassettes and if someone made a mistake you had to start over. Then around 2004 we tried digital learning tracks - and that gave the singers more options to not just learn their part but sing against other parts.

I remember we burned CDs for everyone and said "Here are the CDs and the music. In two weeks, we're going to sing this. We will not teach words and notes here." So, two weeks later I said "OK, let's sing through it" and people asked, "aren't we going to work it?" I said "No, we're going to sing it." (I said it confidently, but I was thinking "Lord, I hope this works!") We sang it and as soon as I cut off, before I could say anything, people were like, "WOW! Did you hear that!?" I mean they reveled in themselves! It's wasn't perfect, but it was pretty darn good. That success helped us make the change and keep going. That was a huge milestone for us as a chorus.

Now when we have sectional rehearsals it's the third or fourth week on a new song. It's not about teaching notes. It's higher level issues: matching vowels, section blend, singing with consistent resonance, etc. ~KW

DIRECTOR WISDOM: Expectations & Requirements

12 Steps to Using Music Learning Tracks
(Shared by Diane Porsch, who said she borrowed from Canadian Showtime Chorus)

This is a twelve-step program to assist you in learning music. It is only a suggestion until you learn your own system that is best for you. The success of this program is contingent upon the effective LISTENING skills of the learner – much more than upon the musical background or ability to read music. Any of the twelve steps may be repeated before continuing onto the next step. BUT remember…EACH step is important to the overall successful results of learning ALL the right notes, words & timing of the new song.

DO NOT ELIMINATE ANY OF THE STEPS because they may appear to be insignificant to you.

1. Listen to the music on the master recording while you close your eyes. (This will familiarize you with notes and timing and general flavor of the song.)

2. Watch the notes on your music while you listen to the recording. DO NOT SING YET!

3. Again, watch the notes on your music while you listen to the recording. DO NOT SING YET!

4. Watch the notes on your music while you listen to the recording. DO NOT SING YET!

5. On a separate piece of paper (or on the back of your music) write down all the lyrics to the new song. Now, watch your own paper while you listen to the recording. NO, NOT YET! DON'T SING, PLEASE!

6. Watch the notes again while you listen to the recording. Remember, NO SINGING!!

7. Watch the words on your music while you listen to the recording. Be careful, not a sound!

8. Try to write down all the words again on a separate piece of paper without looking at your printed music. If you have trouble, listen to the recording again. Watch the words and then try writing them again without looking. Stay on this step until you have all the right words written without looking back at the printed music. Now proceed to Step 9.

9. Hurray! Finally, you can add your beautiful voice! Now, watch the notes on your music while you HUM along with the recording. HUM…HUM! Singing is next!

10. Watch the words on your music while you SING along with the recording. Can you believe this? You're really going to SING this song for the very first time. However, if you have any difficulty, CIRCLE the spot on your music as you go all the way through. Then, go back and listen (don't sing) to those parts again. Happy singing!

11. Put your own practice recording in a playback device. Now, using your own recording device, SING the new part all the way through without looking at your music. I'll bet you can hardly wait to hear this step!

12. VERY IMPORTANT STEP! YOU'RE ABOUT TO GRADUATE! Watch your music and listen to your OWN recording and see if you are correct. You should be wonderful. But, should you have any doubt, go back and check your part again on the master recording. Concentrate on listening to the parts you circled earlier to be sure you have made those corrections.

CONGRATULATIONS!
With a little bit of luck plus all of your hard work, you are now the proud possessor of one more selection of music made beautiful by your additions of all the correct notes, words and timing!

DIRECTOR WISDOM: Expectations & Requirements

When we introduce a new rep song, the goal is to be off the paper in four weeks. Now that's not four weeks of YOUR attendance! Three weeks with music then the fourth off the paper and we can start playing with it. I might change the tag or drop this chord. Then after it's settled, we start working the visual plan.

More often than not, we do not use tracks for competition material. I don't want my chorus to imitating a learning tape voice for competition. (There's also a large expense for songs we know will likely change quickly.)

When I teach a song, I teach it with a keyboard and it's a human, organic thing. It's how most cultures have learned music over the centuries. For a new contest song, we spent an hour before they even heard the arrangement listening to different artists singing it. Then as we're sitting on the risers in sections, I go to the keyboard and play all four parts, slowly. Then I go part by part. They all have their recording devices out and that becomes the learning track. If someone is not there the night we are learning new songs, the members know to contact a friend to get the tracks. I love that about today's technology!

In a CPR (Choosing Personal Responsibility) way, the turnaround time is nearly immediate if you have to miss a critical night. We don't provide it to the members as a chorus. The members connect to each other.

I think if we were to live stream rehearsal, for example, our attendance would suffer. If we had learning tracks and posted them to the site, the members might choose to miss the rehearsal. I think learning tracks and enabling the electronic world is creating a gap in education. We are missing listening skills and learning how to identify intervals when you see a printed page. What every musician has done for centuries! The human experience matters. And you lose that when you say, "here's a track."

That said, we do make learning tracks AFTER a song is solidified, so that new members can catch up. We don't launch a song with tracks. Of course, if it's rhythmically complex, a learning track can be a real boon to make sure the chorus learns rhythms correctly up front. In that case, we do buy the tracks. One year we did ALL new holiday songs for a show, and we bought tracks for all of them to expedite it. It's a situation-based decision. ~JA

> *We are not here to serve technique.*
> *Technique is here to serve us.*
> ~Mo Field

Authentic Performance

How do you balance the need for technical accuracy with the goal of freedom and artistry?

DIRECTOR WISDOM: Authentic Performance

To me those two things go hand in hand. I try to not say "OK, now we're gonna work technique…and now emotion" because then our brain separates those. Of course, obviously there are times you must fix a chord or balance a chord, and then you want to get that <fix> to be second nature and put the artistry back in.

I saw marvelous example when I watched an Ambassadors of Harmony rehearsal in St. Louis. And Jim Henry (talk about role models and idols!) was working some love song with the guys – very technical (diphthongs, tuning, balance, vowels) but then within moments he fell on his knees in front of the chorus and talked about his love for his own wife and how he would take the moon out of the skies for her, and that's what this song was about. Everyone was enraptured…and I thought "that man just went from technical to heart in an instant." He's such a master.

[Q: Why do you think technique and artistry get separated so often?]
It's our emphasis. We want things to be right. Maybe it's a female thing. This is my theory why women don't woodshed as much as the guys do. Because we want it right. We don't want to miss notes. We don't want to make mistakes. I think a lot of us have focused so long on "if that's chord's not in tune I can't go on!" And there is that in my brain too. I feel like something out of tune should not be allowed on stage. Yeah, the technical part has to be there. When a song has a good foundation and a chorus has a good foundation, then laying the artistry, like Betty Clipman says, is like putting icing on a cake. **But you have to bake the cake first!** You can't put icing on batter. If you just do artistry that's what happens. You think you've got fun nuances and emotion in a song, but the cake hasn't been baked yet. ~KB

That's a hard question. I will tell you that the thing to watch out for the most is how close it is to your contest day or your show date. Remember that the performance part of it must be in full mode long enough for the chorus to feel comfortable with it. So, you can't take the technical all the way to the day. I think what most people do is start with the technical then gradually rotate that into the performance aspect. But I happen to believe that it's a better choice to do technical AND performance on the same day. Technical, performance, technical, performance, technical, performance every day, every rehearsal. So that everybody knows the difference, and that they live the difference. As your event gets closer you don't have to try to layer "performance" in. You just run: performance… performance… performance. By then, everybody knows what that takes to be in performance mode. ~KV

I think some barbershoppers conflate "artistry" with "acting" or "showmanship." So, they might say, "We've been working on vowels for twenty minutes; now let's put our faces on." But that's just more technique.

I think there is tremendous value in continually reminding singers that they are musicians and artists themselves, not just keys on the Director's piano, and that the whole point of art is transformation (of self and audience) through communication.

Barbershoppers care so much about craft that it's easy for technique to become an end in itself, and performances turn into displays of competence rather than acts of self-expression. It's the Director's responsibility to always keep the singers focused on the artistic endgame. ~ED

In the life of a song, especially one for contest, we focus at first on technical aspects of singing and bringing the song off the page. We build a strong foundation, then when we go to cut it free – don't think about the basement, think about the house – the house is standing because the foundation is solid. We can't let it soar until we (and that's every individual singer and the corporate unit) are completely solid.

Now sometimes you're battling a deadline for a show – and this happens to everybody whether you've got gold medals or not – you put out a product that's not completely solid. They get on stage and it's a stifled, stiff product. Compared to other songs that have been fully tweaked. We really do try to NOT think about what we're doing on contest stage, just cut it free. That's what you need to get top scores. You can't appear to be worrying about a diphthong. You get up and really entertain and trust your foundation is there. That's why we spend so much time on creating the foundation in the early process of a song.

In our chorus the transition from technical to artistry is called: **Renee Porzel.** I am so grateful for her. She'll come out and coach me and the chorus; work with me on gestures to be sure the chorus feels the phrase like I do. That's not one of my strengths. Once we're into the freedom and message of a song, I love to play at a high level. But I rely on Renee to help us get over that hill from technique to artistry. ~JA

When I'm correcting, I'm constantly talking about the message of the song. I do it together. When we're learning new music, I will say, "You need to put love in your voices as you express this." I don't get embarrassed talking about emotions, all kinds of emotions. We do "power poses." Our big role model is Wonder Woman. My Showmanship Coordinator (Oh that's something else new I did this time as a Director!) coordinates all the visual stuff. That's in addition to a traditional choreographer. Choreographer is under her. The Showmanship category is so much broader. She does something every week. ~BC

DIRECTOR WISDOM: Authentic Performance

I find that I use kinesthetics a lot in my coaching, and I use visual analogies. Here's an example. Imagine Victoria Falls. Can you see it in your imagination? The sound is going to be just like that, it's going to go out and away from you and arc like Victoria Falls going over the cliff. Women think in pictures, so vividly. If you can give them a visual picture, then they'll all be doing the same thing. You can take something very technical and put it into a picture, and they will relate to it. I found couching Rönninge for so many years, it crosses language barriers. I've learned to trust the voice in my head to think of the visual metaphors, they just come to me.

[Do you use this technique with men's groups?]
I have. But there's usually at least one man who wants to analyze and get more technical explanations for things. I'll explain for a while, but then I ask them to try it, to take it on faith. Then they'll either decide they want to use me again <as a coach> or not. ~PG

It's funny because I've always considered myself a performer. But I realize as a Director, I'm a technician. When I turn around to sing with the chorus, I think about singing. I don't think about technique. It's a hard thing to marry. If you're afraid to make a mistake, you never get the freedom needed for true artistry. I try to give my singers some tools to access the artistry side. We do some acting games that get people out of their comfort zones; help them be silly and free. We use video evaluation to give them feedback on where they are performing with authenticity (or not). Sometimes people thinking they're doing something HUGE but it's really not. Videos can show them where they're on the right path but not to the degree it needs to be done.

Artistry can't and shouldn't be constantly monitored. But it does need to be constantly encouraged and promoted and evaluated and demonstrated.

Showing videos of other performances is another way to help, but I think watching videos of yourself has the most impact. I've heard members say, "I thought I was moving a lot, but now that I see the unit around me, I see I'm not." You can't always tell if you're fitting into the visual when standing on the risers.

MNC has a reputation for doing great character work. Sometimes it's easier for members to feel free inside of a specific character than as themselves. We give them parameters and then let them explore within those to create their character. There are a lot of adults who don't know how to play! So, we help them get started and then they create wonderful things. ~KW

My approach is very different, in that I come more from an artistic place to begin with, and then add technique. When we start a new piece of contest music, I spend probably 30 hours in in-depth analysis: Why is this piece of art appealing to me? What do I perceive for it?

With a new song, we sing the music without the lyrics first, because there is always a musical message that many times leaps out of the music before you introduce the lyrics. Each part sings the music on a different vowel, so that they don't try to match vowels. We're so technically trained in this art form to match vowels, to do balance, blend, and cone.

In my opinion, in our organization we've had a lot of information about technique, but not a lot of information about musicality, artistry. I look at my chorus and they're singing with artistry. I want them to experience the music. When you sing all on the same vowel, then they get into technique. They just naturally go there and want to match their vowels. I want them to feel the musicality and the message in the music first. It sounds like an orchestra. I usually do Leads on AH, Tenors on OOH, and both Bass and Baritone on OH. Sometimes I put Bass on EE, but I like the bass clef parts on the same vowel as a foundation and a more open vowel. I developed this approach because I felt we were too technique driven in the organization and there was a lack of musicality and artistry and freedom.

We were training our singers to sing great sound but not how to sing great music. (Can you tell I'm an Expression judge?) Similarly, my concern with learning tracks is we learn note-to-note and word-to-word. But there are musical thoughts, lyrical thoughts, and emotional thoughts. The learning tracks cause us not to have musicality. I'm blessed that my daughter Becky creates our learning tracks and they are highly musical and reflect my interpretation. Even so, our learning tracks are probably only good for about two weeks <because the song evolves.> ~VM

I'm definitely more technical; I'm working on this personally as well. I make sure that I have coaches who have those skills. I've had a lot of Expression Judges as coaches, and Becki Hine and also Mo Field. The chorus calls Mo "life coach" and they adore her. I've skewed in that direction, because I feel like I can handle the technical and we (the singers and I) need coaching on the other side. I constantly touchstone with coaches saying, "help me get back into that headspace." ~JC

A critical way of doing this is to only let them learn 8 bars of a song at a time. And if I need to teach a technical aspect of a song, I will teach it – but only as it relates to something else. Music is a giant bunch of relationships. Small moves make big things happen. It's a mistake to hyper-focus on specifics, "if you sing this vowel this way, you'll get this outcome." Stop worrying about the outcomes. Break it down. ~MF

DIRECTOR WISDOM: Authentic Performance

I try not to teach them separately. When it comes to working the material, it's always layers, always working to marry everything together. This year I've given up running vocal warmups, and for now, it has worked out really well. I'm able to come in and start the night with singing, work craft within the songs. I think that working craft is extremely important, but I also know that once you have a base level of singing with resonance and understanding how to breathe, etc., anything you can do to put them in context is a good thing.

Sometimes my expectation of where the chorus should be does not match where they really are. I might go into my men's or women's chorus on level 10 of an idea or skill and then realize they don't understand. I have not done my job as I should have. So, then we backtrack, but it's backtracking inside of the song itself.

And it never stops. There's never a time in my teaching that I shy away from saying "you need more soft palate lift there" even if it's right before we go to the stage. It's all wound up together – the vocal technique and the messaging. If you're making a bad sound, it doesn't matter how much luster you put on it. ~TD

Early on in my directing, with my chorus I was Mr. Left Brain. When I went to coach other choruses, they didn't see me as Left Brain at all because I brought the ideas and the artistry and the emotion. Because I was coaching what was already there.

It feels better to the chorus to work right brained; it feels better to work the artistry. All of that stuff just sings so much better. I intentionally try to stay there, while quickly getting in all of the nuts-and-bolts that I can get. This is why this nut or this bolt is important – because of the emotional effect it's going to have. I try to reach through the right brain into the left brain.

There's a balance. When I try to stay too right brain it becomes too ethereal, too foggy. Then they want me to be more specific. The beauty, the art, the freedom of the music – I want to get there and stay there as soon as possible. That's why having a really good learning track is important. In years past I would have a learning track that I thought was "good enough" and then we'd spend all this time trying to learn all the things I wish had been on the learning track. If you don't have all the excellence on the learning track, it's hard to get to the fun of the song. ~MG

I'm not sure I know the answer. I get so much into it, I guess I just inspire them to be emotional. I am a resonance box. I feel energy and electricity.

When someone is standing there and just singing and looking like a "fish face" and not involved, I immediately react to that. I try to inspire the individual and if they don't respond, I talk to them and ask why. I say "I get worried when I see you're not inspired singing this. What can we do to make you more emotional?"

When you require a really high level, you are expecting the singer to do both (technical and expression). When we are working on something really technical and I realize we've lost the emotion in it, I immediately go back to the emotion.

We don't want just a square, perfect, technical diphthong. We want an emotional diphthong. ~BB

Artistry . . . needs to be encouraged and promoted and evaluated and demonstrated.
~Kim Wonders

Authentic Performance

When do you fix a problem and when do you let it go?

If you're in performance mode at rehearsal and you hear something wrong, do you just let it go by or stop and fix it?

Well, both. You have to stay in the performance (even in rehearsal). But you have to go back and pick it up next time. I would let them go all the way through the song as a performance and then say I am going to be technical for a moment. You got to work this.

I'm a big believer in working measures, not phrases. Work the measure; work the problem not the whole thing. Instrumentalists work measures; singers want to work phrases. But you've got to get *this* small thing in your brain. This interval in this measure must be fixed. Then you can move it out to the phrase, and then you can move it into the song.

You need to have a keyboard around because people will tell you they can't start there <at the problem measure>. You give them their three notes on a keyboard - just sing those, that's all I need. You get everybody their notes, and you go over it.

I take the words out first, then layer them back in. You find the issue. It could be rhythm, could be accuracy, could be changing vocal quality. Could be a hundred different things. Could be something going differently in every part.

I've always told section leaders, "If it makes you hesitate, if it's hard for you, it's going to be a problem for the chorus. You might as well plan in and be ready to address it." ~KV

Peggy Gram, who is a regular coach, told us before Hawaii to focus on emotional singing. She said that we were technically so good that adding the emotion is going to make our "product". She was right. That gave us, as leaders, the confidence to ignore those tiny discrepancies. You can always hear small discrepancies. You can get too stuck polishing and polishing and polishing. ~BB

I've really had to learn NOT to try to fix things as I'm directing in a performance. I would hear something going wrong and try to get them to lift or something. All it does is make them look tense and wonder why I look tense! I'm trying to stay more relaxed and enjoy the performance. That makes them relax – and they sing better! ~JC

> *You can get too stuck polishing*
> *and polishing and polishing.*
> *~ Britt-Heléne Bonnedahl*

Authentic Performance

Is it important for all singers to have a shared story about a song?

Yes, I think there is an internal message in the music. Some songs call for us having the same character or thought process, some songs we don't have to be the same, but you need some story weaving through your head, something you can attach to the lyrics. We've done acting games to help singers. We've even had a "character night" where members come dressed as a specific character. ~VM

I find it depends on the chorus and their level. For us, I will never inflict another story on a singer. What we want is the truest form of communication. We say, "Here is what we want to communicate." Our new ballad is a powerful story of joyful love. We have explored the idea that psychologists say there are four main emotions: Joy, sadness, fear, and anger. (You may have seen this in the movie "Inside Out.") The other emotions are under those. If we're singing a love song, it needs joy in it that amplifies the loving energy. That leads to freedom and release. We tell our singers, if you are compelled to write that story, great. If the lyrics work for you, great. If you need to think of something else like an actress to get to the emotion, great. We use a lot of tools to keep a unified energy, but we won't say this is our common story. Our last ballad was "If I Had My Way" which has a positive, joyful message. "It's only you for me." But one woman was having a hard time with it. It came out at our retreat that she had been widowed and she was thinking about that husband. So that elicited a different emotional response. She had to go to another angle and make the love about her son instead of romantic love. Then she could amplify the joy. That was great for the chorus to hear and see how she adjusted. I have been known to say: "I don't care if you're thinking about a lover, a child, a dog, or a piece of apple pie…whatever gets it to the audience!" ~RH

Often, we give the chorus members an open door to think about whatever they wanted, for example, about falling in love. Some might be thinking of children, others a spouse. We didn't care as long as you can sing with a high level of emotional impact. For the song "Some Enchanted Evening" we were very careful to look at the historical background of the song. We have done that the last ten years. We look first at when was this song created and why. We try to find the real background for the song, instead of creating our own. We get inspired by that and share links for the chorus to read and watch. ~BB

I prefer each person has their own story that moves toward the same feeling. When we try to have the same shared story, not everyone can connect. We have so many different backgrounds. We used to joke on a love song that you could sing it to whoever makes you feel that way. Maybe it's your spouse, or your child…or your cat. We have a member that comes up with a dialogue backstory that we share with the chorus sometimes, but it's not a requirement that they use that story. ~JC

DIRECTOR WISDOM: Authentic Performance

I definitely think it does need a story. I don't think it has to be the same story. I think it has to be the same feelings. We can't read each other's minds and I really don't care what your story is. I want to believe that the words you're singing to me are honest. I want to believe that you're communicating this story to me. It doesn't have to be the same story. I want them to share the feelings from phrase to phrase. Is this hopeful? Is it sad? Why is it hopeful or sad? We usually come up with different scenarios, but not a story that has to be exactly the same.

We just changed our upcoming contest ballad to "Yesterday I Heard the Rain". As we gave it out, we talked about the fact that we didn't want it to be a horrible sad picture. We want it to be a joyful picture. Then as we went through and worked on sections of the song, we also talked about "what's supposed to be happening here" emotionally. I usually have an outline and I start the conversation. Then the women do a better job of getting more personal and coming up with scenarios and pictures that help my vision of the song. ~MG

When I coach, I talk about left brain triggers that evoke a right-brain response from your audience. Most of the triggers involve word coloring, how you're saying a certain word. It comes up as emotion, but the singer is coming at it from a left-brain perspective. There's also right-brain in the execution. I talk about word coloring, vocal textures, and storytelling…all wrapped into honesty. You care about what you're singing about.

We have a membership age range of 14 to 85. To give all that span of age the same specific story? I don't know that it will hit the same believable button. Maybe a group with a smaller age range or similar backgrounds could do it. But I've always been leery about that. You have a plan for even more emotional chaos. Put one story in front of 100 people and you will have 100 interpretations of that story.

We try to talk over-arching themes. We try to get a more holistic view. Then we can have moments in a retreat or coaching session and call on specific people to ask "what are you thinking there" because their face is amazing. Do that a few times and maybe their ideas resonate with others and the audience will interpret it as the same story. I think it's great that some choruses write out individual stories. I don't think that's a waste of time by any stretch to go that far in what the story means to you. I just think it's a good idea to have some guidelines to it. Maybe give them a starter kit, like "this is about the hope of love…that you long for." It gives more focus to the end results. ~ TD

We used to have one story. We'd try to assign a set of emotions like, "You're sitting at the restaurant with your new love and the song comes on and you remember your lost love."

What I've found is that we are much better singers than we are actresses, for the most part. I started looking more at verbs than emotions. We're better at doing things than we are at unifying how we portray an emotion.

We would go through, and we do this today at Rich-Tones (and can take two evenings), as small groups across the risers. We also mix up the groups so it's not always the same riser-buds. I break the song into lyrical passages, and we talk about the song being a conversation that you're having. What is it that you're doing? What's the purpose? Are you explaining? Are you begging? Are you convincing? Are you questioning? What is it that you're doing? We have a big white board and we go across the risers and write down every one of the descriptions that they have. We go through all of them, and they've gotten really good at it. Some have their thesauruses on their phones to find exactly the right word. Some words are better mental pictures than others. I leave all the words up there but use a different color to circle the word that I think is the best mental picture.

Then Dale gets up and directs it. The song changes. She finds that when we do this right after we've qualified on it (maybe 75% qualified) then nuances come into the phrasing that weren't there before. It's a part of the natural phrasing of the music. Sometimes it's what she wants and sometimes we need to change the verb we chose. It goes into their natural physical expression and unifies it. It unifies their faces.

I teach a class called "Putting the Emotion into The Song" and it does that... but it does it through the verb. When I first taught the class to the chorus and they said "Great! What are the verbs for this song?" and I said "I don't know. It's not my verbs. It's not Dale's verbs. It's our verbs." I'm just the facilitator to get them there. The first time we did it was on "I'll Be Easy to Find" and the song came to life. It was the first time we got an A+ on that song. You can watch video of how we performed it before and after the verb work. There's such a difference. It's so much more believable. ~PG

> *Maybe give them a starter kit.*
> *~Tony DeRosa*

Authentic Performance

How do you encourage singers to get out of rehearsal mode and perform?

That is so important. When you're in performance mode strange things happen! The uptune gets out of sync and it never has before. Or a voice sticks out and it never has before. Or someone overacts and uses their hands too much and you've never seen that before. You've got to get into performance mode every rehearsal. I like to end every rehearsal with a little mini performance, including emcee work. That's when you can practice things like: where do you look when the emcee is talking? What do bows look like? The little things that make a polished performance, but we tend not to rehearse them too often. You might find future emcees. We were very lucky in south Florida because we had a lot of guests every week. Not necessarily prospective members; they were visitors and Sweet Adelines on vacation. Wasn't uncommon for us to have 30-40 guests every week! What a great performing opportunity. But even if you have no guests, turn it into a mini performance every week ~KB

I try to lead by example (by being vulnerable and expressive in my directing when I am asking them to be vulnerable and expressive). I constantly introduce exercises to inspire looser, more emotionally authentic performance: stand in a circle and perform for each other; find things to "steal" from someone else's performance; comment on what you love about someone else's performance; stand facing a small group as though you are about to perform, notice how your body reacts to the always-stimulating experience of "being seen," then discuss that bodily reaction; stand facing a small group and perform one line from any song you know, notice how your body feels, then discuss; and many other exercises. Most importantly, I try to nurture an atmosphere of play and exploration rather than "correct and incorrect." Coaches like Mo Field, Donya Metzger, Cindy Hansen, and many others are brilliant at helping singers feel safe to open up. ~ED

We use a ton of visual aids. Betty Clipman noticed that I was talking a lot in rehearsal, explaining things. Betty stopped me and asked the chorus, "How many of you know you are visual learners?" About 80% raised their hand. She turned to me and said, "You realize you have no visual aids while you're teaching, and you have a chorus full of visual learners?" So, she gave me some great visual aids. One is a vowel chart. While they're singing, all I have to do is point to one of the vowels and they fix it almost immediately without me having to stop and say something. She also encouraged me to start personally demonstrating what I want to hear. She said, "You can explain it all the time, but if you sing it, they will figure out how to create it" without me having to micromanage 60-some individual voices. We have a screen connected to my iPad. I can project the music and rather than calling out a measure and they try to find it in the music (or find their music!), I can just show them all at the same time. ~JC

DIRECTOR WISDOM: Authentic Performance

We would do a lot of analytics viewing and listening not just of barbershop but of all kinds of performances. We rehearsed in a venue that had a little tiny 100 seat theater with a screen and sound system. Before the 2015 International we spent the entire month of June watching performances and singing for only half an hour. We analyzed performances, made the musicians smarter. When I asked them to do something, they had more food to draw upon. They could draw from the bank and replicate. We quickly moved from imitation to assimilation and then very quickly to innovation. ~MF

Visualization. We close our eyes, imagining we're on the stage in our costume, picture someone in the house who loves you and wants you to do well.

Also focus and energy can help get into performance mode. As Sweet Adelines, we are masters at focus – if our brains are in gear, we're able to go there pretty quickly because we're so well trained. ~BH

We've been doing more improv stuff. My chorus has a hard time being vulnerable on stage and I think that's also a reflection on me. I am not an open book kind of person. We're finding our way and the improv games help. You can't be inhibited and play an improv game. We'll do that at retreat. One game is where you have a line of 20 people and you say the same phrase, but you have to say it a completely different way (it can be accents, emphasis, or even language, just not the same as anyone else). We also do communication improv where you whisper something to a person then they have to act it out for the next person. I like "acting out" games to work with big motions. I'm doing more to be open with them. I share my process "this is what I'm trying to do" on my journey as a Director. ~JC

> *I try to lead by example.*
> *~Elizabeth Davies*

Membership

What are the keys to becoming a great chorus member?

When it comes to coaching a singer, there's a hierarchy that starts with posture and breathing before a note is sung. When you think about coaching someone to be a better member for her chorus, is there a similar hierarchy there? What are the priorities?

DIRECTOR WISDOM: Membership

I'd start with attendance. If you're not there, you can't get any of the education. So, getting them to rehearsal is important. But I think that's MY job not theirs. To have the inspiring rehearsal that people don't want to miss! Then you know if they are missing, they obviously had a good reason. That comes in trusting your members. ~KB

---

1) Attendance
2) Preparation (knowing the music)
3) Attitude (bringing your "best self" to rehearsal)
~ED

What makes for a good member? "Good Members" are singers of all different levels so defining a member based on her singing skill is just wrong. Everyone has something to offer and the more valued a singer feels the more she will contribute…or at least try to contribute.

Commitment and dedication to the ensemble and projects undertaken by the ensemble can only be accomplished if every singer is valued and recognized for her contributions. Recognition doesn't cost money. Let the magic happen! Recognize the members and enjoy the benefits. ~DP

Work ethic, without a doubt. You just can't be in our chorus without being willing to work and become a better singer.

And hand-in-hand, attitude: the more positive, the more plugged in they are, the better they do. I'll take a not-as-good singer who will work hard over a great singer who will procrastinate and not work as hard. Those are the main things; the rest will fall into place. ~JC

> *Getting them to rehearsal is important. But I think that's MY job not theirs.*
> ~Karen Breidert

Membership

What tells you that a new member will stay and thrive?

DIRECTOR WISDOM: Membership

You can see the people who are hooked right away, like I was! You see the passion, and they volunteer to get involved in things. Though sometimes that can be a worry. Sometimes they jump in and get involved in too much and burn themselves out. When we bring new members in, sometimes we overwhelm them and scare them off with the money, commitment, costumes, etc. I think, "Easy does it".

But, yes, you can see those people that are hooked. You see that light bulb go off as if it were a cartoon. ~KB

Some people come through the door and just seem like they fit in. They are at home They are comfortable. They want to be part of us. I coached a chorus for several years at their retreat, and last year they had a brand-new member that I had not met before. On Saturday morning, we had a session asking what everyone had learned Friday and how we could build on it. This new member said, "I wasn't sure I was going to be able to handle it last night; it was just so intense." We'd been working hard, and it was high energy. So, I think that when some people visit my chorus, they find it's too intense for them. It is high energy. We have in-house coaches out front asking for specific things. If you're looking for a laid-back chorale, you're not going to find it with us. So, when people come in and are sitting down and seem lost, you can tell it's not a good fit. But the ones that love it, can't wait to come back and they know their audition song the next week! ~BH

I find that people who are cheerful and positive usually click with our members right away. We have some recent ones who are pretty quiet, but they're excited about being there. There's also one that just beams all the time!

We're also finding, and this is a good thing, that some guests find what we do too rigorous too for them. It's good when they recognize it's not for them. But sometimes guests surprise me. Sometimes the ones who seem more negative stay…and become transformed. Sometimes the really good musicians who are more positive find that barbershop just isn't for them. I just had one who said, "I love the chorus, but I don't love barbershop." So that's not a fit either. ~JC

I think new members stay when there are ongoing opportunities for them to feel challenged, to feel successful, to feel valued, and to feel included. ~ED

Two big indicators are their work ethic and how quickly a new member or guest learns music. (Now that doesn't necessarily mean if they don't learn quickly, they can't be successful!) Another indicator is the questions they ask or the terminology they use. That says to me, "They know what we're about."

I also look at the personality. If people come in and they're real negative and make negative comments, then I think they may not fit here in our chorus. It's a fine line, I guess, because our chorus is very good at self-appraising. Sometimes that means pointing out what we didn't do well. But it's not to be negative, it's to process through it and improve. But we don't like to say, "we never do this right" or "we always miss that." That negative frame really hurts the energy. ~KW

When they come in saying, "Where have you been all my life?" "I wish I knew about this before." "This what I'm looking for."

Our biggest stumbling block is getting the word out there. It seems obvious when someone comes in gung-ho and you know they're going to learn the music and fit in. Of course, sometimes the eager people come in and don't last. Even when the commitment, money and time required is explained and documented by the Membership Team.

Every once-in-a-while we see a new member with a different perception of what membership truly means. Perhaps there's a coaching session, weekend retreat, etc. (all of which has been explained and an assigned "big sister" has done her job) and yet the new member is surprised at the cost or the time commitment. I think they are so excited when they become a member and they are so enthralled with the joy in the group, the wonderful sound, etc., etc., that they don't truly "hear" what's been said regarding many things.

It's hard to absorb all the information in the beginning. I'm thinking that we need to be aware of this and proceed with caution with new folks. They truly are overwhelmed at the beginning.

Until they 'live it" with us for the first year or two they really don't understand everything in spite of nodding affirmatively as information is being shared. Becoming a "great member" is dependent upon our understanding of where they truly are…not where we think they are in the process. ~DP

DIRECTOR WISDOM: Membership

How they look at you; if they look you in the eye. Eye contact is a good predictor. There's just a way that people carry themselves that lets you know they're going to be almost instantly successful.

But! Don't count out those others, either. I can't tell you how many people's lives I've seen changed by this organization. How many times I saw people come through the door that were a little unsure of themselves. They didn't know if they could make it, but they got up their courage and they came through the door. They found a safe place and realized how much they enjoyed singing again. They realized it was OK to have something for themselves, to have applause in their lives again.

There is something wonderful about applause and not many people get applause. You just don't. We start out in life with applause – for everything. What do babies do first? (Clap) we teach them to do that when they are delighted. As we get older, we don't applaud. Unless you are going to a performance, you don't put yourself in a position to get applause or to give applause.

I used to have this poster with a giant ice cream confection on it – many scoops of ice cream, strawberry, chocolate, butterscotch, whipped cream, everything – and it said, "I can live on a good compliment for months." Applause is like that.

I think it's one of the secrets of our organization. The kindness of the organization and the effect it has on people – people walk in and here are a bunch of women actually being kind to each other. Guests may think it's too good to be true! There may be a few snarky people, but it generally gets overridden by the kindness. You can never be too kind. ~PG

Some people come in and not only does it feel like they belong here, but it feels like they've BEEN here for 5 years. I'm not sure I can pinpoint what it is…but they engage very quickly, they are excited very quickly, and they get involved. They are thrilled with the music. Other people come in maybe more confused – they can still work out and often do. The ones that I know are not going to work out are the ones who don't get engaged, don't make friends. They always seem to be off to the side. We've found it's very important to get people involved in a smaller group within the chorus. ~MG

When we take in new members, early in the process my Assistant Director and I have an interview with each one away from the rehearsal time. We ask them to come to my home and we spend at least a half hour asking them what they can offer to us and what they are expecting from us. If you aim for singing in a world champion chorus, you should sing well. We follow the regular procedure to ensure there is a vocal quality as well. But we are as careful about what kind of person we take in when it comes to commitment - willingness to develop, willingness to be a resource to the chorus and help out.

Recently we had a lady with a lovely voice who was extremely shy. She was almost floating into the wall in the rehearsal hall. We have such an outgoing attitude in our chorus, we weren't sure she would enjoy it. In the interview we said, "your musical standard is fantastic, AND you will need to be a drama queen at the same time and act out on stage." She said "oh, that might be difficult for me." We talked to her about tools that she might use to develop that and that she would have a period of time to work on that in the chorus.

As a leader, you learn to feel things about the guests. You learn to separate if a person is very cocky and you know it's mostly due to insecurity. If they are very shy you can kind of work to get them out of their shell. Most of our chorus culture is to be aware of the whole human being, not only the singer. We want to see how we can increase your overall well-being, so you can sing even better. But we're not counselors! We keep a frame of what can be done within the chorus, being understanding, generous, warm and supportive. ~BB

> *They realize it is OK to have something for themselves, to have applause in their lives again.*
> ~Peggy Gram

Membership

How do you help new members assimilate into your chorus?

I think we tend to overvalue the difficulty of barbershop. The barbershop style is not difficult. It's specific. It has a specific sound. It's always made easier if the prospect can sing.

I don't mean that rudely. When someone comes into our singing organization and they don't sing very well but they have heart and want to do it – it's going to be more difficult for them. We do have things set in place if we're coming up to contest or show. We're very specific with what material they need to pick up. Hopefully our learning resources and rehearsal media are there, and the person is encouraged to put outside time into it.

There are vocal technique things that every singer needs to hear all of the time, no matter how long been around. No matter how many times you heard something you can realize "yup, I wasn't quite there." That's called being human. My reminders, when reviewing basics, come in the form of "We all need this. The further you are from being a new barbershopper, the more you probably need it."

There's a saying at Disney, "The worst place to rehearse is on stage." You're going through the motions of the song rather than intently focusing on making it your best. That comes from having an open mind for technique you already know and technique reminders.

When it comes to new members, I would much rather have ten never-sung-barbershop-but-can-sing than three who've been barbershoppers somewhere else for 10-12 years. First of all, it's good for the organization, to have brand new enthusiastic members. It's also good for our chorus to be working with brand new people who have no idea what this barbershop thing is. We can absorb them into our culture and belief system, how we do things and how we want to treat people. That's a lot easier to do with brand new people than those who've been to other places. I mean that with no disrespect to any level of chorus out there.

Choruses are different. I wouldn't walk into a Rich-Tones rehearsal and expect it to be like a Toast of Tampa rehearsal. Or Scottsdale or any other chorus. Each has different processes and procedures. There are a lot of different ways to get to a good result.

The learning curve for a transferring member can be interesting for sure. I just ask them to have an open mind and remember there's always something to learn and affirm. There's always something for me to learn. ~TD

DIRECTOR WISDOM: Membership

We started a program in 2017 called Rookie Chorus created by our membership chair and Assistant Director. One Saturday a month any new member (<1 year) is strongly encouraged though not required to come and review music for show or contest.

The new members get more time to be in the trenches, working on the basic musical elements so that we can be working at the highest possible level at regular rehearsal. The Directing Team can explain some of our lingo (target vowel, no breath zone).

We had 9-10 actual rookies and this last time 22 women showed up for the additional time. A great back-to-basics rehearsal. We also encourage Section leaders or teams to attend so there are strong voices to model. ~RH

A couple of months ago, I was up in front of the chorus and I was frustrated about the diphthongs in a new song. "I can't believe I have to mention diphthongs… turn the diphthongs…you're supposed to be an A chorus…" I went from cajoling to nagging to doing stuff to make them laugh. So, then rehearsal's over and we have this 12-year old member. She came up to me, "Miss Betty, what's a diphthong?"

I thought, oh my gosh, how many times have I missed the opportunity to explain to new members. So, the next week I did a whole visual presentation on word sounds. Everyone left understanding it better – even people who already knew it said they enjoyed it and learned from it. That inspired me to go back to 101 for new people but still change it up to not bore the long-time members. ~ BC

> *The worst place to rehearse is on stage.*
> A Disney saying shared by Tony DeRosa

Administration

Do you engage members in the necessity and value of administration?

Sometimes members (or Directors) complain about the administrative side of chorus life. "I just want to show up and sing" they say. Do you encourage members to invest in the admin side?

DIRECTOR WISDOM: Administration

I think you have to start with what they can offer. It could be that at this moment of life that's all they can do. Maybe then our job is to hook them with how much fun it is to be part of the board or the team or a committee. But that isn't something you can force. You can't force joy on somebody.

I'm really into, as I've gotten older, cutting people some slack. When someone says "all I can do is come and sing" maybe that's true for them. Maybe next year, that's gonna be us saying that. You know, there but for the grace of God go I. So, I like to cut people some slack. ~KB

I think there are times in your life when you just need to sing. I think it's OK to let people feel their way into it. You know we can be a bit overwhelming to new folks. I think it's better to let people find their own way, find the things that they can do to help when they are ready to do so.

We need to allow people their privacy sometimes, too. I'll never forget the lady who decided to join and didn't tell us for a while that she was dying. She wanted to sing before she died. She knew she had 18-24 months to live and she wanted this. It was way after a year before she told us. She didn't tell anybody. She didn't do extra things with the chorus because she simply couldn't. We don't know what people are dealing with. It's better if we don't prejudge. ~KV

Before I became a Director, I was lucky to have worked closely with another Director, Ted Chamberlain, from the moment he was hired by the Seattle SeaChordsmen. From Ted I learned that it pays to establish clear boundaries; the Director doesn't do anything that could be done by other members of the chorus.

I also learned from Ted that one of the most important tasks of the Director — maybe THE most important task— is to notice the specific work that individuals are doing, acknowledge it publicly, and express gratitude. It is not enough to thank "everybody" or "the chorus." Individuals are more likely to go the extra mile when they know the Director is paying attention and is appreciative. ~ED

Our philosophy is everyone gets involved to the degree that they can. For instance, there are four people on the membership team. But on the costume and makeup team, two oversee it and then there is a team of 20 people. We have a huge marketing team and a huge team that focuses on non-dues revenue. There's hardly anyone who does not have a job in the chorus. ~VM

JENNIFER PALUS

Administration

How much involvement is too much?

Choruses sometimes overwhelm new members in our excitement to get them involved. How do you handle that?

DIRECTOR WISDOM: Administration

It happened to me when I joined my first chorus. My mom had joined an under 20 member chapter. My first night I was made a baritone, the second week the Lead section leader. Now, I understand need and I was eager to help. But it was a lot when I had no idea what I was doing. Fortunately, I had my mom there so what I didn't understand she could explain. Just simple awareness can make a difference between helping and over-extension. ~KV

There's a high level of competitive spirit; this is a working chorus. So, if you just want to come and sing, it might not be the best venue for you. Because we expect everyone to have a strong work ethic and work at a high level, people tend to self-select out. If they say "I'm not sure I can handle this" <work level, time investment, money, etc.> we've learned that they are probably right…and that's OK! ~VM

There are people who are so ambitious. They want to do everything when they join. We actually try to hold them back, because we know burnout can come from that. But they are new and excited! They can't get enough. I go, "whoa, whoa, whoa, take this in." That's where we've gone wrong sometimes.

Let's face it, when we have a new energetic person who is skilled in an area of need for the chorus and we want them involved, we want their help and they are flattered to be asked. We just have to be careful to allow them to wade in the baby pool first – regardless of what they bring to us. The really eager ones can jump off the deep end getting far too involved too soon. Consequently, they burn out before they even get started. ~DP

Administration

What's your take on Director involvement in administration?

DIRECTOR WISDOM: Administration

That's a good question. Maybe I have a different perspective, because before I became Director, I was a chorus member and I had been on the board, so I had experience at that level. I believe the knowledge and experience that I gained from that has helped me as a Director. I appreciate the administrative side. My perspective might be different than a Director who comes in and has never been on the admin side. That Director might say, "Well, you all just go ahead and plan that." A lot of times our Directors think, "I just want to deal with the music." But if the music and the admin conflict, then we've got to come to terms with that.

The goal of the administration is to support the music so that the music goes on unimpeded. I get that. But it is not the role of the music to just drive right over the admin without respect and regard. You have to have respect and regard for both parties.

I encourage Directors to get involved. If they have a Management Team, then they're part of the process. If they have a Board, I think they should go to Board meetings. I think it's important to either go to the meetings or see and comment on an agenda in advance. Sometimes the admin side thinks they have to decide things and don't want input. But 95% of the time, the Director has influence on the administrative side: how things are going to work within the organization. It makes sense to work together. The only thing I am not crazy about being involved in is finance. I respect it. I'm mindful of the chorus's money and working within the budget, but I trust my financially trained members with this area.

I said years ago, "If it has 'sing,' 'perform' or 'rehearse' in it - then I'm involved as Director."

I think it's important for Directors to be involved in the regional level as well. It gives you a broader perspective of what is going on at the regional level with other choruses. I do think some choruses are insulated. All they think about is what they're doing, and they let "other people" run the region. I like to remind Directors: If you don't do anything to get out there and meet people at the regional level or get involved then you don't have the right to complain. ~KW

I am moderately involved. I am on the regional faculty and have accepted assignments to provide free coaching to a chorus that was struggling musically. I have also helped organize regional events, have taught classes and PVIs at regional events, and have served on one International task force. ~ED

I think it's great to have strong musical leaders directing the course of the organization. However, it's just not everyone's bailiwick. I love organization. I have a very administrative approach to my Music Team. Directors who aren't strong at administration or hate it should get an administrative assistant to help them. ~BC

DIRECTOR WISDOM: Administration

I believe my role is primarily about leadership: Grow a leader, grow an organization. I think this is a huge part of why Skyline has been so successful. I think I'm really good at identifying and growing leaders—and finding people to help me develop leaders. So, I am definitely part of the management team, which helps me fully grasp the overall picture of the chorus and also allows me the opportunity to share my vision directly with the chorus leadership. And, I think it's important for the director to be involved in the Sweet Adelines organization. When the Director is involved, she's more invested in the organization and not just the chorus. It's especially helpful to participate in regional events. I currently serve the international organization as a judge and as a judge specialist—and that's a huge and rewarding job. It allows me the opportunity to experience the entire organization in ways I could never fathom otherwise as well as allowing me to serve my organization. It's important to give back. ~VM

Director involvement in administration is important and timesaving especially under the Management Team concept. The administration has much to do for any chorus with support of the musical product, education, etc. Strong admin is imperative in a successful chorus. Personally, being a part of our Management Team and being a trusted voice in that environment is invaluable to the chorus and to me. It works for us in Buffalo. I can say that I think it's very important that the director is involved because of a need to be aware. He/She, however, should not be "rowing the boat" of other committees…but awareness is key. ~DP

I think the Director needs to be cognizant of his or her decisions as far as the music goes and how that effects the administrative side of the overall chorus. You can't lean back and say, "we're going to have 12 coaches this year" and ignore the fiscal impact. Budgets make an impact on everything. You have to have money coming in and projects that do that. You have to be aware of how much time chorus members have to devote to chorus. The administration needs to hear that most people join to sing not to raise money. It helps the administration and the music for there to be dialogue with the Director.

I think there is a need for leadership at the regional level. It speaks well of a chorus and its leadership to have people involved. It says to your chorus members that you aren't just an isolated group of people. There is a larger structure. You don't just go and compete with other people you don't know. There is a larger organization and you benefit from the regional and international structure. ~PG

I was the YWIH Coordinator in Region 23 and that gave me a sense of the administrative side. I saw so much potential for making a difference at the logistical level. Later I was Education Coordinator and I enjoyed that even though it's a freakishly hard job. I didn't expect to be elected to the IBOD, but it was an honor to be. I'm honestly not that involved in the Admin side of my chorus. We decided to stay with the Board structure, so the Director is not on the Board. Since I'm at a distance, it would be challenging to be highly involved. I think it's important for Directors (and other leaders in a chapter) to educate their members to the larger organization and encourage involvement. ~JC

I was on the Showcase committee a long time ago. A few years ago, I was on the nominating committee for the International Board. Currently I just started in the role of Showmanship Category Judge Specialist. That's a LOT of administrative duty. I read every showmanship score sheet from all the regional contests. After the first couple of weekends of regional contests, you get this stack of score sheets in the mail. It's my job to read every sheet and make notes about how the judge is doing. I evaluate every judge in many areas. It was so time consuming I couldn't believe it. If I want to, I can delegate some of the task in the future, but I wanted to do it myself the first time. I wanted to know every judge's style, the personality of how they write. I'm also involved in the Judge Training program as well. When you apply for the Judging program, if you're not a Director, they like to see that you have leadership skills in your chorus and in your region. It's shows you're interested in your region and you have experience leading teams. I encourage Directors to be involved if they can (and their job and family situations allow). If you have skills and time, you should get involved in regional and international. ~BH

It's good to be involved in the organization. It gives insight into what's going on that makes it easier. You meet so many people and you learn so much from them. I find it very valuable. ~BB

> *I believe my role is primarily about leadership:*
> *Grow a leader, grow an organization.*
> Vickie Maybury

Administration

What do you see as
obstacles and opportunities
for Sweet Adelines in the future?

Earlier I said there were three things that define a good member: show up, pay your dues, learn your music. It's not always easy. Nowadays it's "I'll be there if I can. I'll pay if I have money. I'll learn the music if I have time." There's more static in it now. I think it's cultural. I've talked to so many other friends and other Directors. We (Sweet Adelines) may need to let loose of some of these requirements. Maybe we have to do things a different way? Maybe we need to rehearse less frequently with more intensity. I don't know. How can we make it work?

Mine is a very healthy chorus, but it's challenging to get everyone to attend a regional music weekend, for example. There are always those 12-15 members who attend regional music schools, yes, but many have young children, weekend jobs and/or find it hard to justify taking another weekend away from family life, etc. when we already ask them to be present for retreat weekend, contest weekend, cabaret weekend and one or two coaching weekends a year. Some of the members can't justify the time and expense. Financial commitment for "optional" things is really difficult for many. I've noticed it more so in the last few years.

The "social" part of what we offer seems to be more important now than it might have been ten years ago. There's so much stress in the world today and being with other singers who share the same interest is an important release. That being said, our musical product must be of a high enough standard to attract good singers. We don't want to waste the time of anyone else…yet we need to recognize how important our sisterhood is and to build things into our weekly time together in order to reinforce that as well. It's a tricky balance but an important one. Feed the hearts of the singers and the music will be better.

As a front-line director of three successful Sweet Adeline choruses (and one BHS chorus for 7 years) I often think that it's time to consider retirement – and I have considered it and *almost* done it. But I've changed my mind – at least for now. I'm intrigued by learning different approaches to musical refinement, joy in rehearsals, personal fulfillment, etc. The organization has been evolving and changing since I became a member in January of 1975.

Barbershop music is a unique genre…one which continues to be preserved by Sweet Adelines International. I see us continuing to be the preservationists. At least I HOPE we continue to preserve the artform. This is what makes us unique and viable. Also, we are specific to a singing opportunity for "women". Again…this is what makes us unique and for women who want to sing with other women – WE are the answer.

Inasmuch as contemporary arrangements are fun to sing and definitely draw singers to what we do…it's the true 4-part barbershop chords and the visceral reaction to them that excites our singers…thus our audiences. Yes…we are changing where necessary…but I see US as the only remaining organization singing true barbershop which is, as I see it, one of the reasons we will grow!! ~DP

DIRECTOR WISDOM: Administration

There is a downturn of membership, not just in Sweet Adelines, but in volunteer organizations all throughout the world. Rotary is down, Lion's Club is down, my husband belongs to an antique boat club and that's down. People just aren't joining things like they used to.

How can we stay fresh and thrive and never lose what we've got? One obstacle for membership is money. But it's funny. Someone will say they are not going to join or they're leaving because of money but then we see them doing other hobbies (photography, golf) that are also expensive. For what you get out of singing with your sisters, it's so worth it. When someone says it's just the money, I don't totally believe that. There're other choices going on there.

Membership in the future means attracting young people in everything we do. This last Rising Star contest – oh my gosh – some of those quartets could have won their region and maybe been top 10 at International. We're doing something right to make young singers that good want to be part of us. So, we have to keep doing that.

Those of us that aren't young any more need to understand how different young women are when they join our choruses. They just retain and learn faster. It's possible they don't need to attend every rehearsal to be up to snuff. I watch how young people work and, my goodness, you could give them a change in the wings of the auditorium, and they'll have it! Not so with me anymore! Some of our members need to give young members a little break, that they rehearse differently than we do. We want them; we want to attract them; and we want them to stay. ~KB

Maintaining HQ staff is important for our organization. There has been a huge turnover in the past few years, I think that has a trickle-down effect on our members. We also need to continue embracing young women and looking for opportunities to involve them and learn from them. ~KW

Well, we're still dated. Part of that is our artform and we're not going to give that up. So, we have to find ways to stay true to the artform but make it fresh for new members. Also, as a society, especially the younger people, are less membership and club oriented. They can connect to everything remotely.

But I will say, I was a vocal performance major for three years in college, and I've gotten better vocal education in Sweet Adelines than I ever did in college. Our education is terrific, and it shows in our organization. ~JC

Administration

Is there a book that you give as a gift to inspire others?

If you ask someone their favorite book, they may freeze up. You can almost see their brain flipping through a mental card catalog, as their heart wonders if it's disloyal to say Pride and Prejudice when they also love The Wizard of Oz. The question can make one feel like a contestant in the final round of a game show.

On the other hand, if you ask someone what book they most often give as a gift, you usually get a calm, thoughtful response. For example, I've given away probably 10 copies of <u>Improv Wisdom</u> by Patricia Ryan Madson, a slim book that takes about an hour to read and several months to digest. This question is less stressful because it's not a judgment; it's based on our actual past behavior. And the books we choose to give to multiple people provide a lot of context into what we value and what we think others will appreciate.

This table shows the Directors' most-gifted books and authors. Some included more than one book. Some said they rarely give books as gifts, so they are not on the list.

DIRECTOR WISDOM: Administration

Book	Author	Director
The Art of Possibility	Ben Zander	Kim Wonders Ryan Heller
Balcony People	Joyce Landorf Heatherly	Kim Wonders
Daring Greatly	Brene' Brown	Dale Syverson
Feel the Fear and Do It Anyway	Susan Jeffers	Britt-Heléne Bonnedahl
The Gifts of Imperfection	Brene' Brown	Vickie Maybury
Go for Gold	John Maxwell	Vickie Maybury
The Good Earth	Pearl S. Buck	Jennifer Cooke
Grace Notes	Phillip Yancy	Karen Breidert
Harmony from the Inside Out	Jan Carley	Becki Hine Britt-Heléne Bonnedahl Kim Wonders
Mindset: The New Psychology of Success	Carol Dweck	Elizabeth Davies
The Music Lesson	Victor Wooten	Mo Field
The Perfect Blend: Seriously Fun Vocal Warmups	Timothy Seelig	Kim Wonders
The Power of Positive Leadership	Jon Gordon	Ryan Heller
Reach for the Summit	Pat Summitt	Kim Wonders
7 Habits of Highly Effective People	Stephen Covey	Britt-Heléne Bonnedahl
Shoes Never Lie	Mimi Pond	Becki Hine
Singer's Manual of English Diction	Madeleine Marshall	Michael Gellert
Singing for Dummies		Jim Arns
So, You Want to Sing Barbershop: A Guide for Performers	Billy J. Biffle and Diane M. Clark	Lori Lyford
Tao Te Ching	Lao Tzu	Mo Field Ryan Heller
The Talent Code	Daniel Coyle	Elizabeth Davies
Top Performers	Zig Ziglar	Betty Clipman
Vocal Wisdom: Maxims of Giovanni Battista Lamperti	William E. Brown	Michael Gellert
Zig Ziglar – any of his motivation titles	Zig Ziglar	Peggy Gram

Contest

Do you have a theme or mantra when heading to contest?

DIRECTOR WISDOM: Contest

We always did. I think that is so much fun. We had a cheer for the year, or we had music. For instance, the first time we went to Vegas, we'd play "Viva Las Vegas" to start the rehearsal. It was a cue that we were about to begin. When we competed in Indianapolis, I asked every section to have their own slogan. The leads came up with "We are high octane leads" and they decided their color was red and unbeknownst to me they decided they would wear red to every rehearsal before contest. It's a silly little thing, but you can't imagine what that does to esprit de corp. Slogans like that are really cool. In Choral-Aires, one year our slogan was just the word "Believe": Believe it could happen for us. We had little buttons and in the last warmup room we sang "I believe." ~KB

Yes, every time. This year we used "It's Time!" The theme was refreshing things we've been working on for 18 months and it also worked with the theme of "time" in the performance package. We've had "Enjoy the Ride" and "Just Jump" and "If It's to be It's Up to Me." It is always culture/motivation related and sometimes it ties into the package, but it doesn't have to. ~JA

Yes, but it's usually not something we impose on the chorus; it's something that just comes up. One year I kept telling the chorus I wanted the "A Team" to show up at rehearsal. When we got on stage and the lights came up, I accepted the applause then turned to the chorus and flashed a "A" with my hands. They knew exactly what that meant. They knew how to put themselves in that space.

Choruses like that kind of stuff, things that make them uniquely them. Harborlites still uses one that I did with them many years ago. I said "That was a great wall of sound. Now I want it to come up behind me like Sasquatch. I want a monster sound. I want to stand in the middle of your sound not in front of your sound!" And they could do it; they had the chops. They got this huge lime green (one of their signature colors) teddy bear and dressed it in their costume and called it Sasquatch. I thought it was kind of cool I got to be part of that.

It has to be an insider kind of feeling to inspire the chorus, make them feel special. ~DS

For several years we had "Let's get the party started." It depended on what year it was. Top of the Rock is in the same region with the Rich-Tones and going into Regional contest we like to say, "Let's make the Rich-Tones *nervous*." We always wanted to beat ourselves. The goal wasn't to win it was to sing better than last time. ~PG

I think these happen organically. Someone will say something that resonates with everyone and there it is! Like magic. There's a different one every time for sure. "Do it because you can" was one of my favorites. ~KV

The whole year we were going to Las Vegas (the year we broke into the Top 10 and came in 9th) the theme was trains. I have them all over my desk. Our whole package was "board the A train." We did all kinds of things with trains. I got more little train gifts! Everyone had a train ticket and they got it punched for achieving different milestones on the journey. It was great fun. ~BC

One year it was "Magic 8 Ball." We were trying to get our scores into the 80s. We wanted one score that started with an 8. So, we had the Magic 8 Ball at rehearsal, and someone would ask it a question. Another year it was "Believe" (seems like everyone does that one). If there is a theme for our package, we pull that through the year as well. As we've matured musically, and people have become more responsible about what they're doing overall, we've needed less and less of that kind of theme. We used to do more of that, and it seem to spur a lot of energy, but I think they are more self-motivated now. ~DP

We've being doing the "With Winning in Mind" book which is all about goal setting and affirmations. We had a three-part affirmation that would get us in the mindset. ~JC

For each of our finals packages, which also is on our annual show and becomes our persona for a couple of years, we work to become that character. For the Chicago set, we were in jail. People came up with a character name and a backstory. Several singers were willing to step in front of the chorus and do a short monologue. They did it in costume and shared who they were. A couple of people were so excited, they had their husband video their monologue and shared it with the chorus. We find that when people are super excited about their character and the finals set that we're going to be living for a few years, they do things like sign their email with the character name and call each other by their character name. One of the singers kept her character names consistent throughout several years and packages. When we were Pirates, she was Scurvy Sal, for the Disco set she was Scurvo Inferno, for Fairies in Training she was Scurvella DeVille, for Chicago she was Shoot 'Em Up Sal. Her character names have had continuity since 2006; it's funny. ~BH

We do a retreat every two years called Quest for the Best. We do coaching, planning, and team building. We decide what our finals package will be, and we announce the word or phrase that is our theme for International. For example, two years go our theme was "Feel the Joy." (Our brand logo looks like a person with her arms up, and we call her Joy.) To us, the theme helps define who we are and where we want to be. ~VM

DIRECTOR WISDOM: Contest

Yes, sometimes we tie it into our package. For example, for Vegas 2016 we did a bowling package and the theme was "That's how we roll" with a bowling ball graphic. Sometimes it's more general inspiration. For Baltimore we had a theme with the word *more* ("do more, laugh more, dance more, love more, sing more, perform more. . . in BaltiMORE") The goal is to come up with something that will motivate our singers and remind them that this is a different challenge. I think if everything is the same, same, same - then what is it that's going to make them want to perform differently or perform better? ~KW

Yes. When we went to Seattle as a wildcard, our mantra was "Etch a Memory in Their Hearts." We wanted to reach the audience, and we wanted to do THERE what we did every week at rehearsal. We also have done little buttons that say, "I AM the Scottsdale Chorus." Like, it depends on ME. One year, Betty Clipman talked to us about singing with the lift of a hot air balloon, so that become part of our theme. At our retreat the last night we had balloons with little LED lights, and we stepped outside and sang and then released the balloons. We don't get too carried away with a theme, but some sort of uplifting thing like that. ~LL

We usually have a goal for the contest, what we want to accomplish and how we expect to feel. This year we had a retreat theme "Breaking Records by Winning Hearts." We have a score we want to break through, and we know it can't be achieved by digging for the points. We have to dig for the heart. The points will come when the music is exciting. ~MG

When we compete at International or at Regional, we always take time for relaxation. We always do mental relaxation and then I talk them down to an alternative conscious level and they take out their goal picture and reinforce it. It's been a very, very, very good tool for us to believe that we can do it. It means we are in charge of the quality level. They build that picture of themselves and then they don't want to do anything but the best, because that's the picture of themselves they have created. The trigger for the whole chorus has been "It´s all happening perfectly" for many years! ~BB

> *It has to be an insider kind of feeling to inspire the chorus.*
> ~Diane Porsch

Contest

How do you share your contest score sheets with members?

DIRECTOR WISDOM: Contest

We would meet right after a contest. Frankly that was one of my most fun moments of the year. Even when it's a comment you're not really happy about, the way you handle score sheets as a Director is the way the members are going to. So never mocking the judging or not believing what they said. But sometimes we would have a catch phrase. Once we were called "robust" so that became the word for the year. We loved reading those score sheets. ~KB

Mainly I want the singers to understand that even though the judges write comments on a wide variety of performance-related topics, when it comes to assigning points, they all primarily reward sound. I tell them that they should think of the showmanship judge as a sound judge who also gives tips to improve your visual performance. I don't want them to get so hung up on a comment about an unturned diphthong or messy hair that they start thinking diphthongs and hair matter more than vocal production. ~ED

We always tried to get together and review that day, as soon as we could. Good, bad or indifferent I think that's important. Then when we had the video, we would do a full debrief. ~PG

We knew going into contest what our Achilles heel was, where we were in our overarching long game development. We would know this was just a snapshot in time. We knew where we came from and where we wanted to go, even if we weren't there yet. So, when we got the score sheets back, we would read them out loud. And, with all love and respect to the judges, we could tell which were subjective opinions and which were relevant to what we were working to create as artists. ~MF

At International, I'll read them at our dinner Saturday night (win, lose, or draw). At Regional it's harder, because we don't have a place to all be together. So, we review those at a rehearsal night. One time, Betty Clipman was coaching the chorus. We reviewed the score sheets and watched the video. We watched North Metro, who had finished ahead of us that year. Betty pointed out some of the things they were doing that we needed to emulate. You learn so much watching other performances. Sometimes you learn "I would never sing that song" and sometimes you learn "Wow, I love how they did that!" or "I love how I felt when they did this!" The Internet is so valuable now - for listening, watching, and learning. ~LL

Usually immediately after the contest is over, we have a meet-up place and we review them. Then we email them out and we usually watch the video at the next rehearsal. ~MG

I read them to the members at dinner after contest. That lets me help interpret, especially for our new members. I post them, and I invite them to contact me with any questions. Then we watch the video and talk thru the sheets at our first rehearsal back after contest. ~JC

After contest we usually go over the score sheets together on site. The next week I scan the score sheets and I send them to the chorus. Throughout the year, I refer to them as we're working on things. You know, "The showmanship judge said this or that." Sometimes I'll pull them up and talk about them at rehearsal. I also refer to the JCDB (Judging Category Description Book) to help our members understand what the levels mean and where we have opportunities. Sometimes I fall short in remembering to do that often enough to help our newest members get up to speed. I love that the JCDB is available online for free now. Great resource. ~KW

We share them immediately. Then we put the scores on our private website. Then we review the video and review the scores again. Sometimes we have judges review with us to explain things to us and help us plan what to do next. It's tricky sometimes; we don't always understand what's written. Some judges use phrases that are common to Americans but not to us. Now we have an American girl in our chorus and some members who have lived in the United States, so we have more resources to help us. ~BB

Although most of the Directors said they share the score sheets with their choruses as soon as they can, two said they have learned it's better to wait.

I do not share scoresheets at the event. I think emotions run high, people are not really listening, they hear only the bad stuff. I want the chorus members to have fun Saturday evening, to celebrate the day.

The first rehearsal after contest is a night for reviewing scoresheets and the video. Sometimes we watch it 4 times. Once for each category. This is a great educational opportunity and I'm always looking for those.

If I had to say there was anything that was my "thing" it's this: Teach or learn something at every possible opportunity. Don't ever stop. There is always something else. ~KV

DIRECTOR WISDOM: Contest

We don't look at them right away. After our performance we get together and celebrate. I maybe glance through them and pull a couple positive comments to share. The members know the numeric score (since that's posted). But I feel like it takes a lot of vulnerability to perform and I do not feel that right after is the best time to hear everything you did that wasn't right. I think you're too vulnerable. That can get in your head and in your heart. We wait.

Usually within the next week I put scoresheets out for everyone to read and give access to video. They can sit down and do their own self-analysis. Then we get together and read through the score sheets and we talk about them and answer any questions. They make their own laundry list of what they are excited about and what they'd like to improve next time. ~VM

> *<Scoresheets and videos create> a great educational opportunity and I'm always looking for those.*
> ~Kim Vaughn

Contest

Did you have to overcome any negative contest experiences?

Have you ever had a negative comment written on a score sheet that was hard to handle? Or a negative experience at contest? How did you deal with it and did it change you?

DIRECTOR WISDOM: Contest

One year I made a really bad music choice. For the first time in 20-25 years the chorus dropped out of the top 10. And it was my fault. It was my choice; I wanted to do something really different. And I did, and it fell flat on its face. I think we came in 17th. And I was so embarrassed and ashamed and so guilt-ridden. I was just a mess. The chorus came and got me from my room, and we went down and had this big long conversation. They wanted me to know that they recognized the fact that I was accepting responsibility for everything, but that they were the singers and they were the musical leaders and they could have said something, too, and maybe we could have fixed this. But in the meantime, let's just go home and fix it.

It was the first time I felt completely and totally supported by everyone in the chorus. It changed me. I don't know what it did for them, but it changed me. You know that thing about how good failure can be for you? We had been very, very successful for a very long time, and that failure kicked every one of us in the ass. Every one of us, but especially me. It made me work better within the team. I allowed more people into more conversations. I expanded the Music Team. About every six months, we brought in all the Assistant Section Leaders as well and did some training. We widened everything. I started doing more with Kathleen, to the point where the year leading up to International, I only did the International music and she did everything else. And that's how I knew when it was time for me to go that she was the right answer. ~KV

In a quartet a long time ago, a judge wrote "Tenor is closest to OK" in a particular area. We laughed about that for a long time.

Anything we've heard on a score sheet, I've really taken to heart. And I've learned at contest to not open my big fat mouth and get defensive! Because you read something like "You didn't have a lot of dynamic variance" and my first instinct is to say, "we did too!" then I'd get home and play the DVD and go "Oh. Darn those judges; they're always right." I've learned to not make comments like that until I've really assessed the DVD myself. And then I try to learn from it and try not to get defensive. ~KB

I don't remember if this was chorus or quartet, but one judge said "Well, good, you finally got it going about 16 bars in." Oops. One time the chorus was doing a gospel medley in a package and just really having fun. I remember the judge said, "Ah, too bad you didn't do that on your contest song." ~LL

I don't always agree with everything the Judges say in the moment. But in retrospect, I usually realize they were right. I do remember one International panel where one of the judges was just lower than the rest, and I joked she was watching a different contest. They hear things differently, of course. They're human. It's hard when the words they write seem like one score, but the number is lower. I like when we get specific things to understand the score. And on the other end of that it's really encouraging when they appreciate small things that we've worked hard on: A gesture or inflection. I think it is human nature to remember the negative comments and forget the positive. This year I sent a recap of positive-only comments to members to say, "Remember all the great things we did at Regional!" ~KW

The Judge talked about some abrupt interpretation. That was my interpretation and it was not as artistic as it should have been. And I learned from that. I'm still learning, and that feedback is part of it. ~PG

Early on we got the comment that a song was too difficult for us. That's hard to read as a Director, since you're the one who chose the song. When you make a mistake as a Director it affects the entire chorus. It feels like I let them down by not recognizing that. And the Judge was right. I shouldn't have stuck with that song, but I did. After that we changed songs. ~JC

Music judges have told us something doesn't meet the criteria for barbershop. That's hard to hear, and as I mentioned earlier, sometimes it inspires me to make it work anyway. And a few scores and placements were hard to read. But over the years I've learned to really trust the Judges. They are very well trained and they usually get the numbers right on the mark. We "tell" them what to right down with our performance. In the last few contests, all the numbers and comments have made us very happy. It's been a while since something upset me – but I think we probably deserved it, whatever it was. There is one comment they make that sounds like a good comment, or I <u>used</u> to think so: "You hard work shows." I don't see that as a good thing anymore. I don't want our hard work to show! ~MG

> *I don't want our hard work to *<u>show</u>*!*
> *~Michael Gellert*

Contest

How do you break through a plateau?

Most choruses will have periods where they advance, some where they fall back, and some where they are plateaued. How do you identify and deal with a plateau?

JENNIFER PALUS

Talk to other Directors who have been through it. If they survived it, we can too. Let the chorus know honestly what you're feeling. To be very honest with the chorus and say "I'm just distraught right now because we've lost 10 members in the last couple months. It's all for good reasons, but my heart is hurting. Can you help me with this?" I just think honesty with your chorus gets you thru a lot too. ~KB

When we identify it, we speak to it. We say, OK we've run into this wall. I learned this from Kim Vaughn, when you're dealing with a troubling thing you kill it the way you kill mold: you expose it to light and air. If there's something you need to deal with, you talk about it. Communication probably solved many of those little plateaus.

I do remember one time getting ready for Regional. And in our region, you can never assume who's going to win. There are three very competitive choruses that you will run into (San Diego, Harborlites, and Scottsdale). We're always working our tails off, so don't misconstrue this that we thought we were all just going to breeze into something!

I notice about two weeks before contest, the attitude and effort and the energy weren't present the way I thought they should be. And I said, OK friends I would like you to transport yourself to another time. I would like you to perform now and rehearse for the remaining weeks as if we are preparing for an International. And it was like Transformer time! Vrrrt-Vrrrt-Vrrrt! They elevated themselves. Isn't that powerful? Because that was simply a change of thought.

Changing your thinking about what you're doing alters the outcome much more than changing the way you do something. Because if you change the way you think about it, the way you do it will change. But if you only modify the way you do it, it won't last. ~LL

We certainly always have those times in our lives. Generally, I've looked at myself and asked, "What's going on with me?" Because that's where it comes from, I think. It comes from the Director when the plateaus or ups and downs happen. I don't mean that to sound self-serving, but I think I have a huge impact on why that happens. When I get in that space, I do a variety of things. I've reach out and talked to other friends who are Directors, I've gone into counseling, I've done personal work. I have a mantra that I developed about four years ago: *All things good and abundant are in my life*. When I feel like I'm getting *that* day, I start chanting my mantra and things change. ~VM

DIRECTOR WISDOM: Contest

Plateau is not the word I would use. I would say, "Valley of Depression."

When I took over, the chorus had had quite a ride. It was originally the Elkridge Chorus and the Director of 17 years had just left. She was another icon of Sweet Adelines, Jackie Grant. She had taken the chorus to International several times and made the Top 10. When I took over there were 130 members. (I took over thinking I would be an interim Director. I had been doing opera and loved that. I figured I'd stay a few years and then the real person would show up. And I just celebrated my 25th year!)

Then another chorus started called Pride of Baltimore and they hired Janet Ashford who had been one of my Assistant Directors when I first started. Some of our members started leaving to go to Pride of Baltimore (it was only about 20 miles up the road). So, we were having this very, very slow split over the next ten years. We slowly lost about 60 members. I know that things like that happen around the country all the time. And it feels horrible to be on the end where you're losing members, especially when you're not quite sure why it's happening. And you can't quite get on top of what's going on. There's a depression there.

So as a Director, I started trying harder. I was trying so hard to have meaningful rehearsals. But because I was trying harder the rehearsals got harder. And everyone was in a panic – a slow panic that lasted a couple of years. We got down to the upper 40's I think in membership. There were people who said we were a "dying chorus" – I actually heard that. And we turned it around. Every year I did a State of the Chorus address. I would talk about the most important thing the chorus had to work on. And there would be different themes. One was that the rehearsal must be the most joyful thing that anyone is going to do all week. Something that people look forward to, and the happiest place you can be. When you have that, it's attractive and people join. I think it kind of started there.

When we started to feel a difference, we had a 3-prong goals: Record a CD, be a wildcard to International, and compete and try to win Harmony Classic at IES. We accomplished all those goals and that created momentum. And we've continued to grow from there.

I learned that every chorus is fragile. It doesn't take much to knock it off-kilter. It doesn't take much to have a chorus split. Watch carefully about any problems that are festering. Look at the expressions of people as they walk in the door and the expression of people as they leave. When they walk in the door, there should be a look of excitement and "I'm happy to be here!" If there's a look of "I'm here because I told myself I have to be here," that's trouble. And when they leave there should be a look of exhilaration, exhaustion and happiness when they're leaving. ~MG

We actually had a "fall back" period in our last contest. The score went down, and it just wasn't our best performance. We first dealt with the discouragement and then we set new goals. I don't lead the goal setting. We have a member who does goal setting because we determined if I lead the members say what they think will make me happy. When she leads, they are more honest. We tried to analyze what went wrong, how can we make it better. We tried to stay big picture. I mean, we're contest-oriented, but that's not what defines us. I think the fall back can help us move ahead now. ~JC

I think my chorus is on a plateau right now. We all know where we want to go but we aren't quite able to get up to the new level. But I think we will! The issue is: what got us HERE won't get us to THERE. That's true of any plateau.

That's how life works. You're going to have some flat times and some growth times. If you are always accelerating and you never stall out, then you won't learn. If you're always improving, improving, improving, then there's never any time to look back and figure out, "how did we get here?" and appreciate the journey. Sometimes when choruses plateau, they are happy to be there and stay there. That's OK if everyone is happy there. To continue to rise, there must be a shared desire to improve, to get better as singers, as performers.

There's a balance. The individuals must get better so the chorus can get better as a whole, then the individuals have to get better again. If you never experience the plateau, you might not appreciate the journey as much. ~KW

> *Changing your thinking*
> *about what you're doing*
> *alters the outcome much more than*
> *changing the way you do something.*
> Lori Lyford

Contest

Any advice for choruses who are working toward a regional medal?

Do you have any advice for the choruses working their way up the scores and ranks? How do you keep your focus and enthusiasm in a contest-focused organization if you are not (yet) in the medals or International contests?

Directors that I coach often ask, "How do we get past the B scores?" I tell them to stop directing and let the singers go. The Director is directing too much. You have to test the waters on what the singers need. Sometimes staying out of the way gets a better result. That's usually not possible in the C level; it happens in the higher B levels.

You have to see yourself (as a conductor) as having a direct impact on the quality of what they do. In the beginning they need tons of guidance – literally from your hands. As they get smarter and more skilled, you must be less literal with them, or your literal direction will make good singers sing choppy! They won't sing past what they see.

That's part of why you see me disappear on uptunes. That's something that just happened because of the choreography (there was no room for me on a small stage) and we learned that I could go off stage. The first few times I was off stage thinking "OMG they're doing it without me" and that thought swung from happy to sad and back again! I've never had children, but I've often thought that situation was my parallel to the kids going off to school. It was the start of something that's been very good for the chorus and for me. It made me step further out of myself. Again, you can't take this job and not expect to be changed! ~DS

It's a tough place to be. The more educated you become, the better you'll handle it. You have to become better at analyzing what you hear. You have to be better at tearing things apart. You can't just do it from the beginning to the end. You have to tear it apart.

It's like getting your toothbrush out and scrubbing grout…that little corner you know that never gets clean? You have to clean it. That's the stuff people don't want to do. They don't want to work at that. Some Directors don't work well because they think it's not very fun. I will tell you that for half the chorus it is fun. They love that kind of work. The other half is going to tolerate it because in the end, it's going to sound so much better. But the key is that toothbrush scrubbing time is when you have to tear it apart and figure out: What is the difference between a B and B plus? You look at the judging level sheets: "This one says *most* and this one says *all*. OK, so we're getting most but not all. Where are the ones we're not getting?" and it's time to dig, dig, dig. That's why I would never change two contest songs in one year. I would only change one - if I had to. I'd rather keep a song another year and get my toothbrush out and scrub it. ~KV

I quote Ted Chamberlain: "This is unlike other contests that you might have participated in. It's a celebration of the art form. It's not the kind of contest where you hope the other guy gets food poisoning. It's the kind of contest where you hope the other guy puts on a performance that knocks your socks off." ~ED

DIRECTOR WISDOM: Contest

When I coach, I really try to encourage these choruses. I'm a big proponent of the Harmony Classic. I think one of the best things our organization did was break us into divisions. When I first joined the organization and for many years at regional there were only the top three awards. Then they expanded to five. They only gave one Small Chorus award and that was kind of figured like the formula they use for Harmony Achievement award (highest scoring below a threshold number of singers). I can remember hearing Small Choruses say, "Oh we'll never get to International." Since they divided us into divisions in 1999, and I say this to choruses when I coach, every chorus in this organization has the opportunity to sing on the International stage.

It has to do with your goals as a chorus. Do you want to be the best C+ chorus you can be and sing-out in your community? Or do you want to work on the skills to get into the medals at regional? They give 1st, 2nd, and 3rd in A and AA. So technically there are 12 awards at regional: three in each division, five overall, and most improved. Now often those double-up, but there's 12 opportunities. There are choruses that are ecstatic for 3rd place AA or A medal, and they should be, they worked hard for it! That dollar-fifty-nine piece of medal around our neck is worth so much more than that in self-esteem. ~KW

I encourage people to evaluate based on their score sheets. Find the common elements from the judges. Then pick one and set a path. Maybe that one thing is energized phrased endings. Maybe all the judges mentioned that your intervals are not as clean as they should be. Start setting goals for yourself. Don't set goals that related to someone else. If you say, "Our goal is to be in the top 5", there might be five other choruses who also had that goal. But if your goal is to improve your own level, that's different (and I would focus on level not score). I recommend reviewing the level rubric that we get and explain that to the chorus. If you want to go from C to C+, aim at B-. If you want to go from B to A-, aim for A. "Shoot for the moon, if you miss you still end up in the stars." ~LL

It's important that everyone has a strategic plan in place, so they understand what the culture is and what the expectations are and what the goals are. If all of those are in place, the Director has the freedom to **reinforce** that. When everything is clear and mapped out, you make progress. It's when it's not clear that you have problems. People just don't know. They find themselves making excuses. Then the Director may come on too strong. A plan frees up the Director to reinforce rather than impose the goals. ~VM

One of the tools I use is level videos. I've found that most choruses think they're on a different level than they are. A B- chorus might think they are singing at a B or B+. I have a video of them and then the level videos and I say which are you closest to. I don't tell them the levels until we're done. They usually identify the correct video for their performance, but it's a reality check to know the level. This is not punitive, but it's important for them to understand where they are and what it would take to get to where they want to be. They need to understand what's between one level and another, and they can usually isolate the work. Usually it's vocal skills.

And what's fun, Betty Clipman recently did this same exercise with my chorus on the difference in the A levels. They were able to isolate a whole lot of things. I thought, "I do this when I coach, but why didn't I do it with my own chorus?"

When I'm coaching, I try to remind choruses that the work on vocal production may not be as fun to do, but it has a huge payoff for the audience. They will enjoy the entire performance more when the vocal production is stronger. For Pride, our focus is on eliminating as many distractions as possible for the audience so they can enjoy the ride of our music-making and sharing.

The other thing that's just important for whatever the level is: It's perfect for where you are right now. Don't try to be what you're not. You scored a C+, great. Let's work on getting some glimpses of B-. You shouldn't expect to leap up three levels. The journey is about on-going improvement. **Celebrate that.** ~RH

> *The journey*
> *is about ongoing improvement.*
> *Celebrate that.*
> Ryan Heller

Contest

How do you avoid burnout when you're in the International cycle?

Some choruses are in a 2-year rotation at International. This is exhilarating but can also begin to cause burnout (mental and financial). How do you address this and keep things fresh?

That is tricky. Maybe the snowbird chorus was an advantage. When I was gone over the summer in a way it was like "Oh she's coming next week; we have to get this music ready!" In a way that kept it fresh. When the snowbirds would come back it was like "Whoa, the family's together again!" We just thrived on coming up with entertainment packages. That was always fun and funny and a lot of variety of music.

I think people get burned out when maybe they only work on two songs and they have a year of two songs. Members and Directors get burned out. ~KB

I always gave the same speech before we went to contest: "Understand before we walk out that rehearsal hall door, no matter what happens at competition when we walk back in that door, we're going to be the same chorus. If they put a blue ribbon around our necks it will not change who we are. We're still the same chorus. If we have problems, a blue ribbon is not going to solve them. If it's a red or green or no ribbon at all, it does not change who we are. We are who we are. Right now, we could sit here and write our own score sheets." I would ask them to say what will be on the score sheet and ask, "What can we do about that?" Why wait to see what the judges say if we know what we need to do? ~PG

Things can get very tense when you are getting the same scores over and over and coming in pretty much in the same place every time, even if that place is the top 5 at International contest.

The chorus hired Jan Carley to work with all of us. I was very hesitant and I'm sure I became Jan's problem child – until she came to town to work one on one. Jan insisted on my doing and thinking about things in a new way. I resisted for sure, but she finally convinced me. What did I learn? That she was always on my side and the side of the chorus. She made all of us stretch ourselves to a place we had never gone. I cried more than a few tears in this process but when we won the next year, I knew she had been right all along. ~KV

I try to do music that is fun and entertaining and has NOTHING to do with contest. We did "God Bless the USA" and "Aquarius." We had a show that was a blast. We sang for a graduation ceremony. We sing at a winery twice a year. You're still working on your craft and improving vocal skills and improving characterization and improving visual performance while you're singing a variety of genres. ~BC

DIRECTOR WISDOM: Contest

I often wonder if we should be doing more and different things. Right now, contest and competition has been the thing that has fed the organization. It gives us an opportunity to be on that wonderful grand stage with that amazing, supporting audience. It gives us a chance to circulate repertoire with a specific end goal. You gain a lot of education along the way, in the material you are singing and transferable skills.

Every contest cycle offers a different personality to the overall ensemble because of the membership that's there for that particular cycle. Sometimes there isn't much attrition and sometimes there's big changes (like a class of 25 newbies for contest). It brings a different energy and dynamic. It offers a chance for member flip-flop, which I think is a good thing.

In today's society, people are less and less likely to be lifelong members of things. Members who are 28-50, those are people I want in my chorus because they can afford it, they know who they are, they are there because they want to be. And it also means when they look at going through another two years of what we just did, they may or may not want to. It gives us a chance to continually reform our chorus in the two-year cycle.

Today, many people say, "Oh I can do this for 18 months" and then they move on to something else. It's not the lifelong member thing for those folks. Our organization is going to have to figure that model out in order to continue. There will always be a base of "lifers," but a large part of our membership will be on a revolving door.

If you can offer it as a timeline – here's the resources, the cost, the schedule for this period of time. Now, if they get hooked, great! But if they don't that's OK. We gained from your participation and hopefully you had a great experience. ~TD

With Spirit of the Gulf, even though we were blessed to make the Top 10, it was never a guaranteed thing. We were not Rönninge or Rich-Tones. We had to work hard on the first set. If you work too hard on the final set, you're almost guaranteeing that you're not gonna need it! Working on repertoire songs makes you a better ensemble. Leaving the contest songs and working on something else is never a waste of time. It's making you a better chorus. Every time you do a local singing engagement, that's making you a better chorus. ~KB

Some people do get burned out. You often lose people after an International contest. I think excitement about preparing a new finals package has worked for us. That brings new music, new choreography, new characters, new costumes. We did a package reveal a few weeks ago. I'll be interested to see how people have started to build on the idea for their characters. ~BH

JENNIFER PALUS

We just completed our 6th trip to International since 2008. Our turnover (ten members) after Las Vegas 2017 was the largest loss of membership we have experienced in the past 20 years. Some older members were ready for a new chapter of life or could no longer justify the time and money. Even some really dedicated, long-time members were just "done". Yet…we picked up ten new singers after that and we've only lost two since returning from St. Louis – all while experiencing an influx of 6-8 singers since then! I know that what we do is intriguing to female singers and I expect we'll continue to grow…all while experiencing retirements, people moving away, etc…The more joy in the weekly rehearsal hall…the better chance of maintaining and gaining members.

All choruses go through tough times, however. There are valleys of challenge in our existence…so it's important to guard against those…see them coming…and change things up a bit in order to avoid as many "valleys" as possible. One of the things that seems to help is to secure coaching for weeknights rather than weekends. Also, taking longer breaks during the holidays or perhaps right after spring or international contests, etc. ~DP

First, we schedule downtime to help reduce burnout. We do our holiday show the first week of December, then take off the rest of the month. The singers come back rejuvenated. We always take off a week after our show and after contest. We take off 4th of July.

Second, it's always about starting new music. When we get back from International, there's always a new piece of music ready to be learned so they are excited to come back. They get it while they're off, and then come back ready to go again.

We try to find balance. We have been in the Top 5 for the last 12 years and we're the only one in the Top 5 who hasn't won yet in those 12 years. So, we've been on the cycle a long time. And yet we maintain our numbers and our positive attitude. We're very driven! ~VM

The every-other-year cycle doesn't seem fast paced to us because there was a seven-year stretch where we went to International 6 out of 7 years. It was a combination of winning our region, or wildcarding or going to Harmony Classic, and one year we took the place of Pride of Baltimore because their Director had passed away. ~MG

DIRECTOR WISDOM: Contest

The year we don't go to International contest has a different feel. This year, as an example, we focused on learning new rep songs, doing more local performances, and our big show with 'the BUZZ.' I think that's a different focus than going to International contest. It's still momentum, but not as hard-driving as a contest year. We always try to have fun, but especially focus on fun in the off-year. Some people have suggested we have a lofty goal like singing at Carnegie Hall in the off-year. That would be a great thing to do - but the time and focus and expense make it similar to an International year. We try to provide balance. ~KW

One of the things I do to break the cycle is to do something different, learn something different. If you're in a cycle you're either not improving greatly enough in your skills, or you're not putting it on stage (not "daring greatly").

That part is hard. That's the leadership part of directing. My concern is always "let's up our skills from the last time." Let's figure out what didn't get on stage. If it didn't get on stage, then it's not that they didn't know how to do it – it's that they can't *handle it under pressure.* That has shaped how I picked music and what I need to do differently as the Director, what needs to change about me.

I knew that getting ready for this most recent cycle for International, I needed to change my leadership to be able to get another step better. We did and it's working. I can't guarantee what's going to happen on stage. They're going to be great! But I can't guarantee a placement. Nobody can.

Things have gotten so tight up at the top. I have won by as few as 14 points, but it's still a win! You've got to take that win home and ask, "What would have given me more of an edge?" For me, my work is almost done when I leave town to go to contest. I earn my medal at home. They earn their medal on stage. ~ DS

Right after International, we always ask the chorus "Do we want to do this again?" If they say they do, we start working for regional. We are, and I don't say this arrogantly, in a region where we are our own competition.

After we say we're heading to International we ask, "How hard do we want to work?" We use the risers as a continuum. Far left means "I'm happy where we are. I don't want to work that hard. Let's enjoy the ride." And far right means "I want to work my butt off. Let's push ourselves to the limit."

I tell them to place their bodies to show how hard they want to work. What's cool is, about 90% of the chorus RUNS to the same point...and there will be a few at the extremes. I ask the extremes, "This is the will of the chorus It's not being dictated by me. Can you get on board?"

Over the years, we've lost a few members who don't want to work at the same level. And there are other choruses they can choose from with different things going on, and we don't begrudge them that. And some have gone away and then come back to work hard again. Of course, there is so much happening in the life of the chorus, with the addition of new music, annual shows and other events, and members coming and going that there is always a level of energy flowing.

Pride has been on the international cycle since I started directing in 2003 (and before!). Yes, it can be tiring at times, but continually improving and challenging ourselves to the best the version of ourselves is hugely rewarding. **Be you!** ~RH

It's easy to become complacent, "Oh we've reached such a high level..." then you don't develop further. To make the development a continuous effort, we try to emphasis each person's best. What is your best? We had each member create her own personal development plan and we followed up in small groups.

The phrase we use in Swedish translates to "Practice Your Best." That means we don't allow ourselves to practice sloppy. What you practice is what you get. Our chorus has a limited time together. We seldom have extra rehearsals and we take six weeks off in the summer and three weeks at Christmas. We have to practice at a very high level. But it's fun; we like it! ~BB

> *I earn my medal at home.*
> *They earn their medal on the stage.*
> ~Dale Syverson

Contest

Did becoming a judge change how you direct?

JENNIFER PALUS

Completely 100% made me a better Director in every way. I wish that everyone who directs a chorus could somehow be a part of the program for at least a year. To actually be in a room as we do the level viewing and talking about "why is it B for you" …it gave me such great insight into where priorities should be. Being in the judging program focused me in a completely different direction and took the mystery out of comprehending score sheets. Being a Director/Judge has allowed a better understanding of how and why points are accumulated. Perhaps, down the road, there could be further education available to the directors (if not the general membership) which would allow observation of the Judge Specialists actually doing a video viewing just like we do before we judge a contest? I think it would be sooooo helpful… ~DP

I had a better understanding of how the points were assigned. What it meant to be B- or a B or a B+. We were B and B+ when I was directing, with a few A scores. We got our first A- at international competition in Salt Lake City, our first time in International. I decided that I wanted them to have more fun than they'd ever had and to make an impression on the audience. We did "How Could You Believe Me" and we did a costume change on stage! When we did the ballad, we were in black and silver. On the intro to the uptune, we went from black and silver to red and gold. The entire dress changes in front of you on stage! We got A- in showmanship. At that time, only the top 5 did show packages and I think we came in 8th at International. We sang very well, but what happened was everyone in the audience wanted to know how we did the costume change! My chorus members got treated like stars. And every one of them wanted to go back to International contest. ~PG

I entered the judging program as a way to give back to Sweet Adelines as my membership in this incredible organization has expanded my skills and knowledge. I am so blessed to have been able to learn and serve. It has strengthened my leadership skills and has fostered my even greater commitment to serving this organization so that it may continue to move forward. ~VM

It was so different! How you interpret the score sheets and how you figure out what the judge is telling you. Beforehand, we would obsess about little bitty things like "oh our best category is showmanship and our worst is expression" and maybe it was 4 points. That's not a big deal! It's the same level! You can release that and not use energy on the little things. The better you sing, the higher your score in all four categories. Work on your singing! If you're a C+ level chorus, the comments you see are going to be more general, "you need better vocal production and more visual energy." But in the A- and above you start to see more specific things, "lead singers need more ring in their higher range" or "your basses lost resonance in the bridge." You can begin to understand more specific things to work on. ~BH

Contest

Do you think a chorus can achieve perfection?

Based on scores and performance videos over the years, Sweet Adeline choruses keep getting better and better. Why do you think that is, can it keep going, and do you think we will have to recalibrate the scoring system at some point?

JENNIFER PALUS

I really don't know! My judge friends tell me they do not recalibrate. But I do think now that there are the amazing examples of near perfection, the Judges are getting training on more finite details by watching the leveling tapes. Things that used to be scored as a lump as "amazing" are now different levels of amazing. ~JC

It is amazing. I joked once on the EDC (Education Direction Committee) "Maybe we should just stop all this education, because we're getting too good." It is a little scary. I come home from International and I don't know if I'm inspired or depressed! How do they do that!?! I will leave the question of "recalibrate" to the judging system. I trust the judging system and our judges so much. I'm sure they will have hashed that out. ~KB

I think this is a fascinating question. I think education is a huge component as to why we continue to get better. I also think instant access to video has helped us grow quickly.

I don't know what will happen in the future. We haven't had the perfect performance yet (no 100's). However, I do think that as our scope continues to change and we continue to grow...who's to say we might not explore more numbers or different levels. We are getting into that area. We didn't have to worry about A+ performance in the past, but now we have to really define that. It's very difficult to be in that high A+ area because of the level of vulnerability and confidence that it takes. ~VM

In a way, the new scoring system for the finals package was a recalibration. For the standard 100 points per song, I don't know that they will recalibrate. I don't want to sound braggadocious, but there are a handful of choruses that live in that 95 range. And when you listen you think, "It's almost perfect." Depending on the song or the performance, it's only a few ticks away from perfect.

We might have said the same thing 20 years ago, but champions were winning with scores of 85. Our first championship score would, today, not even be Top 10!

One chorus raises the bar and others chase, and it ratchets upward. The new scoring in the finals round gives more room to differentiate the top choruses. ~JA

We have been very close to the perfect score. Sometimes we giggle and ask a judge "what would it take to get a 100? It's only a couple of points!" Most of them will say, "No, we will not give 100 because we don't know the perfect version. We've never heard that. We know what close-to-perfect sounds like." Now the men (BHS) do give 100s. Some male judges who have seen our performances have said "I would have given you 100 points." I think that's just a difference in the organizations. ~BB

DIRECTOR WISDOM: Contest

Isn't that a great problem to have? I think part of the way that we're approaching that is changing the performance package to make it one contest song and putting more emphasis on the fact that you have to sing everything well. That will level a few things out. Even if you sing a contest uptune or ballad at a 98, you've got other songs now, and there's more of them. I think that will automatically address it.

I think the contest songs will stay as high as they are. The caliber is great, and the competition is wonderful. I think we've learned that contest is not a bad word. It's a helpful thing to compare yourself to others. Not to make yourself feel more-than or less-than, but to figure out how to do more and what to do next.

Competition isn't meant to make anybody feel bad about what they're doing. It is intended to give us a measurement so that we can go further and further. As competitive as I can be it has never been about beating someone. I want everyone to do the best they've ever done - then I want to win!

There are truly lots of ways to "win" and I'm not just saying that. Improvement is winning if that's your goal. And setting goals is SO important for the chorus. ~KV

I think there is an unspoken recalibration. We've been using the same descriptors for years. But here's the thing: 20 years ago, if a descriptor said "vocal skills well established" that's what it meant 20 years ago, but what does it mean today? Without changing any verbiage, it means something different today. It's like "in living color" on old TV shows. It was a big deal and now it's taken for granted. Now it's in 3D, watching the same thing but seeing something else. Without having to change any language, what "well established" means to us has evolved, and will evolve, as we get better.

That's never been said – it's in my head – but I think that's how it happened. Like an old Olympic ice-skating video from decades ago. What was gold medal *then* versus now. Think about the young girls coming up in YWIH and the things they can do. We're chasing our own tails – which was exactly the vision for this whole thing <Sweet Adelines> 40-50 years ago! ~DP

> *One chorus raises the bar and others chase, and it ratchets upward.*
> Jim Arns

The Director's Path

How should a new Director come into a chorus?

Thinking about the beginning of a Director position, what was the experience of stepping into the Director role from your predecessor like? How do you try to ease the transition for yourself and your singers? How long did it take before you felt it was "your" chorus?

DIRECTOR WISDOM: The Director's Path

I've actually had three different experiences. At the Melodeers I was a member before I became Director. That was challenging because I was young and had to gain credibility and authority. Years later Choral-Aires brought me in after they lost a long-time cherished Director. I came in new-to-them and they trusted me from the very first rehearsal; they gave me wings to soar! I learned a lot with them, and it was a truly happy experience - and we earned two international medals together, so that was special. And with Spirit of the Gulf, I was one of the chartering members, so there was no prior Director and I helped shape it from the very beginning. ~KB

Making a clean sweep right away can cause all sorts of problems but the chorus does need to move into a style that works for the director. I think allowing people to retire from a long-held position is a good thing. A great big public thank you is necessary however. Asking a long-time section leader to mentor someone can be very useful. Chapters have more talent in them than is often noticed. Talk to people about their backgrounds and their strengths. Allow them to help when they can. And do lots of training, lots of teaching. ~KV

I think it's useful to say to the singers, "Let's pretend that I have the power to wave a magic wand and change literally anything about this chorus. What would you NOT want me to change? What aspects of this chorus are important to preserve?" It gives the singers a chance to reflect on what is working about the current culture and shows that you want to understand what they really value. ~ED

This is the story of my life before my current chorus. I never came up through the ranks; I always came in from outside as a Director. I never had the challenge of coming off the risers. Every time my chorus changed, it was because I moved. I think many times aspiring Directors who want to move up in their own chorus make the mistake of bucking their Director. "When I'm upfront, we're going to do it my way." Well, that can turn off a lot of members who are loyal to the front-line Director. You need to be a team player and you need to be willing to share, for example, if there are two Assistant Directors. Some people try to be noticed and get attention in the wrong way. They end up causing conflict. ~BC

The Director prior to me had come in to try to help the chorus back from the brink. They were in trouble and she put energy into helping them revitalize for a few years, but she never planned to be there long term. And when I took over, she did not come to rehearsals. She said, "I want you to stand on your own." When I came in, I was pretty timid as a new Director. People from the risers were like, "you're the Director. You make that decision." It took a few years for me to really take charge. My second year taking them to contest, I really felt we were connected on stage. ~JC

JENNIFER PALUS

Time is the key. We had a little Directors get-together one time in region 23, and we looked around the circle and the majority of us had stepped off the risers to become Director. Almost 100%. You have to be patient with the transition.

The first time I directed Song of Atlanta in contest was on the International stage. It was Reno in 1994. We had been 11th in 1989 and 12th in 1992. I just assumed we'd be around 11th or 12th. It was my first contest to direct. I was doing the best I could do. We came in 26th. 3rd from the bottom. Having to read the score sheets to my chorus members that night…when my members are sobbing their eyes out. I remember thinking 'Wow, I really have this job, don't I?'

Right after the contest, no one had gone with me to pick up the scoresheets. I didn't realize I would need support. I remember I bumped into Renee Craig at the table. I pull out the sheets and I started looking around 11 or 12 and I went all the way to the bottom of the list and there we were. I was devasted. I'm alone walking out of the venue, and I run into Marlene Greenough and Len Greenough (who was Roger's partner). I had gotten close to Len during Roger's illness. They asked, "how did you do?" and I burst into tears. They had a car and drove me back to the hotel. I sat in the backseat with my head on the shoulder of the partner of my dead Director. I know that God put the Greenough family in my path that night. I felt loved and protected and I got it out of my system, and I could share it with the chorus. And the score sheets told us what we needed to work on, so we could all regroup. And I knew it was mine. And then when we won the next regional and we scored 615, but I hadn't finished all of the DCP, so I didn't get to be Master Director that year. But I did two years later! ~BH

I can relate to that because 10 years ago I directed Pride of Baltimore for six months as interim when Janet Ashford was ill. I flew out every week. One of the first things I did was get to know the people, especially the musical leaders and administrative leaders. And then you have to wipe your agenda clean. So many Directors go in thinking they're going to conquer the world. They create fractures in relationships. You have to go in and find out where they're at and THEN take them somewhere.

I would go in half an hour early with the musical leaders to learn what was going on. I relied on them and turned things over to them since I was a distance Director and they knew all the players. I'd say it's important to come with goals as a new Director, but not an agenda.

When I started with the Melodeers I went to every meeting of every committee. It was a well-oiled machine, since it had been run by Karen Breidert! But by doing that I learned about the people and the processes, and how people worked together. Of course, fat chance I'm going to a make-up meeting now! ~JA

DIRECTOR WISDOM: The Director's Path

When I started at Fox Valley, there had been an interim Director and just a few members, so it wasn't really taking over from someone. There were two other choruses in nearby cities that started coming over to Fox Valley (Kimberlaire at the time) chorus, and suddenly we were a chorus of 40. It took years before we stopped referring to the members as "the Appleton girls" or the "Oshkosh girls". And some of these chorus members had issues within and across the old choruses. It wasn't the Brady Bunch! But I was oblivious to it! I didn't know the people and I didn't have the history. It took a long time for that to become a blended family. After 9 years we had 80 people and we won the regional contest in 1983.

Then I relocated to southeastern Wisconsin and became the director of the Riverport Chorus. That chorus was already established but had not won regional – always 2nd – 4th. They had won 3rd the year before and wanted to "hold onto 3rd." I said, "Why don't we try to win!?" They were afraid that if they didn't win, they'd be "too disappointed" to deal with it. I said, "Get ready, start saving your money. We're going to win." I wanted to help them figure out what they needed to do next to get to the next level. The next year we were 2nd by only 15 points and then the following year we won. And we ultimately grew to 110 singers.

I relocated to Buffalo, NY in order to accept a position directing a BHS chorus in the area. I did that for 7 years. I had also coached Buffalo Gateway for several years before I relocated, thus I had a pretty good connection with them. The long-term (and only) Director asked me to become a co-Director with her. We did that for a little less than a year competing in one regional contest as a co-director tandem. By the way, that is the only time in my life I've every competed with a chorus on the risers – for one song when she directed. And I realized: it's a lot of work, you guys!

The management team decided having two Directors wasn't really working. And after a planning process they offered me the sole Directorship position. Buffalo Gateway had always been in the Top 5 in regional competition…so coming in 6th the following spring with me at the helm was a difficult thing for this chorus. Needless to say, there was emotional upheaval over the director and chorus culture change. 22 people left. It wasn't personal, but mostly about the new level of expectation. Bottom line…the chorus trusted the changes and we were third place medalists (and mid-size) the following spring. It took a couple years longer than anticipated in order to work through some of the issues, but we managed to do it…. coming in as a wildcard to North Metro in 2007 and placing in the Top Ten for the very first time ever in Hawaii in 2008. ~DP

JENNIFER PALUS

My transition into Scottsdale was interesting because this was a very successful chorus; they already had two gold medals. (They had lost their Director, Bev Sellers in a pedestrian-car accident.) In fact, the very first International I directed them in was November, and I had come in that July. So, I had a lot to learn. I had to learn the repertoire and have a chance to put my influence into the musical product. And to their credit, this successful chorus never said to me once, "Bev didn't do it that way." They followed my leadership. And I had to learn some things through trial and error, but nobody ever told me I was doing things "wrong" and that was such a blessing. ~LL

I was an Assistant Director, and there were a couple other Assistant Directors at the time. When the Director retired, the Director search committee asked me to serve as interim Director while we conducted the Director search. The deadline for search kept shifting, so I was interim from May to August.

Then we had a goal setting session with Ruth Uglow. At the end of the session she asked how long we were going to keep the search going. She said, "If you're happy with what Kim is doing, then make it official." And that's when they hired me.

It was funny, when I interviewed, one of the people on the search committee shared with me, "We always see you every week at rehearsals being funny and lighthearted and fun-loving. How do we know the rehearsals are going to be any different?" At first, I was a little insulted, then I realized it was a fair question because that's all they see of me. So, I explained that they see me having fun on the risers, but in my job as an educator, I have to do a lesson plan every day. And that's been really valuable to me as a Director all these years. I always have a plan. There's room to change and adjust the flow, but I never just wing it. When I came in, I tried to make gradual changes and do things how I envisioned them. My rehearsals were different than my predecessor; I had different energy and stamina.

Now the first year I took the chorus to regional contest, we won the region. That was exciting, but also a real challenge for me! Suddenly I had to prepare us for International and I really wasn't ready to do that yet. I look back now and think about how hard that was, but at the time there was the euphoria of going to International and I just did it. It's like the dog that catches the car— now what!? When we came back, it started to feel like "my chorus" after a year or two.

Then we went through a long period when we were always in 2nd place to one of two choruses in our region. And that caused dissension. People were frustrated and thinking I couldn't take the chorus to the next level. Ultimately that led to a split of the chorus. After that challenging time, after the split, one positive outcome: I knew that the chorus that remained was my chorus and they believed in me. ~KW

DIRECTOR WISDOM: The Director's Path

I had been in the chorus for about a year and was an Assistant Director. Two small choruses had contacted me to try out for Director and I was going to do that. One night I was approached by the Skyline President who asked me not to interview with other choruses, because the membership wanted me to take over at Skyline. After I became Director, I sat down with the President and said, "Here is my vision. This is what I want to do." Then, I sat down with the chorus and said. "This is where I'm coming from; this is my vision." That chorus became "my" chorus within 6 months. It didn't take long. ~VM

The first time I thought "this is my chorus" was my first International competition in 2004, where we were singing all music that I had chosen. The regional that got us there was all music that I inherited. Then I went to the Music Team and said let's take new music with my sensibility. I remember feeling that connection, that sense of ownership. People said, "this already great chorus has become something new." I also think it's important to evolve with the chorus. In 2013 the chorus had the goal of hitting 700 at regional, so that became my focus, my homework. I'll never forget the feeling in the warmup room, which was so full of joy and electricity, it was one of those moments where all the director can say is: "no matter what happens, this has been an incredible ride…now, let's go have fun!" The rest, as they say, is history: we scored a 701, which I learned later, because as soon as I heard "seven" I had burst into tears and was running/leaping to the stage while screaming and bawling! ~RH

If I were to direct another chorus, I would sit down with each member and ask them "What led you to join the chorus? What are your favorite things about singing with the chorus? Where do you see the chorus going? What do you see that needs to be fixed?" Have a conversation to get to know the group. No matter the size, a chorus is composed of different people. Different people have different buttons…and different things they bring to the group.

Every chorus is a tapestry. There are a lot of interwoven threads. Take out one thread and you take out a part of the picture. Respect the tapestry.

When I go in to coach a chorus, I try to be cognizant of the tapestry. I may not do things exactly the way that they do them. The way they do things has led to the tapestry that they are. I want to embellish the tapestry, not take it apart. ~PG

The feeling of "this is my chorus" has happened slowly over the years. It took about a decade. I didn't want to make sweeping or sudden changes, because that can be hard to do and have bad effects. If I was to go into a new chorus tomorrow, I would take everything I have learned about the most important thing and start there. When I first started, I thought the most important thing was making sure they understood how much I knew. I was taking over a successful chorus. They need to know that I know…something. That only lasted a short while! Now, I know the most important thing is that it must be a joyful experience. It has to be fun. Early on, people would tell me "this isn't fun." And I would think "Well, isn't the fun in doing well?" I don't think like that anymore. That thinking means the whole time you're working on it, it is not fun. It's not fun until you have a medal. That's not a joyful ride!

In the beginning when people said they wanted to have fun, I imagined they want to stop and, I don't know, play a few rounds of BINGO in our break. Now I know the fun is in making the music, it's picking out the wonderful thing in the music and making it everything it can be. Find the things that touch the soul – that's fun! That way the entire ride is fun. You're not putting off your fun for a certain goal. ~MG

I think it's important to create your own vision and to be true to that. For example, I've always been very careful about the singing quality. To define what you want as a new Director you need to define what you want. And then be a very good listener to what your members say and how they act. Make them be involved; make them feel important. The more you can work as a leader for everyone to feel they are seen and acknowledged is the crucial thing. Every member you have is a human being. Create an environment that is safe and generous but still filled with a lot of expectations. My members say one of the reasons we have been successful is that they have always felt so clearly what kind of faith I have in their possibilities. My expectations have been reinforcing to them. It comes from trust and faith; not judgment. ~BB

> *Each chorus is a tapestry...*
> *respect the tapestry.*
> *~Peggy Gram*

The Director's Path

How should a Director leave a chorus?

What about the other end of a career, what's your take on Director succession planning? How important is it to have one in place – with whom should it be shared?

JENNIFER PALUS

I think it should always be in the back of the Director's mind, but the need and timing on making it public varies. Directors should always be thinking "what would happen the day that I retire...or get sick...or move away." Looking for those rising stars and grooming them is very important. And not just Directors. Section leaders should be looking for rising stars in the sections and grooming them to be their successors.

In every case that I had to leave a chorus, the first thing I did was talk very privately to my music staff and the board/team. So those people in confidence knew what was happening. And then came the awful night to tell the chorus. There's an order it should be done.

Some Directors stay way too long, and you see indicators like people leaving, talk about a split, people terribly bored with music, nobody wants to serve in leadership roles, just boredom at rehearsal, Director him or herself is bored. When you've lost the joy. Look in the mirror! If there's something going on in you, it may be time to move on. ~KB

It's important to train leaders to be the best they can be. But I think it's seldom you can give it to someone else directly. I can't train someone to be me. For choruses at this level, the relationship with the Director is unique. Jim has a unique relationship with his chorus. Lori with hers; Pam with hers. If anyone else steps out front the chorus sings differently. I know I can't live forever. As I age, there comes an increasing need to look at what's going to happen when I'm not with them anymore, either because I've passed, or it's become too physically taxing. That's not yet. But it's closer than it was 20 years ago.

We're very focused on leadership development in my chorus in all areas. But whomever gets the job after me, the chorus will, and should, turn into something else. And I don't mean worse, I mean different. I think of what Scottsdale was under Bev Sellers and it's an entirely different shade of excellent under Lori Lyford. ~DS

I think you should always have someone who could take over if you were hit by a train. You need to have a trusted back-up for emergencies. But it if was a planned departure, I don't know that I would say "here is my successor." There are places where that has worked, of course, but the ones that make the most sense to me were where there were co-Directors and one person retires or moved on. Then it's very transparent and logical. And there must be chorus buy-in. I've seen situations where the Director says, "here is my successor" and the chorus is like, nuh-uh. It's ultimately the chorus' choice. ~JC

DIRECTOR WISDOM: The Director's Path

I don't have one; I probably should have. I thought I had it all figured out when one of the younger members with good barbershop skills was planning to major in music. I thought I could groom her. But then she changed her major.

I should be thinking about it. You never know - I mean, that's what happened to Scottsdale last time. I remember when I heard about Bev's death. It was so tragic, for the whole organization. She had touched so many people's lives, and she left many open positions because she was so involved. And when I first heard, my immediate thought was for the chorus and how hard it would be. I was very concerned about them and how they would go on. And little did I know that I would be part of the answer.

Looking ahead, I don't know if the next Director of Scottsdale will come from the risers or from outside. But if I were to decide to retire, I would talk to the chorus early enough that they could start to plan. It wouldn't be a secret.

And I would get out of the way of that process. I've heard too many horror stories of someone retiring but not letting go of the reins. It is important to let the new person find themselves. If you resign on your own timing, if you decide to step back: step all the way back! ~LL

Marv Yerkey was directing San Diego when I joined. He believed very strongly that no matter who is up front it was not <u>their</u> chorus. It was always the San Diego Chorus. Therefore, it was not Marv Yerkey and the San Diego Chorus; it was the San Diego Chorus with Marv Yerkey directing. That's different. That's featuring the chorus. That means the chorus must survive. When they found he had cancer and that he was going to die, he made it very clear to all the musical leaders of the chorus that our job was to make sure the chorus survived. The chorus was not to fall apart because he wasn't there. And the chorus survived. Connie Noble became the Director and had the same attitude. Then she and I switched spots, and I picked it up the same way.

While the chorus is a reflection of the Director, I don't think it survives because of the Director. And one of the things I planned when I decided to retire was that the chorus would survive no matter who was in front. It is first and foremost the San Diego Chorus. ~KV

Whether you think of it as succession planning or not, it's important to recognize and groom talent. And if you do that, you have a succession plan. You recognize people who have administrative capability and music knowledge and the ability to impart that knowledge. Then you put them in roles that allow them to do it and see if they are successful. You find out if they have the people skills to do it. And it's a bit at a time, so that they have a safety net and your chorus has a safety net. Don't throw them in headfirst on something where the chorus is going to sink or swim on. Give the feedback. It's grooming. It's what people did for me.

I've often said I would have not succeeded in Sweet Adelines if I had not had mentors along the way who said "that might work better if you…" or "did you ever think about…" ~PG

If a Director knows they're going to move or retire, they should let the chorus know of the anticipated timeline so that they can start planning. In the meantime, development from within is critical.

We should all be training our replacement and/or at least training our Music Teams to facilitate and plan creative rehearsals that would maintain as many members as possible so the transition is as smooth as possible. My own personal past mistakes would suggest that you don't EVER want to leave on a bad note. Don't wait until you get angry and want to quit over something. Leave on good terms. ~DP

We don't have a formal plan in place. Two years ago, for different reasons, we lost two section leaders in the same section at the same time. We got surprised.

More often than not, our Music Team changes gradually over the years. We bring people in who we think will be future leaders, and we move them through roles. To be honest, we don't have a plan for Director succession. I don't plan on leaving for at least another 10 years. I'm not thinking of leaving; this is where I want to be. ~JA

I feel like it's my job to make sure the chorus will go on without me. If I walked away, Song of Atlanta would still exist. There's strong leadership in place. There are several people that I've thought over the years could be the next Director. And my daughter Melody got her music degree and she's now an Assistant Director. She ran her first rehearsal by herself, and I hear she did great. I do hope to have "International Champion Director" behind my name one day before I leave, so I don't plan to leave anytime soon. But if I did, I'm confident Song of Atlanta would continue. ~BH

DIRECTOR WISDOM: The Director's Path

Sometimes it's hard because a potential successor hasn't emerged yet. So, you have to keep training. When you see someone that you think has the potential you can begin grooming them, helping them to round out their skills. And, more importantly, you give them exposure in front of the chorus and give them a chance to demonstrate their skills to the chorus. Members give me feedback about the people I put out front. If I were grooming someone that the chorus didn't respect, I'd have to shift gears because the chorus makes the final decision on who will direct them! ~BC

A plan works well for some. I think it has a lot to do with the chorus. I think there should be a plan, especially, if the Director says, "I'm going to retire next year." There're many ways to do this, and I've seen many that backfire. The chorus must buy into whomever is going to lead from here on. You know, I don't think it's the Director's responsibility to say, "This is the heir apparent. I'm grooming her, and you will accept her." Unless the chorus is aware of it and approves of the person. They must feel good about it, because ultimately it is the chorus' decision, not the Director's.

Having an exit plan is a hard thing to think about as a Director. But I also think there are times in my life when I feel like God has prepared me for the next thing. I hope that I will know when it's time. When I retired from teaching, I thought "I still have a lot of years left in me" but I also felt it was time to move on. I didn't want to be one of these teachers where everyone says, "Oh, she should have left a long time ago." You have to read the situation, know when it's right to leave and do it for the right reasons. I've seen cases where Directors won't leave, or where they want to be part of the search committee and the search just stretches on and on and on. It damages the chorus. I hope for choruses and Directors that there's a trusted voice that can say "maybe it's time to step down." But I don't think there's a perfect formula for handling it. ~KW

If the Director really loves the chorus, they should give the chorus plenty of notice. The Director before me gave the chorus two years. She really loved that chorus. I think the Director can be, if the chorus wants them to be, part of the process of finding a new Director. I would be straight up with my chorus. I would ask, "Do you want me to be part of the search?" And I would respect their answer. ~MG

JENNIFER PALUS

I have a Directing team of four, who are incredible. When I leave attendance does not falter. So first, there is the importance of having a great directing team in place. If you're sick or out of town, you want the rehearsals to be strong and the chorus to know there will be strong direction when you're not there. Second, it's my plan to have someone in place, ready to go. My daughter, Becky, is one of the assistant directors and is generally considered the "heir apparent" by me and the chorus—now certainly the chorus would need to go through a formal process on that but she's getting a lot of important experience!

And I'm going to tell you there is a Director-in-waiting in every chorus. I believe that fully. I think sometimes our Directors are insecure or afraid to even go there. And I say, "You want the organization to continue? Grow 'em in your own chorus! Get 'em! Find 'em!" The people that I work with and coach are all working on that, because I am insistent. I tell them you need to have a backup and here's why: You will become a better Director if you have a strong backup. That shows you care for your chorus. You want them to continue. I feel confident that if something were to happen to me, this chorus would continue and at the level they are at. They won't go backward.

I do have to tell you, it's a little disconcerting to see so many men directing choruses. And it's not that I'm against men! It's that I think there's some strong women that we're not developing. It's us, front-line Directors, who need to be taking care of nurturing and making that happen. Males come in and they have a totally different approach. Not everyone is like Jim Arns! I have a real passion for this – I would love to meet with Directors and say here's how you make this happen. The women on my directing team are powerful and strong and I'm proud to have them and train them. One of them has been a front-line Director and any one of them could be the front-line Director and they would all work together as a team to make it happen. ~VM

I think the first thing a Director should do when they start with a chorus is begin training their successor. People in choruses may feel like little cliques are starting when you nurture those people, so it's important to be open about your desire as a Director. When I started, I said, "I want anyone of you to be able to pick up and keep going if the plane goes down. Some of you will have more desire and more applicable skills and I'll nurture those." It comes down to information sharing. There is a hierarchy in a chorus, but, especially from an education standpoint, there needs to be a matrix organization as well. Matrix means bring out the best in each person with access to education to anyone at any time from the most qualified person. ~MF

DIRECTOR WISDOM: The Director's Path

I think it's imperative to plan. A very smart man said to me, "once you get into your 40's it's your job to start mentoring." There are certain individuals, and I've seen something in them and think they should be cultivated into something. It may or may not be at Toast of Tampa, but they will have opportunities and I want to be a resource for them.

It's an organizational problem. There's all these giants (Directors), but some have left, and some may be gone soon. Where's the next layer? Where's the next level of leadership? You get really focused on doing the job. I've never had anything other than the hope that I should train someone, or someone would come along. But I think you have to be active and seek those people out. Maybe help aim them to the future.

And also, no one else is going to be another "Dale Syverson" or "Betty Clipman". The hope is to spend time with them and have some of their genius rub off on individuals who take it and inspire their own style. It's doesn't have to be youthful talent – just someone that can move up into the next level.

Several of my section leaders have become Certified Directors. They may or may not be front-line arm wavers, but they wanted the education and the certification. Others are looking at that too. It makes them more empowered to work with the members that are currently in front of them. I am happy to support that, but the idea did not come from me. It came from them, and they did it.

Right now, I'm actively mentoring my two kids. Whether in or out of direct barbershop means, I'm encouraging and supporting their growth. ~TD

I think it depends on the chorus. If there is a natural heir apparent and the chorus knows it and approves of it – all of that has to be talked about. I think where choruses get into trouble is not communicating. Whenever it's time for me to go, we'll talk about it as a chorus. Do we want to do an International Director search, do we want Ryan to stay and train the new Director or step away immediately? It's the chorus' decision, and we're lucky to have the Directing Team to help with any transition. Not ever chorus has that. For me, I don't want to create a succession plan because I want my chorus to continue to be singer-driven and it shouldn't have my shadow over it when I'm gone. ~RH

(Ryan's interview was before he announced his departure from Pride; he added this note in 2019)
I am pleased to share that Pride is currently in the midst of a Director search, and as I had shared, it is singer-driven. I am only involved as a resource when the team has specific questions. The chorus is in charge of the next chapter, and that makes me so very proud. Yes, the chorus reflects me as the director, but I am not Pride of Portland, they are! ~RH

You are hitting a soft spot for me. Historically, in 2001 I was very ill. It took quite some time to be back in the chorus. The chorus worked fine in that time with a couple of strong Assistant Directors, but I started to very eagerly try to find someone who could be my successor.

It just happened that the universe conspired to help me. A very well-trained and good Director from another chorus had just left her chorus. I had been her mentor and coach for a long time and invited her to come to my chorus and be Assistant Director. The original plan was after 2005 she would be my successor and I would step back. But that didn't happen because her professional work become more demanding. And we learned she was more a team leader than a single leader. So, we became Co-Directors.

When we have sessions about our future, there's always the question about what will happen when I retire. I'm 72 you know! It's clear that it must happen. I don't want to be a little old lady in front of the chorus. But the conversation stops there. We haven't found a solution. I'm going to have to step aside and make my own decision. But I enjoy it a little too much! Maybe after next International. I don't know. We've discussed it a lot. There are several ideas. It might be the time we have to re-start with new leaders. ~BB

> *If you decide to step back, step all the way back.*
> Lori Lyford

The Director's Path

What are some things you would tell your younger self about directing?

JENNIFER PALUS

Don't let the naysayers get to you. It was very important to me when I was young to have everyone like me and have everyone like every decision. And that just isn't possible! When people would not approve of something I did or said, it really got to me. I would say to my younger self "Toughen up just a little bit and be surer of yourself. If somebody doesn't like what you've done, there's gonna be plenty who are in your camp. Don't let it shake you." ~KB

I would probably tell myself to not push it. Don't be so brash. Relax a bit. It's going to be OK. It's going to all turn out all right. It's going to be the way it's supposed to be. And there will be so many surprises!

You know, I never expected to be a professional Sweet Adeline. I expected to teach college. I wanted to teach vocal production and vocal pedagogy but when I graduated with my Masters, my studio was absolutely full of barbershoppers. I didn't have any regular voice students anymore. There are only so many slots in a vocal studio, so I had become a barbershop voice teacher. Then the chorus did well, and the quartets did well, and I started coaching. Who knew? That's not what I expected to be! But it turned out all right! ~KV

I almost lost the job, almost got replaced, a number of years ago. I think back on that situation and it was people mistakes, not musical mistakes. Members of chorus leadership wanted me replaced; they weren't sure with what. I fought for the job and wound up keeping it, but then the chorus President, Vice President and 15 other members resigned. The chorus was not in a healthy place.

By Roberts Rules of Order, after those two officers' resignations, one of the Secretaries, Jean, had to step into the Presidency until the next election. And the one who got it was someone who seemed like the class clown. She was the tenor on the top row who would always pop off with a funny remark. Turns out I was not sensitive to what she was able to do. And every time she did it was because things had gotten too serious and she could make the chorus laugh. She was exactly what the chorus needed at that time, exactly what I needed at that time. She held a country-wide leadership position for an association of executive secretaries. She had major leadership chops. She taught me so much.

Now, if we're going through any turmoil, I think about what she would do. She taught me to listen to the mood of the chorus. It was a long journey for me. ~DS

DIRECTOR WISDOM: The Director's Path

I would say: All that extra energy that you're pouring into your directing is actually not helping your chorus; it gets in the way. They benefit more from you doing less. Do less.

I would remind myself that "this too shall pass." Don't get too riled up on the small stuff.

It used to feel like it was a compliment when people would say "Oh Lori, I can hardly take my eyes off of you." Then it hit me that that was not a good thing! I'm getting in the way of the chorus. When my chorus sings without me, they are always freer. They are always more expressive.

I have learned to scale back what I do, to allow that freedom to come out, to allow that unity of purpose. When the unit comes together to express the message, it's better than individuals who follow a Director. ~LL

Love the singers. Just remember where you came from. These people are not only volunteers, they are paying to do this. Make tonight worth their while. Make it fun. Make it joyful. Make them feel good about themselves. Focus on what's going on inside these people. What is motivating them to sing? There are so many people who are struggling in their personal lives and Sweet Adelines is their outlet. They're not looking for another job. It's not like, "I want more stress!" We have to temper everything we do with an understanding of why people are here. ~BC

Be stronger in my vision and focus for the chorus. Don't be afraid to have high expectations for my singers. Teach to the fastest learners. I would also give myself a heads up that Directing is more about people care than I thought. I wasn't expecting the amount of nurturing that is needed. I'm fine with it! It was just a little bit of a surprise when I was new. I'd tip myself off. ~JC

Being the front-line director doesn't make you the "boss" of the chorus. It means you are in charge of the musical product and you probably should be managing committees, etc...that are related to the music. This is not an easy thing to do...especially if you are skilled in other areas.

Bottom line: Chorus ownership is critical to the success of the group. And, guidance and suggestions from a director are important...but it doesn't mean that the chorus should do only as you say. Learn to say "no" (lovingly) and encourage growth in others. A strong leader develops others...I'm still learning this, by the way! -- DP

JENNIFER PALUS

When I first started directing, I thought I should go get a music degree. But as the years went by, I realized I should go get a psychology degree! It's a big part of what we do.

I embraced becoming a Director, but I was flying by the seat of my pants. I am a sponge, and I like to learn. But I still don't know it all. I probably would have tried to look at myself as a strong leader instead of relying on my personality. I would have tried to be a stronger leader. Though, I don't know that I could have done that. What I know now I've learned over time. I don't know that I could have sped up that process. It took time. I had to figure it out on my own. ~BH

Don't sweat the small stuff. And essentially, it's all small stuff. To be happy. My younger self was more concerned with keeping everybody happy. Once I got to the age of 40, I decided who gives a rip? I'm going to focus on keeping myself happy and focusing my energy there. ~VM

Calm down! I would have been nicer to my singers. I was focused, and it wasn't balanced by the side that's comical and fun. I would get irritable. I would tell my younger self not to do that. One time, Betty Clipman put a chair in front of me because I was walking too close to the chorus (and the far side couldn't see me). I was irritated. Finally, I kicked the chair. Well, I had sandals on, and a welt started on my foot. And I stood there pretending I wasn't in pain. I wouldn't do that today.

I learned a lot, and not all of it at the Melodeers. When I was 19 and thought I knew everything – and came in last at my first regional contest. That was a wonderful learning lesson. I wish I knew then what I know now about that experience. At the time I knew it was an important slap in the face, a wakeup call. But if I knew what I know now, I would have valued it even more. ~JA

Don't be so darned ambitious. It is the same perspective as being a teacher. It is very easy to be absolutely, totally overwhelmed by how much you can do. And even if you work your butt off to do everything you can, there's always more to do. I worked myself to illness by working too much. It was a very scary experience. When you have had that kind of experience you are always scared you will drive yourself to that edge again. That is the most urgent thing I would say to myself: please don't take yourself so damn seriously. ~BB

DIRECTOR WISDOM: The Director's Path

Don't be a jerk! Don't be a dork! Looking back there was so much talent in my first chorus cycle and I didn't make the best use of it. Pay more attention to how you treat people.

I'll probably say the same thing about what I'm doing NOW if you ask me this is in 10 years. If I look back in 10 years and think "yeah, I got it all right" then I wasted those 10 years. I'm sure I'll look back and want to say, "Don't be a jerk!"

It doesn't mean there weren't accomplishments, but in general you're always learning and wanting to be something different. Something better! I've always been confident in who I am and my abilities, but also always wanting to improve.

When I first started as a men's chorus director, I was 21-22 and had just won my first Men's International and had been a member of the Society since I was 7. But I was new to directing. If I heard a recording of those rehearsals now, I'd probably think "Oh why'd you say it like that?"

I'd always known, from watching my dad, Joseph DeRosa (Papa Joe), that the interpersonal part of directing and teaching was so important. He was way more of a people-person that I am. People loved him because of his passion. He was a chapter grower. He could take a "fixer-upper" chorus and raise it to champion caliber. He was able to relate to people on a very basic level and really do amazing things with them. I want to be better at that as I continue to direct. Whether working at the 'fixer-upper level' (which is always the case) or working more on the artistic elements. ~TD

You can't do everything as a Director, don't expect to. You're going to try. But you can't.

Find out what you're really good at. Figure out how people can mentor you and coach you on those things. Find out what you're not good at and find other people that that's their Zen and let them run with it.

Get unity and agreement between you so you can move forward as a team. Figure out how to choose people who are smarter than you, so you can learn how to do stuff. ~MF

JENNIFER PALUS

Trust my gut more. There are many times I had gut feelings about things, and I gave in. 9 times out of 10, my gut was right, but I gave in to the other voices. That doesn't mean I'm always right. But I would have to tell my younger self to trust more in my instincts.

I would also tell myself to enjoy the ride more. Enjoy the times you have, the celebrations, and the people you learn from. I've always been an avid learner. I would not stop that. But I would want to go back and figure out how I could have grasped some of these things sooner. I was exposed to a lot of good things earlier on. I didn't quite grasp them all at first.

I would probably reach out more to other Directors for advice. I did some, but I didn't always think to ask! I missed out on the opportunity that there is a network out there. When I first started directing, I didn't know those "big" people. Now of course, I have relationships with many of them and feel comfortable talking to them. Maybe that's part of it as well: my comfort level of asking for help. I think at an earlier age I should have asked for more help. It wasn't because I didn't think I needed it. I just didn't know how. ~KW

Don't take yourself so seriously. Trust your gut. It took me a long time to really listen to the voice in my head. I know a lot and my gut reaction when I'm working with a group is usually right. If I just listen to it, instead of trying to pick it apart myself, the sum of what I know rises to the top, and there's a reason why my inside voice is telling me to do that. ~PG

Be happy and joyful now – don't wait. Don't think that this has to happen, and this has to happen…just be happy now. ~MG

> *If I look back in 10 years and think*
> *"yeah, I got it all right"*
> *then I wasted those 10 years.*
> Tony DeRosa

The Director's Path

What lessons did you learn only with time?

Looking back over your career, can you pull out some key lessons that came with time in the job? Or are there any things that you believed early in your career that you don't believe any more?

Now there's a long list. I had to learn to stop directing by using my body so much. I'm a natural mover and I had to learn to stand still so that my arms meant more. My arms and my hands mean more if they are the only things moving. Mike Elliot (directs the Spokane Chorus) taught me that.

I learned from Greg Lyne the importance of the vowel. That the vowel is the basic work unit of all a cappella music. And that when you can't think of anything else to do, work on the vowel because it will fix so much.

As a younger Director, I thought energy meant fast. Now I know that energy does not mean fast. Energy is a physical commitment to what you're doing; it has nothing to do with speed at all. But I certainly believed that early on. I also thought that brighter was always better. And I thought loud, louder, and loudest were three GREAT dynamics.

As I got older, I got better at finesse. I could hear more artistry; I could do more artistic things. I sensed things in words that that my younger self didn't see or didn't hear. And I began to do that. ~KV

This organization has seen in me something I didn't see in myself many times. I've been pushed to do certain things. One time I was asked to teach conducting to the B+ and higher Directors, and I was one of them at that time. I remember obsessing about it. "How do I do this?" The wildly uncomfortable experience of doing that was absolutely pivotal for me. I must have rewritten that class three times at the hotel before I taught it. I was so nervous I couldn't see straight! I walked into the gift shop at the hotel. I don't know why! And I bought this little bunny figurine with a stupid, serene look on her face. I set her under the podium. Any time my nerves were getting the better of me, I went back, and I touched my bunny. She still sits on my shelf. I have so many reminders on my shelves of how I got to where I am. ~DS

The Director's Path

What was an important but difficult lesson you learned as a Director?

JENNIFER PALUS

I've only had a few bad things happen in my 30 years directing. One was receiving a letter from a chorus member that was absolutely vitriolic. It could not have been uglier. And it was anonymous.

I had been the Director for five years or so, and I was absolutely devastated. My grandmother had always been my closest friend. So, I went to my grandmother and she read it. We talked about it, and she asked, in her typical grandmother way, "Kimberly Ann, do you know how to get rid of mold and mildew?" I said "Grandma, this is serious! This is a big thing, and I'm really upset, and I don't know what to do." She said "Kimberly Ann, do you know how to get rid of mold and mildew?" I said I didn't know how. She said, "You put light and air on it." I asked, "What does that mean to me?" and she told me to think about it for a minute. I realized what she meant. I asked, "You want me to read this out loud to the chorus?" She said "Yes, I think you should read it to the whole chorus. It will never happen again if you put those words out there in front of the chorus."

And they were UGLY, very personal words - but I trusted my grandmother and I did it. I went to rehearsal, and I told the chorus that I was going to read something that someone in the chorus had sent me anonymously. And I told them after I read it, I was going to give it to the Board, and the Board would decide if there was anything in the letter that required them to take action.

But I wanted everyone to understand that I would never, ever accept anything anonymous again for the rest of my life. I explained, "You can say anything to me but if you want to say something to me in the future, you will have to say it in person."

Then I read it. Every face was glued to me - except one, who sort of turned her body and looked down. It was really ugly, but I've got to tell you: It never happened again. The Board came back to me a couple of weeks later and said there was no additional action needed, and they destroyed the letter.

I went back to Grandma and said, "Now I know who it is." She said, "Ask her to do something for you. Keep her close. Find out why she's so angry with you." So, I did. It took me a month or so before I even wanted to think about it. I asked her to do a little job for me - something that really needed to get done. And she said yes and ended up doing that job for several years and she did a good job. She didn't leave us until she retired. ~KV

DIRECTOR WISDOM: The Director's Path

A difficult lesson I had to learn through experience was about how to receive feedback. My first year it was part of the chorus culture to have a comments box at rehearsal to let leadership know their thoughts. But it was mostly anonymous, because that method encourages anonymity. And something came in that was just a trite issue. It was like being back on the playground. The Management Team and I agreed we wanted to get rid of the box. We wanted to hear from members directly and have a conversation about topics. So, we had a ceremonial destruction of the box and encouraged members to bring us their concerns. They responded beautifully.

Now, members email or call with ideas and concerns. It can be difficult for a new director to realize the importance of dealing with non-musical issues, but of course, many things have an impact on the chorus. Be approachable, be kind, listen. Delegate as needed, but remember, you're a large part of the reason the singers stay! ~RH

We had a few dark years where we had some administration that was oppressive. I spent those years trying to put out fires.

You don't realize that your singers are not singing as well as they could (because they're unhappy) until years later when you've come out of it. We had years when people were just not happy. We'd stand out front and talk vocal production and energy and try to get people excited, but we just couldn't. Those were hard years.

I couldn't figure out what was happening until some things changed. All of a sudden we sang better. We were coachable again. In hindsight, we realized we made it through a weird time.

If I ever sense we're heading that direction, I will take steps to correct the compass immediately. I'm smarter now about sensing those things. The admin side changes people frequently, but the Music Team stays largely the same. I'm smarter now about how to work with each new admin team. ~BH

> *If you want to say something to me in the future, you will have to say it in person.*
> ~Kim Vaughn

The Director's Path

Do you think the path to Director is different today?

Is it easier or harder (or the same) to become a Director today than when you started?

DIRECTOR WISDOM: The Director's Path

Not sure I know how to answer that. We've certainly given the Directors tools now that we didn't have when I started. Anyone who wants to be a Director and who isn't in the DCP is missing out on great information. The education that we provide for prospective Directors is amazing. When we have a Director Seminar or when your region offers something for Directors, or section leaders, or prospective Directors, take advantage.

In a way, I think that has made it easier. When I began it was all guts and nerve. ~KB

I don't know if it's harder. But it feels like a lot fewer people are breaking in. I see a lot of choruses looking, like when a Director retires or moves, and it seems to take forever to find the right fit for that chorus.

But I don't know that it's harder. I see some of these Directors who came up through Young Women In Harmony and they are doing really well in their early 20's. The next generation is starting to break in. ~JA

My impression is we have a really high need for Directors right now. We have choruses who are going through searches. They are trying to find people and going outside the barbershop world because they need somebody.

I wish we had a deeper stratum of people who are experienced enough to help a chorus or direct a chorus. Some barbershop is better than none.

Now when I started, I was not steeped in barbershop at all. The thing I had going for me was that I could direct. I knew how to wave my hands. I knew how to read music. I knew a bit about vocal production. I was a voice performance major. When I got in trouble, I could get out of it by relying on my own musicality. I learned about barbershop style as I went along. I love being coached; I love learning things.

But truthfully, I think it's to a person's advantage (as a Director) to know about barbershop. And sometimes people eliminate themselves, saying, "Oh, I couldn't do that" but if you know about barbershop, you'll have a better feeling for it than someone who's perfect with their hand movement but unaware of barbershop. ~LL

Hmm. There's more weird stuff to contend with because of society and more distractions. Have to get people to get off their phones and have a 1:1 conversation.

But as far as becoming a Director…people have initiative that's either shown or not shown. But people don't miss real talent that wrapped around true leadership mindset. Being headstrong is not leadership, nor is always being right.

Some people say, "I haven't had the break" but I wonder "maybe you haven't learned to be a true leader." It's way more about managing expectations and personalities, getting people to work through their insecurities, letting them see the vision and want to work toward it. ~TD

I know that my ability to be a distance Director has a lot to do with the technology and connectivity we have today. I don't know that I could have done this 15 years ago. Almost everything the chorus does is on our website or via email. Even some Music Team meetings we do virtually so there's not travel required. ~JC

I think it's the same. Every Director coming in has got to learn how to deal with that particular group, how to make the changes they feel must be made, and how to recognize the people who will stand in the way. They have to create the thermostat for what the rehearsal feels like. I think all of the issues are the same; they are reinvented with each new Director. ~MG

> When I began,
> it was all guts and nerve.
> Karen Breidert

The Director's Path

What are important characteristics for a Director?

What makes a great candidate? And on the other hand, are there characteristics or qualifications that people THINK are necessities but may not be critical to success as a Director?

Wherever you're lacking, fill that void by surrounding yourself with people who have what you're lacking. For example, people would assume you've got to be really good at music theory. Maybe you must be able to play the piano, dissect a chord, know Pythagorean tuning. But I would say if that's not your thing, that doesn't mean you can't be a Director. It means surround yourself with technical people.

I would say I'm pretty good at the rah-rah stuff, the emotional cheerleading stuff. So, I don't need that in a coach. I needed more the technical person in the coach. My background is foreign language not music. So, I brought in, for instance, Betty to work on vocal skills. But I didn't need a spirit cheerleader person. So, you find where your voids are, and you just fill them. ~KB

Self-confidence and/or the ability to appear self-confident. A good director must be prepared for every rehearsal, be people skilled and command the respect of every singer all because of these attributes. ~DP

A great Director needs the ability to know what the group needs at the time. For instance, there's a time to dig into the heavy lifting of a rehearsal and there's a time to let up.

I wish I'd given myself that advice last week! We had some sickness and ice and snow and only had 40 of the 90 people in the chorus. I started working on what we had just done at the retreat. We needed to debrief. But in hindsight it wasn't the right time to do that. I did it anyway and it was a frustrating rehearsal.

As recently as this week, I could have given myself the pep talk that there are different needs at different times. I'll probably raise it with the chorus and acknowledge the frustration and then move on. I don't like to dwell, but I do want them to know I know it was frustration. ~MG

The most important thing is a desire to direct. You have to <u>want</u> to do it. There are some who think you have to have very formal training in order to direct. But in some cases that can actually be a detriment if it gets in the way of a genuine connection with your singers. Then you look at someone like Dale who is not formally trained but you wouldn't know that. She has such a feel for it, such a connection.

I think the key is learning your strengths and weaknesses whatever they may be. Build on your strengths and learn how to develop and strengthen your weaknesses. ~KW

DIRECTOR WISDOM: The Director's Path

People think a strong knowledge of vocal skills and musical skills is a prerequisite. But what's great about our organization is: we'll teach and train all that. If you have good leadership skills, if you have inherent musicality and good ears, that could counterbalance a lack of training. 10 years ago, I wouldn't have said that. I would have said knowledge of vocal skills and how to teach it was critical. But I think if you have the willingness, you're halfway there.

A lot of people think good people skills is the most important. And while I think it's important, I don't think it's the most important because it can be learned. And this is all part of my journey. I spent 2-3 years with Jan Carley, all about the power of positivity from the leadership perspective. Prior to that, from my training, I would tell you the most direct way. It's not my job to control your emotional response. "Hey Sally, you're flat." "Hey Suzy, smile." But people hear "he hates me." So, we made an agreement that I would always try to find a better way. So, if you have a willingness to learn whatever you need, THAT's the most important thing!

The other thing that comes to mind is conducting skills. Maybe you don't have the best gestures, or "beautiful hands," that's okay! Conducting can be learned, and each director needs to find their own style. Can you communicate what you want to hear? Eventually, using fewer words and more gestures can be an ideal way to communicate. I suppose the overall theme here is to be flexible, generous, positive, unceasingly curious, and open-minded. ~RH

There are very successful Directors who don't read music. As a music teacher that drives me nuts. I mean I want to help them understand "this is why" and "this is how." But you CAN do it by having great ears.

I probably compensate for the fact that I don't think I have especially great ears by looking at the paper and saying "this should ring" even if I don't hear it.

Some people think the Director has to be set apart from the chorus making unilateral decisions. I believe the opposite. The more accessible a Director is, the more open the chorus.

And as I've seen as I've been out teaching and coaching: you can't teach personality! I've seen Directors exude no energy themselves and wonder why their chorus doesn't have any. The opposite can be true, too. If I give too much energy, my chorus doesn't think they have to do as much. "Hey, look at her - like a bug in a jar down there doing her thing!"

But there's no one way to do it. For some Directors, it's all about the sound. For others, it's all about the lyric. The Director has to be mindful of it all. But if you don't possess every skill personally, you can surround yourself with those that do. That's how the Directors who don't read music make it work. They have super-strong people around them. ~LL

I've actually talked 3-4 people into becoming front-line Directors. It's not always about the hands or the musical information. People think you can't direct if you don't have amazing musical skills, but that can be learned. What's really important is leadership skills. Most of the people in the organization have great ears. ~VM

People think you have to be able to read music on the fly. It's an asset if you can, but it's not a requirement. What you do have to do is have the ability to have information enter your ear (something be sung), make a diagnosis, and provide a prescription. Assess, diagnose, prescribe. You have to be able to do that at the level your ensemble is at, so they can keep moving. The biggest challenges are the second two. They hear something, but they're not sure what it is and they're not sure what to do. That's why we have Directors' workshop and coaching. That's an essential piece. Some can diagnose but they don't have the tools to fix things. Others pick up a tool at a workshop and try to fix things that don't need fixing! And like any teacher, you've got to be at least one chapter ahead of the class. The educational materials we have in the organization are phenomenal! ~JA

You don't have to have a musical degree. You do need to have a set of people skills. You do have to have ears and an imagination. I discounted my imagination for a long time and thought that idea had to come from somebody else's head. They really don't. They can come from your head.

People ask me to come in and voice place their chorus, and I say, "let's work at it together." And some say, "Oh I'm not skilled enough to do it." And I say "Well, you're not going to learn any younger" (as my daddy would say!).

I remind them when they go out on chorus performances and not all the voices are there, the Director needs to know how to place what's there. So, I work with them to hear what's going on and hear which sound YOU like the best. Let's listen to how voices sound together and learn so you can do it next time. And they realize they can do it. ~PG

Sometimes I think people think a Director needs to straighten other people out. Maybe it's different with a male Director with women. Might be different with a female Director. I know there are times when I definitely stay out of a situation and they want me in. I say "I don't think I should be in this. You need to handle it amongst yourselves." They expect me to be a mentor, and some want me to be a big brother. I have to watch to make sure someone is not looking at me too much for some emotional help and lighten that up real quick. ~MG

DIRECTOR WISDOM: The Director's Path

The most important thing for a Director is to show their undying curiosity for this thing that is greater than themselves and let that humility and vulnerability be seen. "I know what I know, but there is so much that I don't know." Let that be in the room as well. That helps foster a place of curiosity and independence amongst the singers. Natural leaders will start to emerge in that environment. Give them everything they need. The better they are, the more challenged YOU will be; the better leader you will be, and everybody goes up. You lift as you climb. You can let go of control and realize the creative process is not linear, it's a bunch of lateral moves. If you are fostering that in the people that you are asking to be in leadership, they will know what to do if you're gone. ~MF

> *You lift as you climb.*
> Mo Field

JENNIFER PALUS

The Director's Path

What advice would you offer aspiring Directors?

DIRECTOR WISDOM: The Director's Path

Get all the education you can. Attend everything: International, regionals, seminars, everything you can. Go to a show – and instead of enjoying the show as a typical audience member, watch the Director. Look at their responsibilities. Visit as many chorus rehearsals as you can and watch the evening. Visit within your region and outside. Spend the money and fly to Scottsdale to watch rehearsal. Surround yourself with how Directors work. That includes talking to them. Sometimes we feel as though we are alone, and we are NOT alone. There's a big network of people out there who would love to help you. If someone wanted to be a Director and were to call me or Lori or Betty – these people would love to say, "Let's talk about that!" and "Why do you think you'd like to go into this" "What apprehensions do you have" or "What excites you?" You are not alone. Ask people their opinion. ~KB

There is always a way to help. Make sure people know that's what you want to do - help make good barbershop and get it out to the world. Keep your love for the art form out front. Ask for help. You will never be so good that you won't need help. And ask sooner rather than later. ~KV

The two things you must bring to the job are a continuing willingness to learn and the ability to change. Everything else you can learn. But if you are not a life-long learner, you're going to struggle, and you will not be able to keep up. I've been in this organization for more than 50 years, and it has changed. The only reason I'm still at all relevant in the organization is because I changed too. The organization is crazy different than it was when I joined. We make mistakes as an organization, and we're only human beings. But we keep changing and growing. ~DS

Go to every educational event you can. And attend a lot of different performances, not just of barbershop but of all kinds. Research every song that you do. Find every version of it that you can. Listen to the nuances of different performers, listen to the orchestration, listen to the style. You get different ideas, if you take the time to do it. ~PG

Always remember you look at the chorus and you see multiple people. They only see one. You have an untold effect on them. Be careful what you say, because you can't take it back. ~PG

Make sure your Director knows you are interested. Get into the DCP program and get involved. Educate yourself musically and from a leadership standpoint. Find a mentor. ~VM

Don't be afraid to get out front of people and direct. Don't be afraid to make mistakes (that's where I learned most of my big learnings!) Put yourself out there with your chorus and take the journey together. You're leading them but you're also walking with them. Find a mentor. I've had several Directors who really mentored me, and some were standoffish. Find the right ones for you. ~JC

Get a mentor. Find someone somewhere who is willing to say "Yes, I will help you." I'm telling you there are so many people who will. We have 30 some international faculty in our organization who are sitting there to help you. There are master Directors everywhere. And if you are not a master Director yet that means every one of them knows something you don't know, yet. And for the people who haven't gotten to the 500 level yet, we have potential mentors and coaches clearly identified. If you're scoring at a C, you don't want to go for the Bev Sellers of the world. You want to go for the coach who just won the small or medium size medal. Get the one who has gone through where you are! We need to avoid going to "upper management" (top tier coaches) every time. We need to go to mid-management. That's how mid-management gets better, and it's how a mid-level chorus get better. ~KV

Find people who have been where you are, who know things you don't, and learn from them. Directing is a journey, and it had better be one that you enjoy. Now and then remind yourself that you love this! ~KV

Embrace Sweet Adelines, who and what we are. The organization is always changing but there are things we've always stood for: Harmonize the World. I think the organization is a wonderful organization. We're always looking toward the future. The leadership changes, but they always have the best interest of the members at heart. There are a lot of resources that Sweet Adelines International puts out there for anyone who wants to learn – anything. There's a lot of stuff people don't take advantage of. We can all continually be working on things. The DCP program is a great resource for anyone, any musical leader. And they're always updating it. ~BH

Observe, and better yet, join, as many different choruses as you can. There is so much to learn from different Directors, both what to do and what not to do. I recommend that aspiring Directors attend the Director track at Harmony University (BHS). SA does not need to reinvent the wheel, but it would be great if more in SA knew about the fantastic classes for Directors at Harmony U. ~ED

DIRECTOR WISDOM: The Director's Path

The DCP <Directors Certification Program> is wonderful. It's organized; you do it on your own time. Open a dialogue with the Director of your chorus. Could you do warmups or teach a tag in your own chorus. OR keep an ear open at the regional level: is there a small chorus in your area that needs a Director? That's how I started! I took the first thing I found. Years ago, we had an ensemble group that did daytime performances (and I couldn't do them since I was teaching). We had a member who led that group and got to be a Director. There's not just one path. ~JA

It's OK to ask for help. I think sometimes choruses look at Directors like we should have all the answers. And we don't! Therefore, we don't want to tell them what we don't know, because then they may not want us to do this anymore. Sometimes it's hard to vulnerable, but I would encourage them to be more vulnerable early on.

Years ago, a lot of our Directors had the musical skills, but they didn't have the people skills. It's important to remember you're in a leadership role, but you're not the most important person. Surround yourself with people that will be assets to your weaknesses. Surround yourself with people that will say what you need to hear not what you want to hear.

Be open. You have to be open to people making suggestions. The number one thing is to stay focused on the best interest of the chorus. ~KW

You need to learn to be a leader and do what's right for the chorus no matter what anybody says. People come to you with questions about what do about with this or that. The answer is always: Do what's best for the chorus. You were hired to make the best choice for the chorus, and you must do that. That's your job. You agreed to do that. ~KV

Can I put it the opposite way? I have a daughter, a two-time queen, she's mesmerizing in front of the chorus, she's fantastic – and she doesn't want to be a Director. I have not been able to inspire her to shift that. That would be my ideal dream: to have her as my successor. She wants to sing! I think I look more to the idea that you can learn how to wave your hands, but it's damned hard to learn to be a good leader. To learn how to be a good person in front, to learn strategies of how to work with the group. That is so much more challenging. You can always get help musically and with technique. It's very hard to get work on how to handle a group. I've learned so much from all the Directors' Seminars and coaching sessions. At the same time, you have to be open to learn as a Director. You need to be ready to learn, eager and curious. If you think "I don't have more to learn" you are in danger. I still learn a lot...but I forget it sooner (ha)! ~BB

None of this is really about you, although you pay a key role in facilitating the opening of something that's greater than all of you. You can't underestimate your role, but at the same time you can't claim successes that come with it, per se. If their success isn't about you, then their failure isn't about you. And that's hard as a leader. If they are not successful, you feel like you failed them.

If someone's not there on a rehearsal night you feel like you're not offering enough to make them prioritize it. You take everything personally. But you're responsible for facilitating their opportunities.

If I attach my ego to their success – such as "yay, we got a medal" – than I also am stuck attaching myself to the failures when we don't achieve. But the reality is, there is so much subjectivity in music, we cannot be in charge of how it is received. If I have my ego involved and someone comes into the room to observe, maybe it's a mentor I want to impress, and the chorus misses a beat, and I try to assert myself, try to make it happen, well that's never going to work – I'm never going to get the music out of them because now my ego is in the room, taking up too much space. The chorus responds, or not, to this imperceptible energy shift, and never positively. Sure, there's room for ego in the music, but the music happens in the moment and then it's gone. You are either fully surrendered to that moment and dwarfed by it, so much larger than any of you or anyone who walks into the room… or you're trying to impress someone. You cannot be that generous and try to get a reward at the same time. It's impossible.

You're either there for self-interest or there to use the best of your selfishness in a selfless way. I'm so addicted to music because it makes me feel good, and that's a selfish quest. But I'm selfless in it because I've surrendered to the fact that I'll never achieve what I hope. I'll find glimpses of it and that will thrill me and encourage me. And hopefully anyone watching will feel what I'm feeling, because of the music, not because of me.

So, for new Directors: check your ego. It's going to try to take a contract out on you in really suspicious and unpredictable ways. You may not notice until you start to feel angry and upset. As an artist you're going to be passionate and you're going to be frustrated from time to time - and you're allowed to be those things! They are fuel to the creativity. But when your ego is in the way, you're going to find yourself tangled in expectations, ambition, and disappointment. Keep those things in check.

~MF

DIRECTOR WISDOM: The Director's Path

Be open. Don't worry about making mistakes. You're going to make mistakes. Admit it. Don't let people intimidate you because of what you think they think about you or your decisions.

Be willing to get outside your comfort zone. But in the process, don't drown your chorus because you decided to jump into something really difficult.

A good product will grow your membership. If you bring in lots of people who are not really qualified, you won't have a good product or a good culture. It is more difficult to create your sound and your culture with lots of people. You don't need to start with lots of people. Start with who's there, help them learn, and they will draw others. Get performances, get out in the public. Your members become proud of their product and they start inviting people. But it's not all about numbers. You don't have to be big to be great.

Keep moving your bar, move your expectation. When you feel like your chorus is getting bogged down or not doing what you want them to do, don't overdo it for them.

To have high expectations for your chorus, you have to provide solid education. Try to have as much musicality (phrasing, dynamics, etc.) as possible front-loaded into a new song. That's why I want my chorus to learn music quickly and accurately, so that we can get to musicality much sooner.

Try to move at the pace of your fastest learner, rather than slowing everything down. If the fastest learners know that they're going to be rewarded for their work, then they're more inclined to keep working. One of our dear members who has had to resign due to cancer, Charlie, would learn her music in a week. Every time. I would say, "We're going to sing this all the way through because I know Charlie knows it." And she'd be off the paper, just singing away. Always keep your finger on the pulse of the fastest learner and reward them in some way. Acknowledge them. "Wow, Daren, I see you are recording again. Do you guys know she records every week and listens to herself?"

Be willing to make the tough decisions.

Put the meaning into your standards.
~LL

Make sure that your musical convictions work hand-in-hand with what you're presenting from a humane perspective. Help people be better people, while helping them become better singers and performers.

As I've gotten older, I think so much about "gosh this person drives 3 hours to be here" – there better be more than just some good chords tonight! There must be some visceral human connection with what they're singing, who they're singing with, and what they're being asked to do. The Director needs to think about the holistic of the "WHY" – so that people feel fulfilled in what they are doing.

Being open to when you just shanked something! My dad said to me a long time ago, "Just be honest. Stop the chorus and say, I don't know what's wrong, but that's not right." The more honest you are, the more grace they will give you.

If you're always the King of the Answer, people will either always look to you for the answer rather than learning themselves OR they shut down and stop listening. Sometimes I say, "that was really good, but I think you can do that better." I could have said four different specific details how – but you don't always need to give the answer.

Be open with your singers and open to their ideas.

Be smart about what you pick for your singers. Show off their strengths.

Know who you are. And know who you are WILL change!

Have a clear vision and follow it through.
~TD

If it was a young female Director taking over a chorus, I would tell her to be confident in her skills and that it's all about the joy they're having rehearsal to rehearsal and all of that will add up to weeks and months and years of things going in a great direction.

If it is a male, I would also say Make sure you learn their rules. They think differently. Don't insist on how you think because you don't think the same. And don't dare get involved with one of them. Because if you do, there are going to be problems! ~MG

DIRECTOR WISDOM: The Director's Path

Be approachable. Be genuine. Be your truest self.

Prioritize the chorus at as high a level as you can. If you have a young family and the chorus is 2nd or 3rd, don't try to hide that – share it and ask for help.
Don't try to do everything yourself. Surround yourself with a great team.
If you think you don't have those people – take the time to seek out the strength and nurture the team. Be open minded. Be willing to try new things.

Seek the advice of coaches and mentors often.
Make use of this incredible network that we have – I always say I'm available and I get questions but not nearly as many as I think I would.
It OK to say, "I don't know."
Remember: It's my fault. Take ownership.

As much as possible, be able to model what you want. If you can't do it vocally, find someone who can and take the time to teach and train them.

For a male Director, immerse yourself in all thing Sweet Adelines. Don't try to bring the BHS details to SA. Learn about the categories. Learn about the female voice. Learn that working with women is different than working with men. Embrace those differences. Don't try to be anything inauthentic in front of the chorus.
When it's feels like you're speaking two different languages, it's because you are.

Ask for feedback. It's always good to have someone on the risers giving you feedback. Someone who will just be brutally honest. Positives and negatives.

Be a student. Go to as many things as possible. Listen to barbershop. Know what you love and why. Know what you don't love and why. Spend time on the craft. Listen to a lot of different things so you can understand the differences.
Be realistic about our members. They are only human. They are paying to be there! As Carol Kirkpatrick always said to me: We want them to show up. We want them to know their music. We want them to be kind. We want them to pay their dues. Four rules. It doesn't need to be more complicated than that.

If things are spiraling negative – step back and figure out what's getting in the way of the joy.

When it comes to music selection – pick what you respond to. Don't pick something you think is good for the sake of being good. If your Music Team gives you an idea that they love but you don't – don't do it. It won't work. If you're not on board in your bones, it's not going to work for the chorus.
If you love a piece of music, but it doesn't work with your chorus – go back to the drawing board. Find something new. Keep lists – keep lists of songs all the time. Keep notes as you listen, it's a great resource for you and your team.

Remember: It's all about THEM! ~RH

My favorite thing about directing is sculpting sound. Your hands sculpt the sound that you want to hear. It's so cool that we get to do that. ~KV

You can't imagine how rewarding it is to stand in front of a group and feel like they are hanging on your hands. To feel that connection, that communication with the group. That is almost spiritual. The group is in your hands. It's a powerful thing. You have to do what you have to do to get that.

Feel gratefulness about that and never take it for granted. ~BB

> *As Carol Kirkpatrick always said to me:*
> *We want them to show up.*
> *We want them to know their music.*
> *We want them to be kind.*
> *We want them to pay their dues.*
> *Four rules.*
> *It doesn't need to be*
> *more complicated than that.*
> ~Ryan Heller

ABOUT THE AUTHOR

Jennifer Palus is a proud member of Metro Nashville Chorus, her only chorus since joining Sweet Adelines in 2004. She is a marketing consultant by day, and previously wrote a business book called Centered Presentations, available on Amazon. Her cat, Mezzo Forte, is responsible for (and deeply repentant about) any typos. If you want to point out his proofing mistakes so they can be corrected in future versions, or if you have comments or questions about this book, please email JLPalus+DirectorWisdom@gmail.com.

> *Author's note for July 2019 Revision:*
> *A HUGE thank you to Master Director Julie Starr (Bay Area Showcase Chorus) who reach out to say she loved this book, but the typos were driving her crazy. She is a retired technical writer and graciously reproofed it for me. Thank you, Julie, and apologies from me and Mezzo for the errors in the first version.*

Made in the USA
Coppell, TX
20 November 2019